The
LEVY FAMILY
and MONTICELLO, *1834-1923*
SAVING THOMAS JEFFERSON'S HOUSE

The
LEVY FAMILY
and MONTICELLO, *1834-1923*
SAVING THOMAS JEFFERSON'S HOUSE

by Melvin I. Urofsky

THOMAS JEFFERSON FOUNDATION

Monticello Monograph Series

2001

Library of Congress Cataloging-in-Publication Data

Urofsky, Melvin I.
    The Levy Family and Monticello, 1834-1923 : saving Thomas Jefferson's house / by
Melvin I. Urofsky.
        p. cm. -- (Monticello monograph series)
    Includes bibliographical references and index.
    ISBN 1-882886-15-1 -- ISBN 1-882886-16-X (pbk.)
        1. Monticello (Va.)--History. 2. Jefferson, Thomas, 1743-1826--Homes and haunts--
Virginia--Albemarle County. 3. Historic Sites--Conservation and restoration--Virginia--
Albemarle County. 4. Historic buildings--Virginia--Albemarle County--Design and
Construction. 5. Neoclassicism (Architecture)--Virginia--Albemarle County. 6. Levy, Uriah
Phillips, 1792-1862. 7. Levy family. 8. Thomas Jefferson Memorial Foundation, Inc.--History.
9. Historic Preservation--United States--Case studies. 10. Antisemitism--United States--Case
studies. I. Title. II. Series.

E332.74 .U76 2001
973.4'6'092--dc21
                                                                                    2001029645

ON THE COVER
Inset portrait: Uriah P. Levy, courtesy of the United States Naval Academy.
Background images: text from Uriah P. Levy's estate inventory list; Monticello's East Front,
c. 1870, courtesy of the Holsinger Collection, Alderman Library, University of Virginia.

This book was made possible by the generous support of the
Honorable John Langeloth Loeb, Jr.

Designed by Gibson Design Associates.

CONTENTS

PREFACE

$\mathcal{A}$merican concern about historic preservation grew gradually during the course of the twentieth century. Public and scholarly interest in particular sagas of historic preservation, meanwhile, have blossomed notably during the past quarter century. The Bicentennial of the American Revolution in 1775-6 provided a notable stimulus for both preservation activity and for interest in how the nation's most significant sites came to be regarded as a heritage requiring restoration and protection. We have become curious about the preservation process itself: how do sites worthy of preservation come to be identified as such, where do we find the resources necessary to facilitate preservation, and what has been the relationship between the private and public sectors in "saving" historic sites and structures for future generations? Above all, perhaps, we now want to know how places that have really mattered in our past are perceived, presented, and interpreted for visitors.

As interest in collective memory has increased, there has been a growing desire to be more inclusive when we describe significant episodes in the national narrative. Consequently the role of slaves in life at Mount Vernon, Monticello, and Colonial Williamsburg is being explained to a degree not envisioned a few decades ago. The same is true of the part played by Chinese laborers in building transcontinental railway lines during the post-Civil War ear, and by Texans of Mexican descent (Tejanos) in battling to defend the Alamo in 1836. For a very long time the Society for the Preservation of New England Antiquities (founded almost one hundred years ago) concentrated most of its efforts on saving eighteenth-century structures, and to a lesser degree, ones from the nineteenth century. The colonial period enjoyed a kind of privileged status. Not long ago, however, the SPNEA made the innovative decision to preserve and interpret the ultramodern 1938 home in Lincoln, Massachusetts, of Walter Gropius, founder of the

Bauhaus movement in art and architecture. Thus the stories presently told by means of properties owned by the SPNEA have become far more inclusive than its founders could have imagined.

Melvin Urofsky's account of the Levy family and Monticello deserves to be appreciated in the context of these expansive developments in the preservation movement and historical inquiry about it. The reader should be aware, however, that this book actually covers more ground than the dates specified in the title, 1834-1923. The reader will learn how Monticello came into being and underwent transformation during the half-century between the 1770s and the 1810s; why the estate left the possession of Jefferson's family after he died deeply in debt in 1826; but also why the two men, uncle and nephew, who did so much to "save" Monticello from physical disintegration for almost a century, were relegated to virtual oblivion from 1923 until 1985, when Uriah Levy, a career officer in the United States Navy, and Jefferson Monroe Levy, a real estate entrepreneur and member of Congress, finally received public recognition for their role in preserving a unique architectural masterpiece. Only in the past sixteen years have the official guidebooks to Monticello and the tours given there by interpreters told a full and balanced story of Jefferson's home—its literal ups and downs, possessions and attempted dispossessions amidst changing attitudes toward Thomas Jefferson himself, toward the value of historic preservation, toward the place and role of Jews in American life, and toward the responsibilities of government and the private sector in saving American "shrines."

I use the words "full and balanced" very deliberately in the preceding paragraph because the word "complete" must be reserved for this book. Professor Urofsky has researched the story exhaustively in many different archival repositories and provides us with a comprehensive story filled with dramatic incidents, partisan conflicts, and legal tangles that required years (sometimes decades) to resolve. We are fortunate, for example, that Professor Urofsky's background in legal history enables him to guide us through complex changes in American laws governing charitable trusts. As for melodrama, we learn that three months after Jefferson Monroe Levy ultimately sold Monticello in 1923 (following decades when he refused to sell because he so loved the place he had owned since 1879), he died of heart failure. And for profound irony, we learn that once the Thomas Jefferson Memorial Foundation took over the property in 1923-24, Jews played a very prominent role in getting the Foundation started and kept it on an even keel even as anti-Semitism utterly obscured the conscientious role played by Uriah Levy and his nephew at a time when large numbers of Americans were less devoted to Jefferson's principles and memory than they once had been.

Ironies abound in this narrative. When Uriah P. Levy died in 1863 following a distinguished career in the navy (despite its attempt to dismiss him in 1857 because of his determined opposition to the horrific maritime tradition of flogging), he actually wished to leave Monticello to the people of the United States; but the courts determined that he could do no such thing with a will written in New York concerning a property located in Virginia which at that time was in the hands of the insurgent Confederacy! Besides, what would the people of the United States actually do with such a property? Could the federal government eventually serve as some sort of custodian on behalf of the people of the United States? Apparently not. So went the prejudices of Americans at that time about government ownership and maintenance of historic places; and those prejudices seem to have run along a parallel path to the anti-Semitic ones directed against the Levys, despite their willingness to pour hundreds of thousands of dollars into the preservation of Monticello and despite their welcome to all sorts of visitors who arrived unannounced to see the home of the nation's third president, the man who drafted the Declaration of Independence and had the vision to make the Louisiana Purchase and to found the University of Virginia.

Visitors to Monticello between the 1820s and the 1880s repeatedly described the site as one of "desolation and ruin," and they were not entirely wrong, though Jefferson had actually built his home so well that it was structurally able to withstand decades of negligent resident caretakers and to respond successfully when Jefferson Monroe Levy began to nurse it back to health in the 1800s. Those very same words, "desolation and ruin," had also been the incantation of visitors to Mount Vernon until the 1860s, when a private association of women obtained control and responsibility for the property—a development that not only prompted the genesis of historic preservation in the United States, but also provided the precedent that such responsibility ought to reside with the private sector rather than state or federal government.

Readers of this book will also encounter the fascinating (almost bizarre) saga of the statue of Jefferson commissioned by Uriah Levy and then given by him to the United States, the anomalous abuses and relocations suffered by that statue which nevertheless stands in the U.S. Capitol today, the only statue in the building donated by a private citizen.

Perhaps the most arresting irony among many contained in this volume will be found in Professor Urofsky's evidence that Jefferson, remembered historically for his public statements on behalf of freedom of worship and toleration, actually left assorted traces of apparent anti-Semitism in his private writings. As the author indicates in chapter two, Jefferson seems to have considered Jewish ideas of God and his attributes "degrading & injurious" and their ethics often "irreconcilable with the sound dictates of reason and morality" and "repulsive & anti-social as respecting other nations." Corresponding with John Adams, Jefferson approved of the works of Johann Brucker, which denigrated Jewish philosophy and ethics. And in writing to Connecticut's Ezra Stiles, a prominent cleric and president of Yale College, Jefferson declared that "I am not a Jew" and then misrepresented Jewish views concerning punishment.

Uriah Levy knew nothing of these feelings when he repeatedly expressed lavish praise for Jefferson. Here is a forthright extract from Levy's statement at his trial in 1857 when the navy sought to discharge him: "My parents were Israelites, and I was nurtured in the faith of my ancestors. In deciding to adhere to it, I have but exercised a right guaranteed to me by the Constitution of my native state and of the United States, a right given to all men by their Maker, a right more precious to each of us than life itself. But, while claiming and exercising this freedom of conscience, I have never failed to acknowledge and respect the like freedom in others." As Professor Urofsky suggests, this declaration might well be described as "Jeffersonian," or at least, our customary image of Jeffersonian values.

Thomas Jefferson's reputation has arguably undergone more ups and downs than that of any American president. His achievements and versatility were astonishingly great. His shortcomings and flawed views he managed to keep private.

Historians and the public have admired him greatly and without stint in some periods while expressing grave doubts about certain aspects of his character at other times. With the passage of time a more judicious, realistic, and balanced assessment is bound to emerge. In the pages that follow, he appears as a somewhat impractical idealist—especially imprudent about expenditures, particularly during his retirement years when he compounded his own debts enormously by signing notes on behalf of others who sought his good name as protection against risky schemes of their own. Had Jefferson been more prudent about financial matters, the history of Monticello after his death might very well have turned out rather differently.

But we must write history as it happened, and not as we might wish it had happened. The narrative in this book, filled with unexpected twists and turns, is history as it happened rather than what might have been if Jefferson had been superhuman rather than a brilliantly gifted but mortal visionary who lacked guile at times and perhaps needed guidance when it came to the realm of household finance and estate management. One last irony: Uriah Levy's shrewd investments in New York real estate made it possible for him and his fiercely determined nephew to achieve considerable wealth and succeed in holding and perpetuating Monticello, which Jefferson could not. It is that compelling account that follows.

—MICHAEL KAMMEN
Cornell University

INTRODUCTION

*A*lthough I did not know it at the time, I first became involved in this project nearly twenty years ago. On a winter morning in 1984, I read in the *Richmond Times-Dispatch* that Daniel P. Jordan, my friend and colleague in the history department at Virginia Commonwealth University, had been named director of the Thomas Jefferson Memorial Foundation, now the Thomas Jefferson Foundation, the private, nonprofit corporation that owns and operates Monticello. I had barely finished my coffee when the phone began to ring and people I knew in the Jewish community both in Richmond and elsewhere wanted to know two things: what kind of person was this new director, and would he do right by the Levys?

I had no problem answering the first question. Dan was and is a good historian, a fine administrator, and above all, a gentleman. No question existed in my mind that he and Monticello would be a perfect fit. As to the second question, I had a little trouble. At the time I was in the process of transferring my research and teaching interests from American Zionism (primarily a twentieth century phenomenon) to American constitutional history. I had no idea what one had to do in order to "do right by the Levys." Saul Viener, a Richmond businessman, amateur historian, and past president of the American Jewish Historical Society, told me how many Jewish scholars and community leaders were upset by the fact that although the Levy family had literally saved Monticello—not once but twice—in the nineteenth century, and had actually lived there longer than Jefferson did, memory of their tenure and their contribution to the saving of Mr. Jefferson's home had been ignored or minimized by the leadership of the Thomas Jefferson Memorial Foundation. Moreover, many scholars also overlooked the Levy ownership, and claimed that "a century of ruin and neglect" marked Monticello between Jefferson's death and its purchase by the Foundation.

When I got to school, I immediately congratulated Dan and warned him about the Levy issue. Dan thanked me, and I did not think about the Levys and Monticello again until I received an invitation in 1985 to the rededication of the Rachel Phillips Levy gravesite at Monticello (the details will be found in chapter six). By that one gesture, Dan won the trust and gratitude of the Jewish community. After the ceremony I wandered around Monticello for a while, and, like so many other visitors, marveled at the beauty of the house and its surroundings. Then I left, and again gave no more thought to the Levys; I thought the issue had been resolved.

But Dan Jordan had more in mind. Although the interpreters at Monticello now included some information on the Levys, he wanted the full story published in the Foundation's monograph series. In the spring of 1998 I met with Dan and Susan Stein, Monticello's curator. They invited me to do a book on the Levy family and Monticello.

Although I protested that I was not a nineteenth-century scholar, in the end I agreed to do it, and the Honorable John Langeloth Loeb, Jr., graciously provided the funds to support the research, writing, and publication of this book. His generosity is extraordinary and most appreciated but not necessarily surprising. Ambassador Loeb has long been supportive of many worthy causes, and his philanthropy has been notable for its enlightened proportions. His personal involvement with the Levy story dates from a trip to Monticello while visiting his longtime friend, Felicia Warburg Rogan; at the time, Ambassador Loeb was disturbed that there was no mention of the Levy stewardship on the mountaintop. Subsequently, he supported the reprinting of a booklet from the dedication ceremony of the gravesite of Rachel Phillips Levy at Monticello. This booklet contains a number of scholarly articles about the Levy family and its remarkable history. He also took part in the Thomas Jefferson Memorial Foundation's seventy-fifth anniversary program at the Morgan Library in New York City in December 1998, at which it was announced that he was underwriting this book. At all stages, Ambassador Loeb has been encouraging and supportive.

I have enjoyed writing this small book immensely. It has been a challenge (we twentieth-century historians are not used to reading hand-written documents), but it has also been the type of work I have always liked, where I have learned something new and have been challenged by the task. And for that I must thank Dan.

The story of the Levys and Monticello is a story of the blending of cultures and personalities, of Yankees and Virginians, of Jews and Christians, of city folk and rural people. It is the story of the power of a symbol, and how in America such symbols cut across lines of religion and class and ethnicity. And behind all of this is the towering presence of Thomas Jefferson.

Because we are still so relatively young a nation, we have had to manufacture our national symbols when we can, rather than let them evolve over centuries. The historic preservation movement in this country is really only a little over a century old, but its work has had enormous significance. Americans go to Mount Vernon or Orchard House (home of the Alcotts) or Monticello to learn of their past, and it is hard for us to realize that some of these houses have had rather long interim histories. Mount Vernon, for example, was not acquired by the Mount Vernon Ladies' Association until 1853, long after Washington's death in 1799. Nearly one hundred years passed between the death of our nation's third president and the purchase of his home by the Foundation; it would be many years more before Monticello would be restored to what we believe it was like in Jefferson's time.

Each year more than a half-million people go to Monticello in part to marvel at the house and surrounding beauty, and to pay reverence at the gravesite with that unique and marvelous epitaph. What we are really doing is taking a history lesson; we are learning about what sort of people we were, who were our leaders, and what ideas and ideals they contributed to the making of America. I think there is no more appropriate day for Monticello than July Fourth, not because on that day in 1776 a group of patriot rebels signed the Declaration Thomas Jefferson had drafted, but because each year it is the site where scores of new Americans, immigrants who have come here to join us, take their oath of allegiance and become citizens of this country. Had it not been for the Levys, there would be no Monticello today, there would be no chance to pay homage to Jefferson, there would be no history lesson—for us or for our new brethren.

A number of people have helped me in this work, and it is a pleasure to acknowledge their help and to thank them for it. Susan Stein and William

Beiswanger of Monticello read the manuscript with extreme care, and saved me from countless errors regarding Monticello's history and design. Saul Viener, Harley and Richard Lewis—all of whom played a role in bringing the Levys back—shared their memories with me and also read the manuscript. Professor Philippa Strum of the City University of New York is an ideal reader, asking all of the right questions and pointing out errors of style as well as substance. Professor James Oldham of the Georgetown University Law Center and Professor William LaPiana of New York Law School read chapter three and helped me refine the story of New York law in the nineteenth century. One of Bill's students, Donna Curcio, spent some time at the Hall of Records digging up material relating to Uriah Levy's will. Needless to say, any mistakes remaining in this volume I managed to make by myself.

I have been extremely fortunate in having Emily Catherine Duke, a history student at the University of Virginia, as my primary research assistant. Emily is the ideal assistant, needing little direction and having the historical sense to track down leads and find material of which I had been totally unaware. My debt to her is boundless.

Much of the manuscript research for this book took place at the library of the American Jewish Historical Society in New York, and I am very grateful to the executive director, Michael Feldberg, and his staff for all the help and courtesy they showed me. In the other libraries I worked in—the New York Public Library and Columbia University in New York, the University of Virginia Library in Charlottesville, the Virginia Historical Society, the Beth Ahabah Museum and Archives, and Virginia Commonwealth University in Richmond, and the archives of Congregation Mikveh Israel in Philadelphia—the staffs made my work ever so much easier by their friendliness and their knowledge of materials. Kevin Proffitt, the chief archivist at the American Jewish Archives in Cincinnati, utilized that institution's excellent index to identify and copy for me all Levy-related material in its holdings. W. Robert Ellis, Jr., the archivist in the Old Military Branch of the National Archives in Washington, D.C., similarly identified for me where all of the Uriah Levy and related files could be found. And last but not least, Dr. James Horn, the Saunders Director of the International Center for Jefferson

Studies, served as general project manager and producer, aided by Beth Cheuk and Gaye Wilson. To all of these people a heartfelt "thank you."

Finally, this book is dedicated to Saul Viener. Saul was one of the first people to welcome my wife Susan and me when we moved to Richmond in 1974. He and I have worked together in the American Jewish Historical Society and the Southern Jewish Historical Society, as well as on a number of local enterprises. As readers will discover, Saul helped make it possible for the Levys to receive their due. This book is dedicated to him both for his friendship and for his devotion to all things related to Jewish history.

The Thomas Jefferson Foundation dedicates this volume to Ambassador John L. Loeb, Jr. It does so because he has been a loyal friend of the Jefferson legacy and of the American Jewish tradition over the years. Throughout his successful career as an investment banker, environmentalist, wine-maker, and ambassador to Denmark under the appointment of President Ronald Reagan, he has been warmly supportive of causes related to his faith. The ambassador's Jewish roots in America go back to Colonial times and are intertwined with some of this country's most distinguished families. In addition to his faithful commitment to the Levy story, he most recently made a significant gift to advance the preservation of Touro Synagogue in Newport, Rhode Island, as well as the planning of a visitors center there.

It should also be noted that his childhood friend, the late Rodman C. Rockefeller, was a stalwart member of the Monticello Board of Trustees and also a firm believer in sharing the Levy stewardship with a broader audience. Ambassador Loeb was present when Mr. Rockefeller spoke passionately on the subject at a Monticello event held at the Knickerbocker Club in New York in the spring of 1999. John Loeb is a consummate gentleman, and the Foundation is proud to call him a friend.

—MELVIN I. UROFSKY
Richmond
October 2000

Monticello West Lawn (Thomas Jefferson Foundation, photo by Leonard Phillips).

Chapter One

THOMAS JEFFERSON BUILDS A HOUSE

"And our own dear Monticello. Where has nature spread so rich a mantle under the eye? Mountains, forests, rocks, rivers! With what majesty do we ride there above the storms! How sublime to look down into the workhouse of nature, to see her clouds, hail, snow, rain, thunder, all fabricated at our feet! And the glorious sun rising, as if out of a distant water, just gilding the tops of the mountains, and giving life to all nature!"

—THOMAS JEFFERSON[1]

The beauty that Thomas Jefferson described over two centuries ago is still very much in evidence at Monticello, the house he built near Charlottesville, Virginia, and one can even today get a sense of what Jefferson saw and loved in his own time. Standing 867 feet above sea level, one looks east from the house over the Rivanna River to the gentle hills of Albemarle County. Facing west one can spend hours watching the shifting light patterns on the Blue Ridge Mountains. And if one stands on the north terrace, one can see the University of Virginia in Charlottesville, and recall how in his old age Jefferson established the University and watched its construction through a telescope. Surely this natural beauty constituted one—if not the chief—feature that attracted Jefferson to the spot when he chose it to be the seat of his estate around 1768.[2]

The land on which Jefferson would build his house and working plantation[3] had been in the family since the Crown had patented it to Jefferson's father Peter in 1735, and lay not far from Jefferson's birthplace, the house at Shadwell. Following Peter's death, his son came into a large amount of land, including several properties in Albemarle County. A month after his twenty-fifth birthday,

Jefferson entered into an agreement for leveling the top of a gently sloping hill on one of those parcels so he could build a house there. He already had chosen a name for it, "little mountain," or in old Italian, Monticello, and in 1769, the same year he first entered the Virginia House of Burgesses, he put men to work digging a cellar in the hard, red Virginia clay.[4] It would take him more than forty years before he finished building and rebuilding; the house took its final shape around 1809, but in many ways Jefferson never stopped tinkering with it. As he told a friend, "Architecture is my delight, and putting up and pulling down, one of my favorite amusements."[5]

Most Virginia planters of the eighteenth century built their plantation houses on the plains near the James or another river, so they could easily ship their tobacco and other products to sea. Jefferson, who had no formal training at all in architecture, chose the top of a mountain for it and planned the design himself. Monticello would be a working farm, but tobacco and other cash crops would be grown on the additional properties that he owned. Jefferson certainly knew about the great houses in the colony, such as Rosewell, Westover, and Carter's Grove, and often visited their owners. But he did not like Georgian architecture and wanted something else. He immersed himself in books about architecture until he discovered the neo-classical works of Andrea Palladio—not the monumental creations, but the smaller country villas designed by the great sixteenth-century Italian architect. He had in his library several copies of Palladio's *Quattro Libri*, which he referred to as "the Bible," as well as studies of the master's English disciples, James Gibbs and Robert Morris. Jefferson did not slavishly imitate Palladio; rather, he adopted the Italian's cool, clean lines to meet his own tastes.

Little had been done on the mountaintop when a fire destroyed the Shadwell house, after which Jefferson moved to a small one-room dwelling, believed by some scholars to be what is now Monticello's south pavilion. In 1771 he wrote his friend James Ogilvie, "I have but one room which, like the cobbler's, serves me for parlour, for kitchen and hall. I may add, for bed chamber and study too …. I have hope, however, of getting more elbow room this summer."[6]

Yet the following year, when Jefferson married Martha Wayles Skelton, he brought her back to a small and still unfinished house. Over the next ten years

Jefferson's family expanded as Martha bore him six children (three of whom died in infancy), and work proceeded slowly but steadily on the house. His workmen were still making and laying bricks when Jefferson rode off to Philadelphia in the spring of 1776 to write the Declaration of Independence, and in 1778 he contracted for stone columns. One of our earliest accounts of Monticello comes from a German officer serving with the British who had been captured at Saratoga and later imprisoned at the Barracks outside Charlottesville. Jefferson, then governor of Virginia, extended the hospitality of his home to the officers. The unidentified man wrote home, and his letter was published in a Hamburg newspaper. Jacob Rubsamen, a German-speaking Virginian, sent a translation to Jefferson in December 1780:[7]

South Pavilion at Monticello (Thomas Jefferson Foundation, photo by Peter J. Hatch).

> The Governor possesses a Noble Spirit of Building, he is now finishing an elegant building projected according to his own fancy. In his parlour he is creating on the Ceiling a Compass of his own invention by wich he can Know the strength as well as Direction of the Winds. I have promised to paint the Compass for it .... As all Virginians are fond of music, he is particularly so. You will find in his House an Elegant harpsicord Piano forte and some Violins. The latter he performs well upon himself, the former his Lady touches very skilfully and who, is in all Respects a very agreable Sensible and Accomplished Lady.

When the British rode up the mountain in 1781 they found a still unfinished house.[8] The following year Jefferson's beloved wife died, and construction on the still unfinished house stopped, with Jefferson too disconsolate to proceed any further.[9]

There are really two Monticellos, the first one that occupied Jefferson from 1767 until 1782, and a second and larger house that he began early in 1794 after retiring as secretary of state. The two houses differ significantly in design. The earlier version is clearly Palladian, while the second represents Jefferson's more mature architectural thought as well as the knowledge of French architecture he gained in the 1780s when he served as the American ambassador to France.

Jefferson's drawing of the first Monticello (Thomas Jefferson Foundation).

The first house consisted of three discrete connected buildings, which Jefferson termed a "middle building" and "wings." Two semi-octagonal bays were later added to the wings. This plan allowed Jefferson to build any one part of the house and to use it while constructing the other sections. So he started with the dining room, which the newlyweds desperately needed, since they could hardly entertain in the cramped quarters in which they slept and that was jammed with furniture, books and clothing.[10] In its near-final form, the first Monticello consisted of an entrance hall which led into a large parlor with an octagonal wall facing west; above this room stood Jefferson's library. On the south side of the parlor was the main bedroom, and on the north side the dining room, each ending in an octagonal bow end. It is assumed that additional bedrooms were located on the second floor. The parlor opened onto a broad lawn, with service buildings and slave quarters on each side.

On most plantations these "dependencies" would be in plain view, but Jefferson's plan, conceived in the 1770s but not constructed until after 1800, called for a beautiful garden and lawn as well as a house, and so he devised a unique design to hide the necessary adjuncts of his household—the laundry, stable, and other workrooms. He took advantage of the hilltop terrain to place the dependencies behind and below the house, thus leaving the view of the house from the lawn, as well as the view of the lawn from the parlor window, unobstructed. Nor could one see the comings and goings of the slaves, since they entered the work-rooms from the outside and below the sightline of a viewer on the house level. Jefferson also used the roofs of the dependencies to form L-shaped terraces brack-eting the lawn. This allowed for one side of each dependency room to be open to air and light, and for the slaves to walk under cover to the main house in inclement weather.

Much more than the later house, this first effort is very Palladian in form and decoration. Indeed the design for the dependencies followed Palladio's advice to hide the "meanest" rooms. Drawing an analogy to the human body, the Italian praised God for ordering the members of the human body "so as to make the finest of them to be the most exposed to sight, and concealing them that are not seemingly so." So in a building "the finest and most noble parts of it be the most exposed to public view, and the less agreeable disposed in byplaces, and removed from sight as much as possible."[11] Jefferson also relied on the writings of the English architect Robert Morris, whose counsels of moderation matched Jefferson's own tastes. "I think a building, well proportioned, without dress, will ever please, as a plain coat may sit as graceful and easy on a well-proportioned man …. But if you will be lavish in your ornament, your structure will look rather like a fop, with a superfluity of gaudy tinsel, than a real decoration."[12]

We know relatively little about how Jefferson furnished his first house. The stream of visitors who later left detailed records of what they saw, viewed not the first, but the second house. The Hessian officer noted the presence of musical instruments and some interior decoration. One visitor who did see the original house in as complete a form as it would take was the marquis de Chastellux, a member of the French Academy and an officer in General Rochambeau's army encamped at Williamsburg in the spring of 1782. A well-traveled man learned in the arts, the marquis recorded the following observations:[13]

> The house, of which Mr. Jefferson was the architect, and often the builder, is constructed in an Italian style, and is quite tasteful, although not however without some faults; it consists of a large

square pavilion, into which one enters through two porticoes orna-mented with columns. The ground floor consists chiefly of a large and lofty *salon*, or drawing room, which is to be decorated entirely in the antique style; above the *salon* is a library of the same form; two small wings, with only a ground floor and attic, are joined to this pavilion, and are intended to communicate with the kitchen, offices, etc, which will form on either side a kind of basement topped by a terrace. My object in giving these details is not to describe the house, but to prove that it resembles none of the others seen in this coun-try; so that it may be said that Mr. Jefferson is the first American who has consulted the Fine Arts to know how he should shelter himself from the weather.

Jefferson's public career kept him away from Monticello for long periods of time, but none longer than the five years he served as the young nation's repre-sentative to France. When he returned in 1789 he practically tore down the old house, which had fallen into disrepair during his absence. But even if the build-ing had been superbly cared for, it no longer met Jefferson's needs or tastes. After

Maison Carrée at Nîmes (courtesy of Musée du Louvre).

living in Paris and visiting its great public buildings as well as the city and country houses of the nobility, Monticello seemed small and provincial to him.[14]

Given Jefferson's penchant for "put-ting up and tearing down," he appears to have taken every opportunity to visit dif-ferent types of houses. He admired the Roman ruins in the south of France, espe-cially the Maison Carrée at Nîmes, draw-ings of which he had already used as a

model for the Virginia state capitol in Richmond.[15] But the houses French noble-men built in the last years of the reign of Louis XVI especially attracted him.

Relatively small compared to the great manor houses popular two generations earlier, these homes, in the style of French Roman classicism, emphasized comfort and privacy. He declared himself "violently smitten" with the Hôtel de Salm in Paris, now the Museum of the Legion of Honor across the Seine from the Louvre. He went to look at it often from the Tuileries, and this one-story town house with a dome certainly influenced him as he set out to remodel Monticello.[16] Though by no means abandoning his admiration of Palladio, he had, as Dumas Malone suggests, outgrown him. Jefferson "was disposed to be more eclectic and less rigid in domestic architecture than in public, but he remained a classicist in both fields. In France his classicism was revitalized, as he caught up with the fashion."[17]

The plan that Jefferson settled upon catered not only to his aesthetic taste, but to his personal comforts as well. From the west the house appears to be only one story tall, topped by a dome in the central portion, and students of architec-

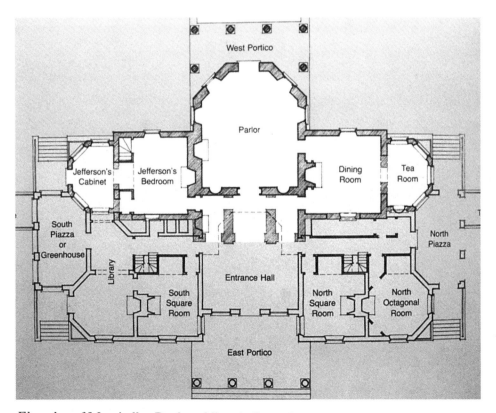

Floorplan of Monticello. Darkened lines indicate the outline of the first Monticello (Thomas Jefferson Foundation).

ture claim that from this view the house looks most Palladian. On the east he pushed out the portico and added a large entrance hall, which is now the first room that visitors to Monticello enter. On each side he placed a square room and a bay—or bow—room corresponding to the ones already in the first house. He claimed one of these bay rooms for his own study; it stood next to his bedroom, the square room on the south side of the parlor. In fact, the whole south side of the first floor formed a large suite, with three additional rooms being given over to his library, one of the largest private collections of books in America at the time.[18] On the north side of the house, the square room corresponding to Jefferson's bedroom served as the dining room, while the bay room was used for tea and light repasts. Two other rooms on the north side served as bedrooms for guests. Throughout the first floor one found light everywhere, streaming in through the tall French doors, or the equally tall triple-sash windows that Jefferson designed himself.[19]

Instead of a large second story and two attic wings, Jefferson planned a mezzanine floor that contained four bedrooms corresponding to the new rooms below. Still another bedroom could be found above the southeast octagon, and higher up on the third floor, and wholly invisible from the outside, were three bedrooms with skylights but no windows. The space under the dome provided a large room, but there is no agreement as to what purposes the room was put.[20] In nearly all the bedrooms Jefferson provided alcoves for beds, following the style he had seen in France. He even designed the curtains. Anna Thornton, who visited the house in 1802, wrote "when we went to be bed we had to mount a little ladder of a staircase about 2 feet wide and very steep, into rooms with beds fixed up in recesses in the walls—the windows square and small turning in pivots. Everything has a whimsical and droll appearance."[21]

Walking through the rooms a visitor could not have failed to be struck by the eclecticism found there, reflecting Jefferson's wide-ranging interests. In the parlor stood not only the harpsichord played by his wife and later his daughter, but also several musical instruments and a large collection of musical scores, ranging from pieces for voice and accompaniment by Vivaldi, Corelli and Haydn, to popular songs and ballad operas. One entered the parlor from the entrance hall through double glass doors that opened simultaneously, with the chain mechanism that he devised concealed beneath the floor.

In his study was a high-backed swivel chair made for him in New York. Jefferson also had a polygraph made by the artist Charles Willson Peale and Isaac Hawkins, which made copies of his letters even as he wrote them. Throughout the house were prints, maps and paintings, many of which were copies of Old Masters, which had been bought in Paris.

An amateur scientist, he had all the necessary instruments for measuring weather —thermometer, barometer and wind vane—and he faithfully recorded the daily weather season after season, year after year. The rod of his weather vane extended through the portico roof to a dial on the ceiling below so that it could be read from the portico or glimpsed from the entrance hall. Clocks galore, of all kinds and descriptions, populated the rooms, but none so striking as the seven-day clock in the entrance hall that still fascinates visitors. Jefferson had it built to his specifications in Philadelphia. Its escapement and chiming

mechanism are driven by two cannonball-like weights suspended by two cables that run from the clock to pulleys in the corner and then down the walls. The weights on the south wall tell the day of the week as they pass markers. There was no room for Friday and Saturday, so Jefferson had a hole cut in the floor, and Friday afternoons the weights passed into the basement, where they stayed until Sunday morning, when a slave rewound the mechanism.[22]

The two-story entrance hall, through which visitors still enter Monticello, then and now is one of the most striking rooms in any American house. George Ticknor, who visited in 1815, described the hall, or as he termed it, a "museum," as follows:[23]

Cabinet at Monticello (Thomas Jefferson Foundation, photo by Robert C. Lautman).

You enter, by a glass folding-door, into a hall which reminds you of Fielding's "Man of the Mountain," by the strange furniture of its walls. On one side hang the heads and horns of an elk, a deer, and a buffalo; another is covered with curiosities which Lewis and Clark found in their wild and perilous expedition. On the third, among many other striking matters, was the head of a mammoth ... containing the only *os frontis*, Mr. Jefferson tells me, that has yet been found. On the fourth side, in odd union with a fine painting of the Repentence of St. Peter, is an Indian map on leather, of the southern waters of the Missouri, and an Indian representation of a bloody battle, handed down in their traditions.

As Susan Stein notes, the hallway served to highlight one of the *leitmotifs* of Jefferson's scheme for Monticello, that the selection and arrangement of objects be educational rather than decorative. "He believed that the future of the United States absolutely depended upon the informed involvement of each citizen." For the people to make informed choices, they had to be edified, "and Jefferson seized every opportunity to advance his cause."[24]

Although the layout, decorations and conveniences suited its owner perfectly, in many instances they detracted from what some architectural students view as the purity of the building. It is, according to Dumas Malone, inferior as an architectural design to Poplar Forest, the house Jefferson later built in Bedford County, and Malone claims that the various parts of Monticello "do not hang together," even though he achieved "pleasing and impressive results downstairs and outside."[25]

But Monticello is not just an architectural relic, nor do a half-million visitors a year go up the mountain to admire just the aesthetics of the house. It captures our attention because it is not just the house where Jefferson lived, but a place—house and plantation—that reflects his spirit and tastes. Monticello is an extension of Jefferson; its comforts and conveniences suited his own tastes and in many ways are quite modern, a sensibility that form should follow function, that a house should have pleasing lines and also suit the needs of its occupants.

Jefferson himself recognized the flaws in the house he so loved. To Benjamin Latrobe, an American architect whom he greatly admired, Jefferson wrote shortly after leaving the presidency and returning to Monticello: "My essay in Architecture has been so much subordinated to the law of convenience, and affected also by the circumstances of change in the original design, that it is liable to some unfavorable and just critiques. But what nature has done for us is sublime and beautiful and unique."[26] And at Monticello nature and art lived in majestic harmony.

And there he had been, and always would be, happiest. In 1780 he wrote: "Abstracted from home, I know no happiness in this world." Seven years later while in France he declared that "I am as happy nowhere else, and in no other society." A full year after leaving the presidency he expressed his great joy at being home again atop the hill. "I am retired to Monticello, where in the bosom of my family and surrounded by my books, I enjoy a repose to which I have long been a stranger."[27] In August 1809, as he showed Margaret Bayard Smith around the grounds, he explained that his "long absence has left a wilderness around me," and then joyfully expounded on his plans for the gardens.[28]

A visitor in 1802 thought the house would never be finished. Anna Thornton thought Monticello "quite a handsome place," then went on to note: "Mr. J. has been 27 years engaged in improving the place, but he has pulled down & built up again so often, that nothing is completed, nor do I think ever will be."[29] Despite Mrs. Thornton's doubts, by 1809 Jefferson had finished the interior of the house roughly as it is today, but the porticoes on the exterior were not completed until 1823. Jefferson would tinker with pieces of the house nearly until his death on July 4, 1826. Long before that day, however, the house had begun a slow slide into disrepair. For at least the last ten years of his life, Jefferson did not have the financial resources to maintain Monticello properly. A visitor in 1824 noted that the "house is rather old and going to decay; appearances about his yard and hill are rather slovenly."[30]

Why would a man who had inherited over 5,300 acres of land, and who at the time of his death still owned 130 slaves, be reduced to near bankruptcy? Did Monticello swallow up his fortune as he indulged his desire to "put up and pull down" buildings? Did his extravagant purchases while in Paris push him over an edge from which he never recovered? Was he simply foolish when it came to managing his estate? After all, as he wrote shortly before his death, "A Virginia estate requires skill and attention. Skill I had nil, and attention I could not give.

Thomas Jefferson by Gilbert Stuart, 1805 (jointly owned by Monticello, the Thomas Jefferson Foundation, and the National Portrait Gallery, Smithsonian Institution. Purchase funds provided by the Regents of the Smithsonian Institution, the Trustees of the Thomas Jefferson Foundation, and the Enid and Crosby Kemper Foundation).

That was engrossed by more imperious calls, which after acceptance had a right of preference to all others. The wonder rather is that I should have been so long as 60 years in arriving at the ultimate, unavoidable result."[31]

To some extent this claim is correct—while his neighbors paid attention to their plantations, Thomas Jefferson served his country almost without interruption from 1774 until 1809. During the time when his countrymen were recouping their fortunes after the War for Independence, Jefferson was in Paris serving as minister to France. And while from 1789 on he was able to spend periods of time at home and looking after his affairs, he could never devote all of his energies to that task. Having agreed to the service of the country, it had "a right of preference to all others."[32]

About a year before he retired from the presidency he wrote to his daughter that "I now have the gloomy prospect of retiring from office loaded with serious debts, which will materially affect the tranquility of my retirement."[33] Nonetheless, in March 1809 as he prepared to return to Monticello, Jefferson believed that he had sufficient assets to pay off all of his debts. In the summer of 1809 he estimated that his property was worth at least fifty times a debt of $4,500 that might ultimately be charged against his estate. Whether this is true or not, Jefferson believed then and for many years after that his assets greatly exceeded his liabilities. But the problem lay in realizing those assets—consisting almost entirely in property and slaves—at anywhere near their supposed value.[34]

Without going too deeply into all the twists and turns of Jefferson's finances, we can chart a road that began early in his adult years and continued until his death. It is a road marked by an ignorance of market conditions, an attention to detail that gave him a false sense of security, unwise decisions, excessive expenditures, and a selling off of assets that never managed to keep up with his debt.[35] One should also note that southern planters in general were continuously in debt, and never saw it as a sign of moral or financial inadequacy. They were after all, both gentlemen and farmers, two groups who habitually borrowed money. In addition, except in the most prosperous of times, there was never an abundance of hard cash in the South. Planters borrowed against their crops, and in good years paid off their bills on time; in bad years they renewed the unpaid balances. Debts were part of plantation life, and very often the son who inherited the land also inherited the debts on the property. Gentlemen did not worry about money, and Jefferson, who had to worry about money a great deal toward the end of his life, shared his fellow southerners' attitude toward debt as a way of life.[36]

At the end of the Revolution, Jefferson, like many Virginians, found his personal finances in a shambles. The English markets that had bought Virginia tobacco were now closed to Americans, and although the planters did not have to pay back debts owed to British merchants — at least not immediately — neither did they have much in the way of income. Most planters grew foodstuffs for their own households and sold off what surplus they might have in local markets. By the time this economy revived, Jefferson was away, and did not have time to pay close attention to his lands until he left the State Department in early 1794.

Never a great fan of tobacco, Jefferson grew the crop only on his Bedford County lands, and tried to grow grains, especially wheat, at Monticello and on his other holdings.[37] The inveterate tinkerer also experimented with new ideas in farming, such as crop rotation, and the duc de la Rochefoucald-Liancourt, an experienced agriculturist himself, praised Jefferson at the time of a successful wheat harvest in 1796. "His superior mind," the duke wrote, "directs the management of his domestic concerns with the same abilities, activity, and regularity which he evinced in the conduct of public affairs."[38]

But just as Jefferson's plans stood on the verge of success, a severe drought in the fall of 1796, accompanied by a particularly severe winter, combined to destroy his next wheat crop. Fortunately, tobacco then brought high prices, and the output from his Bedford farm managed to pay immediate bills and taxes. Then Jefferson returned to public life, and for the next several years had to leave management of his estates in the hands of others. His son-in-law Thomas Mann Randolph, to whom Jefferson entrusted his properties, seems to have been good at growing crops, but not at the business of farming. Beyond that, many of the things that Jefferson tried at Monticello in terms of crop rotation and fertilizing techniques would not have been cost-effective in the short run, would not have increased his profits, and would not have added to the value of his estate.[39]

Thomas Mann Randolph (photo courtesy of Virginia Historical Society; location of original unknown).

Throughout these years, even as Jefferson tried to manage his estate, he found himself getting ever deeper into debt. When his father-in-law died, much of the Wayles land came to Jefferson through his wife, but so did enormous debts that took Jefferson years to pay down.[40] He began selling off parcels of land, but while he managed to keep afloat this way, land values in Virginia were in a steady decline during this period. Jefferson's evaluation of his property was always far greater than it was actually worth.

Had he been a good manager, his salary of $25,000 a year for his eight years as president should have allowed him to eliminate his debts, perhaps even accrue a surplus. But it did not, and he returned to Monticello in the late spring of 1809 more deeply in debt than ever. He planned on devoting one-half the annual income of $2,500 from his Bedford estates to paying off the debt. However, declining economic conditions in Virginia in general, and in the tobacco market in particular, combined with bad weather, the market dislocations of the War of 1812, and his own spending habits, to put him more deeply in debt. By 1815 he owed over $50,000, and the sale of his library to the national government for about $24,000 eliminated less than half of the claims against him. There was little he could do after that, and even selling off land proved impossible after the economic recession of 1819, which saw property values plummet.[41] Although the Virginia legislature offered him an $80,000 interest-free loan, Jefferson felt compelled to refuse because the money was "wrung from the taxpayer."[42]

During all this time Jefferson kept minute track of his income and expenses, but nonetheless appeared to be "profoundly ignorant of his own financial condition."[43] In a letter to his former secretary, William Short, from whom Jefferson had regularly borrowed money over many years, he enclosed a statement of how much he owed Short, and the amount astonished him. "For tho' I kept such exact entries in my daily memorandum book as would enable me, or anybody else, to state the account accurately in a day, yet I had never collected the items, or formed them into an account, till within these few days." When he did so, he discovered that he owed $10,000 more than he had previously thought.[44] The editors of the *Memorandum Book* suggest that the very act of writing down his daily accounts contributed to his problems. The recording of minutiae gave Jefferson an "artificial sense of order in his financial world" which, combined with his eternal optimism, prevented him from taking the hard but necessary steps that might have saved him.[45]

The blow that crushed him, however, was in large measure not entirely his fault, and that part of the blame that can be laid upon him resulted from his generous nature and desire to help his family. In June 1817 Jefferson went to Wilson Cary Nicholas, a former congressman, governor of Virginia, and now president of the newly opened Richmond branch of the Bank of the United States, and Nicholas helped him secure a loan of $3,000 with assurances that it would be renewed. There was little reason for Nicholas not to help the former president; his daughter Jane had married Jefferson's grandson, Thomas Jefferson Randolph, and the two families knew each other intimately. That fall and winter the bank renewed the notes, and although an infestation of the Hessian fly all but ruined his wheat crop, Jefferson managed to make the interest payments on his various loans. He recognized, however, that he would need additional funds to meet obligations due in May. So he turned once again to Nicholas, who arranged for a second loan of $3,000 from the Bank of the United States, and further obligated Jefferson to him by voluntarily endorsing the former president's note.

A few weeks later Nicholas asked Jefferson for a favor, namely that Jefferson endorse two of the banker's notes, each for $10,000. Nicholas told him that the endorsement would be needed for at most a year, and in any case his estate, worth at least $350,000, would easily cover the obligations. The banker explained that he was then engaged in extensive and complicated business transactions, and that he would never have turned to Jefferson "but under the most entire confidence that you can never suffer the slightest inconvenience from complying with it."[46] Nicholas told Jefferson not to sign if he had any doubts at all, but sent along the notes and thus put Jefferson in a most awkward position. After all, Nicholas had twice helped him, and had on his own endorsed the second note; in addition, how could he say no to his beloved grandson's father-in-law. Although burdened by his own large debts, with great reluctance, Jefferson agreed.

Warning signs of the Panic of 1819 first appeared in the summer of 1818, as the Bank of the United States, concerned about the amount of money borrowed for land speculation, began to rein in outstanding loans. It informed its borrowers that all notes up for renewal would be restricted by 12½ percent; each of Jefferson's notes for $3,000, therefore, could only be renewed for $2,625. "The notification is really like a clap of thunder to me," Jefferson wrote a friend, "for God knows I have no means in the world of raising money on so sudden a call."[47] But Jefferson managed to scrape together the needed funds to pay interest, and, perhaps thanks to Nicholas, the Bank of the United States renewed the two notes at their full amount in September. Nicholas also sent along a request for Jefferson to endorse the renewals of his own notes for $20,000.

In the spring and summer of 1819 Jefferson's fortunes took a sharp downward turn. Economic conditions throughout the country were bad, and in Virginia crop failures augmented the general economic distress. The master of Monticello had to borrow money from one bank to repay notes due at another, and then came a blow from which he would never recover—Wilson Cary Nicholas defaulted. The former governor's estate, which he had told Jefferson amounted to more than $350,000, would not bring in enough to pay the more than $200,000 in debts held against him. As Jefferson later told James Madison, although his own debts had become considerable, they were "not beyond the effect of some lopping of property, which would have been little felt, when our friend Nicholas gave me the *coup de grace*."[48]

And so Thomas Jefferson's debt increased greatly at a time when his assets—as well as those of his fellow planters—shrank. Before the year ended he complained that selling a farm would not bring in even a year's normal rental on the property. The final years of his life would see the elderly Jefferson trying to make ends meet, selling land or borrowing money just to meet interest payments on his ever-increasing debt.[49] In April of 1823 he figured that his debts, including the amount due on the Nicholas notes, amounted to over $70,000. The ruin of his son-in-law, Thomas Mann Randolph, put additional strains on Jefferson, as he now had to assume the expenses of his daughter Martha's family.[50]

Had Jefferson been a younger man, he might have done what many other Virginians did at the time—move west—but by then he was well into his seventies. Apparently he and his family did consider moving away from Monticello, perhaps to Philadelphia or even Paris, but these could hardly have been serious alternatives. He was devoted to the plantation and hoped that it would remain in his family. He managed to stave off creditors, and when necessary sold off still another parcel of his land holdings. One should note that for loans due to individuals rather than to banks, his creditors rarely complained if he failed to pay his debts on time. According to one scholar, Jefferson was well treated by the business leaders of Virginia and elsewhere. Frequently a warm letter would be sent to him granting more time "to the Author of the Declaration of Independence." Their willingness to accommodate him made it possible for Jefferson to live out his years at his beloved Monticello.[51]

Toward the end of his life, he launched one final plan to rescue his finances. Lying awake one night, Jefferson came up with an idea he believed would stave off bankruptcy and save the family fortunes—a lottery, with lands he owned as the prize. He was not asking for charity, he told James Madison, although he clearly expected that people would buy tickets as much if not more out of public gratitude than in expectation of riches.[52] Similar lotteries had been common

Jefferson Lottery Ticket, 1826 (Thomas Jefferson Foundation).

before the Revolution, usually to aid institutions or public causes, although there had been occasions when such schemes had been utilized to dispose of private property.

Jefferson proposed to put all of his lands up for the prize, although he would be allowed to live at Monticello for the remainder of his life, as well as retain the Bedford estate (the only profitable piece of property he owned) and his slaves. Such a scheme needed legislative approval, and at first the Virginia assembly balked, in part because many of his friends and admirers considered it degrading to the man they idealized as one of the founding fathers of the Republic. Eventually the legislature passed the bill, but no tickets had been sold by the time Jefferson died on July 4, 1826.[53] He was buried as he wished, on the slope of the hill not far from the house, and according to his instructions his tombstone carried the record of the three things in his life of which he was most proud—author of the Declaration of Independence and of the Virginia Statute for Religious Freedom, as well as the founder of the University of Virginia.

❦

About a year before he left the presidency, Jefferson wrote to his daughter Martha Randolph, and in discussing his financial affairs told her that the only reason he did not want to borrow money against Monticello was in order "to leave it as a provision for yourselves and your family." He proposed to sell off all of his lands except Monticello and Bedford in order to pay off all his debts, and then to live within the income of the Albemarle estate, using the income from Bedford to aid his grandchildren. Martha immediately refused the offer, declaring that "I can bear anything but the idea of seeing you harassed in your old age by debts or deprived of those comforts which long habit had rendered necessary to you."[54]

In his will, written in March 1826, he left Monticello and his residual estate in trust for his daughter Martha; he employed this procedure, as he explained in the document, to avoid any danger that his property would fall into the hands of his son-in-law's creditors. The will also contained the normal stipulation about the payment of debts, which a full accounting revealed to be more than $100,000.[55] The amount of his assets is unclear, since in his will he waived the usual requirement for an executor to inventory and appraise the estate. He owned 149 slaves, and except for the five he freed, the others were to be sold to help pay his debts. The listing in the Albemarle County records list these as worth $33,655. He owned nearly six thousand acres of land, but it is unclear what its true value would have been. Monticello, for example, brought in far less than the executors believed it to be worth.[56]

If austerity was never a part of Jefferson's life—he had indeed become accustomed to certain "comforts"—in his last years it had become the norm for Monticello. Jefferson just could not keep up all the payments that his creditors demanded as well as put sufficient money into the maintenance of his estate. The house normally held not only his immediate family, including Martha and her children, but a constant flood of visiting relatives, friends, and political acquaintances. Ever since the Washington administration European and

Jefferson's drawing for his grave and epitaph (Library of Congress).

American visitors had come to visit the master of Monticello, and faithful Democrats had trekked up the mountain to get his advice on current problems. In the later years of his life admirers flocked to Albemarle, and Jefferson turned no one away, offering hospitality to his guests that would have been a strain on even a rich man's purse.

In terms of the house, one cannot have dozens of people walking on the floors, rubbing against the walls, opening and closing doors and windows without inevitable wear and tear. Outside the high humidity took its toll on the wood-work, which stood vulnerable to dry rot and insects. Had Jefferson had the resources, he no doubt would have done as any householder does, paint and repair on a periodic basis. To maintain the exterior properly, it should have been com-pletely repainted every five or six years, but there is nothing in Jefferson's exten-sive record books to indicate that this was done.

The innovative terraces, beautiful as they were, also required extensive maintenance. The decks and rails, exposed to heat, cold, rain, ice and snow 365 days a year needed constant attention; they should have been painted each year, and rotting planks and support beams replaced with new lumber. Here again there is no record that Jefferson undertook these tasks, and sometime after his death the terraces rotted away and collapsed onto the dependencies below them. By the time of his death the house could no longer hide its age and neglect, and a visitor com-mented sadly that the house was "old and going to decay." A year after its owner's death, a visitor to Monticello found himself far more interested in the vistas from the lawn than by the house.[57]

It should have been clear to one and all that Martha Randolph, much as she may have wanted to, would not be able to stay at Monticello for long. Her son Thomas Jefferson Randolph, Thomas Jefferson's namesake and eldest grandson, had been named executor of the estate, and as such he also inherited the debts. He began selling off the outlying properties, but the proceeds went almost entire-ly to service the debt; the principal would not be fully extinguished until 1878, after the settlement of Randolph's own estate. While well-wishers raised a special fund to help Martha remain at Monticello, it proved too little. Six months after Jeffer-son's death, the family held a public auction on January 19, 1827, to sell off 130 slaves, the furnishings of the house, and the farm machinery.[58] What was left of Jefferson's library was later sold, while some of the important art works were sent to Boston in the hope that merchants there would have a finer appreciation of painting and sculpture, as well as deeper pockets, than Albemarle farmers.[59] The auction did well, mainly due to the prices fetched by the slaves. The executors were able to pay off $35,000 on the principal of the debt, and another $12,840 against interest and arrears.[60] But it was not enough.

In July 1828 a Richmond newspaper carried a notice for the sale of "Valuable Lands" signed by "Th. Jefferson Randolph, Exec'r of Thomas Jefferson, dec'd." The sale would be of "MONTICELLO, in the County of Albemarle, with the Lands of the said estate adjacent thereto, including the Shadwell Mills, will be offered on the premises …. The terms will be accommodating, and the prices anticipated low."[61] The family initially asked $70,000, but no one stepped forward. Most Virginians who might have wanted the estate were already land-poor, and Jefferson's egalitarian ideas had not endeared him to people of wealth.[62]

Mrs. Randolph had left the house after the auction of the furnishings in 1827, and eventually went to Boston for a time to stay with her daughter. "We have quitted Monticello," one of her daughters wrote, "and are doing our best to reconcile ourselves to our change of abode … for as yet our hearts refuse to give the title to any other spot on earth than the one we have just given up."[63] Martha Jefferson Randolph was a "truly pathetic figure" when she left her birthplace, nearly 60, widowed, penniless, and homeless save for "the affectionate considerations of her children." In her notebook at the time she wrote "there is a time in human suffering when succeeding sufferings are but like snow falling on an ice-berg." Word of her condition aroused widespread sentiment, but no results other than the state legislatures of South Carolina and Louisiana each presented her with $10,000. She died in 1836, and is buried in the family plot at Monticello.[64]

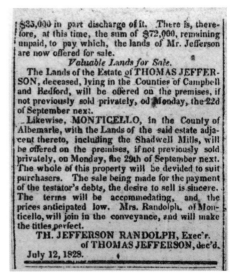

Richmond Enquirer, July 22, 1828 (Thomas Jefferson Foundation).

In the winter of 1830, Anne Royall, a Washington journalist, found the house empty and in disrepair. Mrs. Royall and her escorts pushed in to find the sole occupant "a great course Irish woman," who along with her family had been hired to watch over the house. Despite the fact that Mrs. Randolph had left word that visitors should be allowed to see the house without charge, the caretaker would not budge until she had been paid fifty cents. She and her companions wandered through the frigid house, and as she wrote, "it was much plainer than I expected."[65] The house remained empty and the victim of souvenir-hunters and vandals. *The Virginia Advocate* reported that intruders regarded "the domicile and its contents as though it was an inn ... to rummage everything from garrett to cellar, run their noses into every corner that was open or could be opened." A visitor in May 1830 reported the place empty and desolate, "the spirit which once dwelt within ha[ving] fled." The hearths were cold and cheerless, the walls "naked," the rooms unfurnished except for an occasional fragment of furniture, a chair here, an old harpsichord there.[66] In a desperate effort to save the house, General John H. Cocke, an old friend of Jefferson, suggested renting the house for a school to be set up by a Presbyterian cleric, but nothing came of this plan.[67]

Jefferson Randolph, who knew the condition of the property better than anyone, wrote to his brother-in-law that "in a year or two the house would require extensive repairs," and then the estate would be "unredeemably insolvent." It would be a good thing, he admitted, just to give up the house if a buyer could be found." He would take $10,000 for the house and one thousand acres of land, he declared at the end of 1829, but still no buyers appeared.[68] Finally, in 1831, the house sold, not for $70,000, but for a fraction of that amount.

❦

The new owner, a twenty-four-year-old druggist named James Turner Barclay bought Monticello and 552 acres of surrounding land for $4,500 (the remainder of the original 5,682 acres of the estate had been sold off separately).[69] In the deed, signed on November 1, 1831, the Jefferson family reserved the graveyard and free access to it, a condition that applies to this day.

There are two conflicting stories about the Barclays' relatively short tenure at Monticello. In her old age Barclay's wife Julia wrote an account of her life there. It was "entirely natural that Dr. Barclay should want Monticello," she declared, and noted a "long and intimate relationship between the Barclay family and the name of Jefferson." Her husband's grandfather had been a "devoted friend to Washington and

Jefferson," and she claimed that when he went as first consul to Morocco in 1791, Thomas Barclay had taken with him a little ebony writing desk given to him by Jefferson.[70]

According to her recollections, the Barclays did some restoration on the serpentine walks and terraces, and planted new trees. Mrs. Barclay was such a model housekeeper that Jefferson Randolph, "a frequent visitor," said that she kept the wooden floors in far more beautiful condition than they had been in his grandfather's time. The old gong clock that Jefferson had imported from Europe had long since stopped working, but Dr. Barclay tinkered with it until he had it fixed. The only fly in the ointment, it appeared, was the never-ending stream of visitors that plagued the Barclays, wanting to see the house, hear about

James Turner Barclay (photo, Thomas Jefferson Foundation; location of original unknown).

Jefferson and visit his grave. When Mrs. Barclay's mother visited them, she was appalled at the number of visitors. "Julia, I wouldn't live at Monticello if you'd give me the place," she declared, and advised them to sell.[71]

Despite the relationship Barclay's grandfather had had with Jefferson, other stories suggest that the grandson despised him and his egalitarian ideas. One anecdote says that upon moving into the house, Barclay found a bust of Voltaire by Houdon, and immediate pitched it into a field, declaring Voltaire to be an "antichrist." Barclay cut down some of the poplar, linden and copper beeches that Jefferson had planted, and then, as Mrs. Barclay remembered, did plant new trees. But they were all mulberries, since Barclay entertained a deluded scheme to turn Monticello into a silkworm plantation. He destroyed the lawns, tore out the flowerbeds, planted vegetables near the house, and kept his worms in the greenhouse.[72]

The year after the Barclays moved in, Jefferson's friend and admirer, William Barry, the postmaster general of the United States, made a pilgrimage to Monticello, and he sadly wrote to his daughter: "The late residence of Mr. Jefferson has lost all its interest, save what exists in memory, and that is the sacred deposit of his remains. All is dilapidation and ruin, and I fear the present owner,

Doctor Barclay, is not able, if he were inclined, to restore it to its former condition."[73] That same year, John Latrobe, the son of the distinguished architect Benjamin Latrobe, who had served President Jefferson as superintendent of federal buildings in Washington, drove up the hill and reported that "the first thing that strikes you is the utter ruin and desolation of everything." On the north terrace he found a pedestal, deprived of whatever had once surmounted it, and nearby lay a capital of a column. Yet the natural beauty of the place managed to blot out, at least temporarily, the disrepair of the house. "Take it all in all, Monticello is a spot on which one might well be contented to dwell."[74]

The following year, Eliza Leiper reported the house "out of repair," but still showing signs of its former elegance. The beautiful wooden floors were "highly varnished," and the ingenious glass doors to the parlor still worked properly. Barclay also took Mrs. Leiper around his silkworm farm, and showed her more than twenty pounds of cocoons about to be reeled, and she watched in fascination as the "little workmen," as she termed the worms, performed their various functions. Barclay also pointed out the great number of mulberry trees he had planted, and Jefferson Randolph, the late owner's grandson who apparently spent a great deal of time at Monticello, "told us many things concerning the old Gentleman which were interesting."[75]

Barclay ad for sale of Monticello (Thomas Jefferson Foundation).

But the Barclays were not destined to dwell at Monticello. The silkworm idea predictably failed, and within two years Dr. Barclay put the property up for sale. In his advertisement, Barclay claimed that "The buildings, with the exceptions of the terraces, are in excellent preservation."[76]

Chapter Two

LIEUTENANT LEVY CLIMBS THE LITTLE MOUNTAIN

"I consider Thomas Jefferson to be one of the greatest men in history—author of the Declaration of Independence and an absolute democrat. He serves as an inspiration to millions of Americans. He did much to mould our Republic in a form in which a man's religion does not make him ineligible for political or governmental life."

—URIAH PHILLIPS LEVY[77]

Hardly anyone in Virginia, or indeed in the nation, would have imagined that less than a decade after Thomas Jefferson's death, his mansion would become the property of that rarest of species, a Jewish officer in the United States Navy. Had he never owned Monticello, the career of Uriah Phillips Levy would still be the stuff of heroic stories—pugnacious, a Jew in a service that remained known for its bigotry until well after World War II, a fighter of duels, and a man court-martialed—and ultimately exonerated—six times. His life abounds with mystery, not the least of which is why and how he came to own Jefferson's estate.

There are three stories regarding his purchase of the little mountain. Two of them appear to have no basis in fact, but were repeated often enough that some people came to believe them. One version has the young naval lieutenant visiting President Andrew Jackson in the White House in 1836. In the course of their meeting the conversation turned to Thomas Jefferson and Monticello, which James Barclay had recently put on the market. The fate of the house worried both men, and suddenly Levy told the president: "I have been thinking about buying Monticello, in honor of Mr. Jefferson, whom I love." General

Uriah P. Levy. Undated photograph (courtesy of American Jewish Historical Society, Waltham, Massachusetts and New York, New York).

Jackson eagerly responded: "I order you, sir, to buy it." "Mr. President, I always obey the orders of my superior," Levy replied, saluting.[78]

While it is a charming story, there is no evidence that Levy and Jackson ever met, or that the president would tell a young naval officer to go and buy private property. The second version is equally fanciful but not as charming, and is laden with implicit anti-Semitism.

Friends of the Randolphs in Virginia and elsewhere supposedly planned to raise a sum of money to buy back Monticello and present it to Jefferson's daughter Martha as a home for her declining years. They sent an emissary, a Mr. Hall of Fredericksburg, to Boston where Martha was living with her daughter, Ellen Coolidge. Hall asked Mrs. Randolph if she would accept their gift, and on her agreement, he then enlisted the financial support of a number of wealthy Bostonians, who agreed to raise the necessary amount to buy Monticello from Barclay. Hall then turned home toward Virginia, but he stopped off in New York, where he met Uriah Levy at a dinner and told him about the plan. Levy expressed great interest in the scheme, and asked to be informed of Barclay's terms, with the story intimating that he did so to lead Hall to believe that he would also make a donation. Hall visited Barclay, learned his terms, and headed back north to inform the Boston donors how much the house would cost. He stopped again in New York and told Levy what he had learned. The next morning as Hall went to Boston, Levy sped south to Charlottesville where he purchased Monticello for a fraction of its value before anyone knew about his plans. The "fast-moving" Jew had thwarted the plans of the noble philanthropists.[79] A variation on this theme is that $3,000 had been raised, not in Boston but in Philadelphia, and that a young man named Vaan had been entrusted to deliver the money. His companion in the stagecoach turned out to be Uriah Levy, who got young Vaan drunk and then hurried ahead to negotiate a deal with Barclay.[80]

Here again there is no evidence that any such group of patriots existed, nor that a messenger went to see Martha Randolph in Boston (there is certainly no mention of such an offer in Jefferson family correspondence), nor that Levy acted so energetically. In fact, Barclay by then had had the property on the market for a long time, and one would not have needed a major solicitation to raise the necessary funds. Beyond that, it is highly unlikely that interested buyers would have been found in Boston, where many still hated Jefferson for his Embargo Act and democratic ideas. Further, since Boston was currently the center of a vigorous abolition movement, few of its denizens would have been eager to purchase his estate, once home to more than two hundred slaves. Before we turn to the third, and most plausible explanation, we need to know something about Uriah Phillips Levy.

❦

Jews had been in the United States since colonial days. A Prague metallurgist named Joachim Gaunse (or Jacob Gans) had been part of Sir Walter Ralegh's ill-fated Roanoke expedition. When the English tried again in the early seventeenth century, settlers arriving in Jamestown on the *Abigail* in 1621 included Elias Legardo. Throughout the colonial days one can find instances of individual Jews throughout Virginia, but not until after the Revolution did there exist a nucleus large enough to found a congregation.[81] In the northern colonies, with their small cities, Jews early on founded synagogues. Jews arrived in New Amsterdam in 1654, and despite the opposition of Peter Stuyvesant, were given permission by the Dutch governors in Holland to remain, which they did even after the British conquered the colony. By 1729 the community felt large enough and prosperous enough to build its first synagogue, Shearith Israel, and it remains the oldest continuous congregation in the United States.[82] Jewish communities also grew in Newport, Rhode Island; Charleston, South Carolina; and Philadelphia, where the local community established Congregation Mikveh Israel in 1740.[83]

Rachel Machado Phillips Levy, 1769–1839. Portrait attributed to Adolph Ulrich Wertmuller, c. 1795 (courtesy of American Jewish Historical Society, Waltham, Massachusetts and New York, New York).

It was in Philadelphia and into Mikveh Israel that Uriah Phillips Levy was born on April 22, 1792. His mother, Rachel Phillips, belonged to an old and distinguished Sephardic[84] family that had been in the country for several generations.[85] Her father, Jonas Phillips, had been a prominent Philadelphia patriot and in 1787 had petitioned the Constitutional Convention not to impose any religious oath on office-holders in the new Republic.[86] Her great-grandfather, Dr. Samuel Nunez, had been physician to the king of Portugal. Escaping from the Portuguese inquisition, he arrived in the Oglethorpe colony in George in 1733 in time to help stem a deadly epidemic. Other members of her family had long been prominent in the leadership of the New York and Philadelphia Jewish communities, and sometime before the Revolution Jonas had moved his family to Philadelphia where he had stayed, along with other patriots, when the British and their Hessian mercenaries invaded the city.[87] George Washington had been a guest when her father, Jonas Phillips, had married Rebecca Machado. When Rachel married Michael Levy in 1787, Dr. Benjamin Rush, the famous physician and one of the signers of the Declaration of Independence, attended the ceremony.

Less is known about Uriah's father, Michael Levy, and information on him is both sketchy and at times contradictory. He was born in England in 1755, and came to America at about the age of ten; it is possible that he lived in Richmond or Norfolk before moving to Philadelphia, because there is one reference to him as "Michael Levy of Virginia." He had grown up in a merchant family, and was involved in various mercantile firms throughout his life. He served with the patriot army during the Revolution, possibly before moving to Philadelphia.[88]

During the 1780s he apparently traveled for his firm, Levy & Tucker, several times to Aux Cayes, Haiti.[89] There is also a Michael Levy in the Philadelphia city directory, listed as a clockmaker; it is possible that they are one and the same man. Although his wife and her family were prominent Sephardic Jews, it is possible that Michael followed the Ashkenazic ritual. The records of the German congregation founded in Philadelphia in 1802, Rodeph Shalom, list him as one of the charter members.[90]

The fourth of ten children, from early childhood Uriah spent his days playing around the docks watching the great sailing ships come into port to unload their cargoes. At the age of ten he ran away to sea as a cabin boy. There is a charming but apocryphal story that he first informed the captain that he would have to be back in two years so he could prepare for his bar mitzvah, the ritual Jewish boys perform at age thirteen to mark their entry as adults into the community.[91]

When he did return two years later his family and friends urged him to give up the sea and join the family's mercantile business, but Uriah refused. His father, recognizing that he would never make a shopkeeper of his son, apprenticed him to John Coultron, one of Philadelphia's leading ship-owners, who sent him out on several voyages on his fleet where Uriah learned navigation and other skills. The embargo imposed in 1807 by Jefferson against shipping with England brought American mercantile shipping to a stop, so Coultron had young Levy go to a school for navigation conducted by an ex-lieutenant of the British navy. When the embargo ended, Coultron's fleet resumed sailing and by the time Uriah turned eighteen, he had made several profitable voyages as a mate from Philadelphia to the West Indies.[92]

In 1811 Uriah purchased a one-third share in a new schooner, named the *George Washington* (not, however, after the president, but from the first names of his two partners, George Mesoncort and Washington Garrison). By this time, he wrote in his memoirs, "I had passed through every grade of service—cabin boy, ordinary seaman, able-bodied seaman, boatswain, third, second, and first mates, to that of captain ... I had become familiar with every part of my profession."[93] He may have been, as one writer suggests, the first commander in the history of American shipping to nail a *mezuzah* outside his cabin door; it was a gift from his proud mother.[94]

Here his adventures began. He took command of the ship on behalf of his partners and himself, and on the second leg of his trip, while Levy was enjoying the hospitality of another captain in the Cape Verde Islands, the crew mutinied and stole the vessel with a cargo of $2,500 in gold and fourteen cases of Tenerife wine. While most nineteen-year olds might have thrown up their hands in despair, Uriah went after the mutineers, caught them, brought them to court and saw them convicted of piracy, although he lost the boat. When he returned to the country the War of 1812 had just begun, and in October of that year Uriah entered the United States Navy as a sailing master, one rank below lieutenant.

From available reports, he was one of only five or six Jewish officers in the navy at the time.[95]

He first served aboard the *Alert* in New York harbor, and then in May 1813 reported to the brig *Argus* as a supernumerary, or extra, sailing master. The first challenge facing the ship involved running the British blockade of the continent and delivering America's new minister to France, William H. Crawford, to his post. After successfully accomplishing this assignment, the *Argus* became a raider, hunting and sinking ships in the English and Bristol channels and up and down the British and Irish coasts. Eventually the British navy captured the *Argus*, but Uriah Levy was not on board. A few weeks earlier the *Argus* had captured the *Betsy*, laden with a hold full of valuable sugar, and rather than sink it, the captain detached a small prize crew led by Uriah to sail it to France. On the second day, the unarmed ship encountered a British frigate. Resistance was futile; Uriah surrendered and spent the rest of the war as a prisoner on parole in the town of Ashburton, Devon.[96] By the time he was released at the end of the war, Uriah had taught himself to speak French with the help

Commodore Uriah P. Levy, 1792–1862. Artist unknown, c. 1816 (courtesy of American Jewish Historical Society, Waltham, Massachusetts and New York, New York).

of French prisoners, learned how to fence, and studied a book in his possession, *The American Practical Navigator*, until he knew all it had to teach him.

Uriah returned to Philadelphia and the joyous welcome of his family and friends. They urged him to resign from the navy, since as one friend told him, nine out of ten of his superiors might not care a fig about his being Jewish, but the tenth could make his life hell. According to his later memory, Uriah replied: "What will be the future of our Navy if others such as I refuse to serve because of the prejudices of a few? There will be other Hebrews, in times to come, of whom America will have need. By serving myself, I will give them a chance to serve."[97] He decided to stay in the navy, and his troubles began almost immediately.

Dancing in full uniform at Philadelphia's Patriots' Ball, Uriah brushed shoulders with another naval officer, Lieutenant William Potter. A few minutes later, Potter ran into him, this time with more force, and when Potter did it again, Uriah turned and slapped him in the face. Potter, who had had far too much to drink, shouted "You damned Jew!" Several of Potter's fellow officers made apologies for him and took him off the dance floor. Levy resumed dancing and assumed the incident closed. The next morning, however, an emissary from Potter appeared on Levy's ship, the Franklin, carrying a written challenge to a duel. Levy later wrote that he "wanted to be the first Jew to rise to high rank in the Navy, not the first Jewish officer killed in a duel." But the code of honor left him no choice; so he accepted, seconds negotiated, and weapons were chosen—pistols.

A goodly crowd gathered to view the spectacle. Uriah stated that although a good shot, he would not fire at his opponent, and suggested the ridiculous affair be closed. Potter shouted "Coward!" at him, and then took his first shot, which missed Uriah by several feet; Levy raised his arm straight into the air and fired. By the code duello, this could have ended the match, with honor satisfied on both sides. But Levy's gesture had enraged Potter, and he demanded a second round. The madder Potter got, the poorer his aim, and three more times Levy fired into the air. As Potter reloaded for a fifth try, Levy called out to Potter's friends— "Gentlemen, stop him or I must." On Potter's fifth try his bullet nicked Uriah's left ear. Levy's patience had reached an end, and he shot his opponent square in the chest. The attending physician announced him dead on the spot.

Nearly everyone agreed that Potter had acted very badly and that Uriah Levy had behaved extraordinarily well. But in the eyes of the navy, an enlisted man had killed an officer. In the eyes of some people in Philadelphia something worse had happened, a Jew had killed a Christian. The navy commodore assigned to investigate decided that Levy had acted properly, and dismissed the case without action.

A few days later Lieutenant Bond, a friend of Potter's and an officer on board Levy's ship, the *Franklin*, called him a "damned Jew" and provoked a fight. Perhaps because he faced a climate hostile to Jews, Uriah Levy throughout his career was combative and sensitive to insults. He had a strong sense of personal honor that was considered a hallmark of gentlemen in that time, and he would never allow a slight or insult to pass without a forceful response. Levy would face discrimination throughout his naval career. Much of it can be attributed to anti-Semitism, but in the class-conscious navy of the time, there was also an inherent prejudice against those who had been promoted to the officer corps from the ranks of enlisted men. At the court martial that followed, both Levy and Bond were eventually reprimanded for "un-naval behavior." But even while the court martial proceeded, Levy received a promotion to the rank of lieutenant in March 1817, and about the same time a civil jury acquitted him of the dueling charge.

From his promotion to lieutenant in 1817 until mid-1827, Levy served aboard five ships, ranging from the seventy-four-gun *Franklin* to the sloop *Cyane*, each for a period ranging from a few months to two years. He left each ship after some petty dispute had blown up into a major quarrel, and each incident led to a court martial. In all five trials, the court found Levy guilty, but usually reprimanded his accuser as well.[98] And although in each case superior officers overturned the conviction, Uriah Levy was getting weary of fighting these battles.

In June 1825, Lieutenant Levy reported to the U.S.S. *Cyane* at Gibraltar, and for the next two years served on that ship, first as part of the Mediterranean Squadron and then later in the Brazil Squadron. At the end of June 1827 the navy granted him one month's leave, and he entered the naval hospital in Philadelphia for an unspecified illness. On July 24, he reported no immediate prospect of relief, and the doctors wanted to wait until cooler weather in the fall to perform and operation. The problem could not have been life-threatening, since Levy requested and received three months' leave to travel. He received extensions of this leave, but apparently did not depart for France until August 1828. Whatever health problems he may have had apparently cleared up in Paris, and the navy actually sent him orders—which for some reason never arrived—for him to report to Commodore William Crane for duty in the Mediterranean Squadron.

Over the next few years Levy divided his time between America and Europe; he requested, and the navy granted him, one extension of leave after another, an arrangement that seemed to suit both the navy and Levy at the time. (When his captain suggested the leave could be extended indefinitely, Levy asked him if it was because he was a Jew; the answer was affirmative.) While in Europe Levy studied advanced naval tactics in France, and reported on what he had learned to the secretary of the navy. He also tried, unsuccessfully, to get a model of a new British gun carriage but managed to forward drawings of the device. While in America, Levy settled in New York and apparently went to Washington from time to time to maintain his connections with officials in the Navy Department.

Although Levy had some money, he was not a rich man, and he set off to correct that problem. He moved to New York, and began to invest in real estate at a time when the city was undergoing a major population expansion. Philip Hone wrote in his diary in 1831 that "real estate, up and downtown, [is] equally high; houses in great demand at advanced rents." A few years later he noted that "real estate is high beyond all the calculations of the most sanguine speculators. Immense fortunes have been made within the last three months."[99] Uriah first bought three rooming houses, and within a few months sold one for a substantial profit. He then bought more property, and for the next three decades he was one of a group of highly successful speculators who kept a few steps ahead of the northward movement of population, buying cheap when the area was sparsely populated, holding for a few years, and then selling dear as the growing population pushed north from lower Manhattan. At one point three of his rooming houses brought him an income of $3,500 a month, when the average American working man earned $600 a year. He kept some properties until he died and realized exceptional rents from them. Despite his growing wealth—by 1846 he was

listed in *The Wealth and Biography of the Wealthy Citizens of New York*—Levy at the
time lived modestly in a hotel on lower Broadway, eager to get back to sea.[100]

❦

Since the navy had not seen fit to give him another assignment, in 1828 Levy
hired a real estate manager to handle his properties, and went off to England and
France to study their fleets and to learn something about the latest in naval tactics. He stayed for two years, and from time to time relayed to the Navy
Department the information he acquired. He also enjoyed a fairly full social life,
and outfitted himself in the latest style at a London tailor. He returned to New
York in early 1832 to check on his business ventures, and about this time came up
with an idea to honor Thomas Jefferson.

It is unclear when Uriah Levy decided to do this, but he explained why in
a letter to John Coulter written from Paris (to which he had returned) in
November 1832:[101]

> I consider Thomas Jefferson to be one of the greatest men in history—
> author of the Declaration of Independence and an absolute democrat.
> He serves as an inspiration to millions of Americans. He did much to
> mold our Republic in a form in which a man's *religion* does not make
> him ineligible for political or governmental life. A noble man—yet
> there is no statue to him in the Capitol in Washington. As a small pay-
> ment for his determined stand on the side of religious liberty, I am
> preparing to personally commission a statue of Jefferson.

Why did Levy idealize the builder of Monticello, and did Jefferson deserve
it? The answer is neither clear nor simple. That Jefferson authored the Virginia
Statute for Religious Freedom is undeniable, and throughout his life he opposed
religious bigotry. Jefferson in large measure made it possible for Levy, in address-
ing a naval review board in 1857 to declare: "My parents were Israelites, and I was
nurtured in the faith of my ancestors. In deciding to adhere to it I have but exercised a right granted to me by the Constitution of my native State and of the

United States, a right given to all men by their Maker, a right more precious to each of us than life itself."[102] Surely Jefferson could not have said it more passionately, and yet, at the same time Jefferson seemed to harbor an animus against Judaism as fierce as any of the bigots Uriah Levy confronted in the navy.[103]

Jefferson first became interested in religious liberty while a member of the Virginia Assembly, and he later called the controversies over his views—which lasted throughout his career—the severest of his entire life.[104] Jefferson opposed the very idea of an established church, with the state forcing non-believers to pay taxes for its support. There had been established churches of one form or another since antiquity, and the general view had been that just as one could not have more than one government in a polity, so one could not have more than one church. Thomas Aquinas described church and state not as warring opponents, but as allies, two swords in God's service. There had been an established church in England since medieval times, and the colonists had brought the idea with them to the New World in the seventeenth century.

Jefferson apparently objected to the establishment of an official religion because he regarded religion as a strictly private affair. "Say nothing of my religion," he reproached a correspondent. "It is known to my god and myself alone."[105] As he wrote to Margaret Bayard Smith in 1816, "I never told my own religion, nor scrutinized that of another. I never attempted to make a convert, nor wished to change another's creed. I never judged the religion of others … for it is in our lives and not our words that our religion must be read."[106] But Jefferson went far beyond this simple toleration of other views, and in fact rejected a good part of Christianity itself. He certainly believed in a moral foundation of the universe, but he could not accept either the divinity of Jesus or the notion that God had written the Bible. While he did not publicize his views, his extensive correspondence led to rumors about his beliefs, and his opponents condemned him for his views on religion far more vociferously than they did his ideas on democracy. Many believed Jefferson to be an atheist, a fact that damned him in their eyes as unfit to hold public office. In the election of 1800, a New York minister, William Linn, warned that once "my neighbor persuade himself that there is no God, and he will soon pick my pocket, and break not only my *leg* but my *neck*. If there be no God,

CHAP. LXXXII.

A BILL for establishing religious freedom.

SECTION I. WELL aware that the opinions and belief of men depend not on their own will, but follow involuntarily the evidence proposed to their minds; that Almighty God hath created the mind free, and manifested his supreme will that free it shall remain by making it altogether insusceptible of restraint; that all attempts to influence it by temporal punishments, or burthens, or by civil incapacitations, tend only to beget habits of hypocrisy and meanness, and are a departure from the plan of the holy author of our religion, who being lord both of body and mind, yet chose not to propagate it by coercions on either, as was in his Almighty power to do, but to extend it by its influence on reason alone; that the impious presumption of legislators and rulers, civil as well as ecclesiastical, who, being themselves but fallible and uninspired men, have assumed dominion over the faith of others, setting up their own opinions and modes of thinking as the only true and infallible, and as such endeavoring to impose them on others, hath established and maintained false religions over the greatest part of the world and through all time; That to compel a man to furnish contributions of money for the propagation of opinions which he disbelieves and abhors, is sinful and tyrannical; that even the forcing him to support this or that teacher of his own religious persuasion, is depriving him of the comfortable liberty of giving his contributions to the particular pastor whose morals he would make his pattern, and whose powers he feels most persuasive to righteousness; and is withdrawing from the ministry those temporary rewards, which proceeding from an approbation of their personal conduct, are an additional incitement to earnest and unremitting labours for the instruction of mankind; that our civil rights have no dependance on our religious opinions, any more than our opinions in physics or geometry; that therefore the proscribing any citizen as unworthy the public confidence by laying upon him an incapacity of being called to offices of trust and emolument, unless he profess or renounce this or that religious opinion, is depriving him injuriously of those privileges and advantages to which, in common with his fellow citizens, he has a natural right; that it tends also to corrupt the principles of that very religion it is meant to encourage, by bribing, with a monopoly of worldly honours and emoluments, those who will externally profess and conform to it; that though indeed these are criminal who do not withstand such temptation, yet neither are those innocent who lay the bait in their way; that the opinions of men are not the object of civil government, nor under its jurisdiction; that to suffer the civil magistrate to intrude his powers into the field of opinion and to restrain the profession or propagation of principles on supposition of their ill tendency is a dangerous fallacy, which at once destroys all religious liberty, because he being of course judge of that tendency will make his opinions the rule of judgment, and approve or condemn the sentiments of others only as they shall square with or differ from his own; that it is time enough for the rightful purposes of civil government for its officers to interfere when principles break out into overt acts against peace and good order; and finally, that truth is great and will prevail if left to herself; that she is the proper and sufficient antagonist to error, and has nothing to fear from the conflict unless by human interposition disarmed of her natural weapons, free argument and debate; errors ceasing to be dangerous when it is permitted freely to contradict them.

SECT. II. WE the General Assembly of Virginia do enact that no man shall be compelled to frequent or support any religious worship, place, or ministry whatsoever, nor shall be enforced, restrained, molested, or burthened in his body or goods, nor shall otherwise suffer, on account of his religious opinions or belief; but that all men shall be free to profess, and by argument to maintain, their opinions in matters of religion, and that the same shall in no wise diminish, enlarge, or affect their civil capacities.

A Bill for Establishing Religious Freedom (courtesy of Library of Virginia).

there is no law, no future account; government then is the ordinance of man only, and we cannot be subject for conscience sake."[107]

Jefferson may have eschewed organized religion, but he was no atheist. He believed in a great moral force in the universe, a god, but thought that each person had to deal with that god as one saw fit. Deism, as this view came to be called, was part and parcel of eighteenth-century rationalism, and Jefferson shared it with many of the leading philosophers of his day.[108] It took concrete form for him in the bill he wrote and introduced to disestablish the Anglican Church in Virginia. The eventual success of this bill, the Virginia Statute for Religious Freedom, remained for him one of the crowning achievements of his life, and he asked that it be one of the three things listed on his tombstone.[109]

Jefferson first drafted a bill for religious liberty in 1777, but by then, according to Dumas Malone, he already was the "foremost advocate of the entire separation of Church and State in Virginia." As a result of the bill, he "became the major symbol of complete religious liberty."[110] For many Americans, including Uriah Levy, he would remain that symbol throughout his life, and indeed long afterward. The bill itself took almost a decade to win passage. It faced the opposition of the entrenched Anglican Church; furthermore, many non-Anglicans wanted not separation, but for their churches to receive part of the state tax. Jefferson disagreed, believing that forcing a man to support even a church of his own choice remained a deprivation of liberty. Slowly the idea of full separation won out, and because the Anglican Church so closely identified with the hated Crown during the Revolution, it became a simple and logical step to disestablish it. But not until 1786, with James Madison adroitly leading the campaign, did Jefferson's bill for religious liberty finally win legislative approval.[111]

The bill has a fairly long preamble, beginning with the majestic phrase "Whereas Almighty God hath created the mind free." It then goes on to declare that any efforts to control how or what men believe, or force them to support or attend any particular type of church, goes against the divine mandate. This section is not a list of specific exclusions, but rather a comprehensive statement designed to cover all possibilities:[112]

> We, the General Assembly of Virginia do enact that no man shall be compelled to frequent or support any religious worship, place, or ministry whatsoever, nor shall be enforced, restrained, molested, or burthened in his body or goods, or shall otherwise suffer, on account of his religious opinions or belief; but that all men shall be free to profess, and by argument to maintain, their opinions in matters of reli-

gion, and that the same shall in no wise diminish, enlarge, or affect their civil capacities.

Jefferson was in France when he received word from Madison of the bill's passage, and it gave him the utmost gratification. The measure, he told his friend, had already been translated into several languages and was inserted in the Diderot's new *Encyclopédie*. "It is comfortable," he stated with content, "to see the standard of reason at length erected, after so many ages during which the human mind has been held in vassalage by kings, priests & nobles."[113]

The Virginia Statute would prove a model for similar laws in other states, as well as for the Religion Clauses of the First Amendment. Although some religious conservatives continued to denounce Jefferson for his alleged atheism and lack of religiosity, most Americans then and now credited him as the father of religious liberty in the United States, a claim that also goes too far. But certainly to the small number of Jews and other dissenting sects in the United States during the Revolutionary era and early Republic Jefferson stood as a hero,[114] one, in Uriah Levy's mind, whom the nation had failed to honor properly. One wonders if Levy would have been so enthusiastic if he had known how Thomas Jefferson privately felt about Jews?

Jefferson had some knowledge of Judaism, and in 1776 he suggested as a seal for the new nation the children of Israel in the wilderness following a cloud by day and a pillar of fire at night.[115] In Charlottesville a Jew, David Isaacs, owned a dry goods store on Main Street, and it is said that he sold Jefferson the ball of twine that the latter used to lay out Pavilion VII, the first building of what would be the University of Virginia. In addition to providing Jefferson with meat, butter, cheese, and other items, Isaacs also undertook to furnish the master of Monticello with books and pamphlets on Judaism.[116]

When Jefferson founded the university, his plan included the then-radical notion that there should be no sectarian religious studies required of the students, at a time when students in American colleges not only had to take such courses but also had to attend chapel on a regular basis. Jefferson's desire to make the university a true center of intellectual inquiry, and not a home for denominational indoctrination, can be seen in a letter he wrote to Isaac Harby in 1826: "I have thought it a cruel addition to the wrongs which that injured sect [Jews] have suffered that their youths should be excluded from the instructions in science afforded to all others in our public seminaries by imposing on them a course of theological reading which their consciences do not permit them to pursue, and in the University lately established here we have set the example of ceasing to violate the rights of conscience by any injunctions on the different sects respecting their religion."[117]

When the new synagogue of Shearith Israel in New York was consecrated in 1818, Mordecai M. Noah (a cousin of Uriah Levy) delivered an address extolling the freedom that Jews had found in America. He sent a copy of the talk to various political leaders, including Jefferson, who responded with praise for Jews:[118]

> Your sect by its sufferings has furnished a remarkable proof of the universal spirit of religious intolerance inherent in every sect, disclaimed by all while feeble, and practiced by all when in power. Our laws have applied the only antidote to this vice, protecting our religious, as they do our civil rights, by putting all on an equal footing. But more remains to be done. For altho' we are free by the law, we are not so in practice. Public opinion erects itself into an Inquisition, and exercises its office with as much fanaticism as fans the flames of an *auto da fé*. The prejudice still scowling on your section of our religion, altho' the elder one, cannot be unfelt by yourselves. It is to be hoped that individual dispositions will at length mould themselves to the model of the law and consider the moral basis on which all our religions rest ....

In letters to other Jewish correspondents Jefferson assured them of his high regard for their creed, his regret that their people had been persecuted by misguided Christians, and his hope that religious equality would be inscribed in American hearts as well as in the nation's laws.[119]

Although Jefferson denied the divinity of Jesus, and defended the right of Jews to believe and practice their faith unmolested by others, he also strongly attacked Judaism. He considered Jewish ideas of God and his attributes "degrading & injurious," and their ethics "often irreconcilable with the sound dictates of reason and morality" and "repulsive & anti-social as respecting other nations."[120] The man who championed natural rights and freedom of worship wrote to Joseph B. Priestly that Jewish beliefs and morality "degraded" Jews and noted "the necessity they presented of a reformation."[121] To John Adams he wrote approvingly of the works of Johann Brucker, which denigrated Jewish philosophy and ethics,[122] while to Ezra Stiles he declared "I am not a Jew" and then misrepresented Jewish views on punishment.[123]

But this aspect of Jefferson's personality remained unknown to all but a few of his contemporaries, and would not become widely recognized until nearly a century after his death. In the early 1830s Lieutenant Uriah Phillips Levy, like most of his fellow Jews and indeed most of the nation, saw Thomas Jefferson as the paladin of religious liberty, which in fact he was; they just did not see his dark side.

❦

Once he had decided to memorialize Jefferson with a statue, Levy next decided on the sculptor, Pierre Jean David d'Angers, then France's most celebrated artist. Levy had seen and been mesmerized by David's *Condé* at Versailles, and in 1832 he paid a visit to David's atelier, where the artist accepted the commission.

During one of his earlier trips to France, Levy had met a man whom he and many other Americans idolized, the Marquis de Lafayette. Levy now returned to La Grange, Lafayette's estate outside Paris, to tell him about his plans to honor Jefferson. The aging Frenchman was delighted. He had met Jefferson before Yorktown, and the two had become good friends during the time Jefferson had served as American minister to France. In 1824 Lafayette had returned to tour America as a guest of the United States government, and had visited Monticello in December. On the east lawn an honor guard stood at attention as these two old friends walked slowly towards each other and embraced, while the crowd of around four hundred spectators burst into applause.[124] Lafayette lent Levy his own portrait of Jefferson by Thomas Sully, one of the few portraits of himself that Jefferson liked, and David used the Sully portrait as a model for the sculpture.

Uriah stayed in Paris for several months, visiting the atelier on a daily basis. On January 15, 1833, he wrote to the Navy Department stating that due to an unfortunate accident to David, completion of the Jefferson statue would be delayed by several months. As the "only responsible person," it would now be necessary for him to remain in Paris to supervise the completion of the work.

One might have assumed that given this time on his hands, Levy would have visited the city's cultural sites and participated in its social life. Perhaps he did, but even in Paris Levy seemed to have a knack for getting into trouble; he still took quick offense at any perceived slight, not only to himself but also to his country. As an example, nearly every American in Paris attended a great banquet on July 4, 1833, and we can let Uriah described what happened in his own words:[125]

Thomas Jefferson by Thomas Sully; copy painted in 1856 after the life portrait made in 1821 (Thomas Jefferson Foundation).

On the 4th day of July 1833, I was present in Paris, at a banquet given by the American residents of that city in honor of the day. The Hon. George Erving, formerly U.S. Minister to Spain presided and Gen. Lafayette, Gen. Barnard and others were present as invited guests. Among the regular toasts was one in honor of Washington, —then followed "Andrew Jackson president of the U.S. like Washington firm and patriotic; like Washington happy in the union of men and principles." I proposed nine cheers; will it be believed this toast in an assemblage of Americans in a foreign land, instead of being cheered, was received with groans and hisses! And though repeated attempts were made to drink this national toast, in the modified form "Andrew Jackson, President of the U.S., nine cheers," the major part of the company persistently refused to drink it with cheers. Although the French National toast "The King of the French" was drunk with three times three and one more. Regarding the chief magistrate of the Union as the Representative of my country's sovereignty, I promptly resented this insult to her and to him; and on its first outbreak threw to one of the most prominent in the outrage (a glove merchant) my glove with an invitation to the Champs Élysées the next morning—an invitation not accepted. A similar proposal to another, drew from him, the next day, a written apology to me, which I have yet in my possession.

Instead of bringing him another court martial, Lieutenant Levy's actions made him a hero. Not only papers in Paris, but in Philadelphia and Washington carried the story; even those who had little use for Andrew Jackson agreed that the nation's honor had to be maintained. Levy's neighbor at the banquet table, Charles Pond, later wrote that Uriah had "resent[ed] the indignity in such a spirited and gallant manner. He was an honor to his country ... he denounced the insult to his government in the terms it deserved.[126]

Finally David finished the statue in early 1834, and had the large clay sculpture cast in bronze by Honoré Gonon and Sons of Paris. After making arrangements for its shipment, Levy returned to the United States and commissioned a pedestal from Struthers of Philadelphia. On March 19, his official transcript reads: "Addressed at Washington ... informed that Commodore Hull had been requested to furnish the conveyance for the statue of Jefferson. Requested to tell the driver of the oxen what wharf to go to, and the box to be ready on his arrival."[127] When Hull's flagship docked at Norfolk, Levy stood on the quay with the ox-cart, and supervised the unloading of the crates. He rode horseback alongside the wagon as it made its way slowly to Washington.

On March 23, Uriah sent a letter to the House of Representatives, begging leave to present "a colossal bronze statue of Thomas Jefferson." After detailing its provenance, he wrote: "It is with pride and satisfaction that I am enabled to offer this tribute of my regard to the people of the United States through their representatives, and I am sure that such disposition will be made of it as boasts correspondence with the illustrious author of our Declaration of Independence and the profound veneration with which his memory is cherished by the American people."[128]

The David statue portrays Thomas Jefferson standing with a quill pen in his right hand, and in his left a scroll in which the entire Declaration of Independence is inscribed. Between his feet are two books with a laurel wreath. On one side of the base are the words "Presented by Uriah Phillips Levy of the United States Navy to his fellow citizens, 1833," and on the other side the name of the sculptor and the foundry.

The Speaker of the House, John Bell of Tennessee, laid Levy's letter before the House, which referred it to the Joint Committee on the Library. Senator Asher Robbins of Rhode Island, chair of the Joint Library Committee wrote to Levy to thank him for the statue. Eventually, Robbins noted, the people's representatives would have ordered such a statue, but "You, sir, have only antici-pated their action and have manifested, in doing so, a devotion to the principles con-tained in [the Declaration], equally felt by all classes of your fellow citizens."[129]

But not everyone proved so gracious. Once again Levy had managed to twist some tails in the Navy Department, who thought the act pre-sumptuous for a mere lieutenant, and some members of the House agreed. On Friday, June 27, 1834, Congressman Edward Everett of Massa-chusetts, a member of the Committee on the Library, reported that the committee recom-mended that the statue presented by Lieutenant Levy be placed in the square at the eastern front of the Capitol. William Segar Archer of Virginia immediately objected. If Congress wished a stat-ue of Jefferson, it "would be more consistent with propriety to procure one for themselves, than to be indebted for it to any person whatever." In addition, since Congress had recently resolved to erect a statue of "the great and good father of his

Thomas Jefferson by P. J. David d'Angers (courtesy of United States Capitol).

country," no other statue ought to be erected until that of George Washington had been completed. Another objection came from Charles Mercer of Virginia, who claimed that David had not made a good likeness.

The nitpicking continued until Amos Lane of Indiana somewhat sarcastically noted that he trusted the House would not reject the statue because it came from a lieutenant instead of a commander. After Clement C. Clay of Alabama reminded his colleagues that accepting this statue would not prevent them from erecting another one in the future, or changing its site, the House finally agreed to the recommendation of the committee, but by a vote of only sixty-nine in favor against fifty-five opposed, and in fact did not formally accept the statue.[130]

Although the Jefferson statue stands today in the Capitol—the only sculpture there donated by a private citizen—it had its troubled years as well. Without being officially accepted, it stood in the Rotunda of the Capitol for a dozen years. Then in 1845, with the permission of President James K. Polk, the statue was moved to the north lawn of the White House, where it remained exposed to the elements for more than thirty years, and the once bright bronze gave way to a dull gray-green patina.

It might have remained there even longer had not Jonas Levy, Uriah's brother, written to Senator Justin Morrill of Vermont, the chairman of the Committee on Public Grounds and Buildings in 1876. He noted that Senator Charles Sumner of Massachusetts had recently introduced a resolution for the formal acceptance of the statue and that steps be taken to preserve it. Jonas pointed out that the old objections could hardly matter any more, and that there should be no problem accepting a gift from a man who had served his country meritoriously for more than fifty years. But, he went on:[131]

> If the statue is not accepted by Congress I have to request as one of the heirs to the said property and its recent owner, that the statue be turned over to us, with as little delay as possible, and in as good condition as it now appears in, besides it being one of the only things except the Declaration of Independence in respect to the memory of the Great Statesman in the nation's capitol, we will preserve it that it

may bring to generations to come the memory of the Great Men of our Great and glorious Union.

One doubts if this "threat" had much influence, but not long afterward, Congress ordered the statue of Thomas Jefferson, a gift of Uriah Phillips Levy to the people of the United States, moved back to the rotunda of the Capital, where it stands today.

Levy also presented a patinated plaster model of the statue to "the people of New York." Before the city fathers set up the statue in City Hall, Uriah exhibited it at 355 Broadway, and charged admission to view it. He then used the proceeds to feed the city's poor, purchasing and distributing some 1,200 loaves of bread. For his gift, Levy received a gold snuff box and the Freedom of the City of New York, an honor previously given to, among others, George Washington and John Jay. The statue still stands in the Council Chamber in City Hall.[132]

❧

The great bronze statue in many ways led Uriah to Monticello. One day at La Grange, Lafayette told Levy that he had been distressed to learn that his friend Jefferson had died practically penniless. He asked where Martha Jefferson Randolph had gone and about the condition of Monticello, which he had visited in 1824 during his triumphal tour of America. Levy said he did not know, but promised the marquis that he would undertake to find out upon his return to the United States.[133] A man who always kept his word, Levy set out to discover what had happened to Monticello.

What he found atop the little mountain appalled him. According to one modern source, the house had become "just another untended old home." Already in poor condition before Jefferson's death, part of the main roof had fallen in, the terraces had collapsed, and the stately columns had begun to deteriorate. Barclay had abandoned the silkworm enterprise, and he and his family had moved to another home. Vandals and weather furthered the damage. People still made pilgrimages to Jefferson's home, but found little to admire. One Jefferson devotee wrote "All is dilapidation and ruin."[134]

Had there really been any plan to buy Monticello back for Martha Randolph, it could have easily succeeded. Barclay had put the property up for sale in late summer 1833, just two years after purchasing it. According to one news item, Monticello "is again offered for sale ... [and] no property in Virginia will be more cheaply disposed of."[135] Although the seller declared that "such an edifice, hallowed by so many ennobling associations, ought not to want a purchaser in the Old Dominion," in fact Barclay faced the same problems as had Jefferson's heirs, although several more years of wear and neglect now made it even less appealing.

The morning after he arrived in Charlottesville, Uriah Levy hired a buckboard and drove the three and a half miles to Monticello. He no doubt stopped at the family cemetery to pay homage to Mr. Jefferson, and would have found it overgrown with weeds, the obelisk over Jefferson's grave defaced by souvenir hunters. The house was deserted, the lawns a jungle, the flowerbeds that Jefferson had so carefully planned all gone to seed. Windows were broken, and shutters hung askew.

There seems to be no evidence that Uriah Levy had gone to Charlottesville intending to buy Monticello. Apparently he knew no more about the condition of the house than he had earlier when Lafayette had asked him about it. One can surmise that he recalled his promise to Lafayette to look into the matter. Upon learning that Barclay wanted to sell, Uriah had probably acted on impulse, a habit that had gotten him into trouble more than once. But there may have been more. He did admire Jefferson, and had gone to rather great expense to have France's finest sculptor make a large statue of the third president. If Jefferson's contributions to the religious freedom of Jews in this country merited a colossal statue, then surely it would also be worth saving his beloved Monticello from ruin.

There is some confusion over exactly when Levy visited Monticello and offered to buy it from Barclay. Fitzpatrick and Saphire indicate that Levy did not go until the spring of 1836, and they base this on the fact that the deed of sale is dated May 1836.[136] In fact, the two men struck a bargain on April 5, 1834, in which Levy would receive the house and an indeterminate amount of acreage for $2,700. This date makes sense in that Levy had been in Washington in March to deliver the statue, and since the navy had no orders for him, he was free to spend a few days traveling to Charlottesville. The earlier date is further confirmed by a notice in *The Niles Register* in 1834 that Uriah Phillips Levy had acquired Monticello, and that the naval officer, who recently inherited a fortune, intended to restore the house to its original condition.[137] The reason the deed of conveyance is dated two years later is simple—it took a lawsuit to establish what property Barclay still owned.

Monticello at the time of Jefferson's death had comprised the house and 5,682 acres of surrounding land. Most of this had been sold off at auction, so that Barclay had received only 552 acres, and then he had sold parcels out of that. No one, even Barclay, knew exactly what remained, and Levy's own experience in real estate led him to insist on clearing title before he paid over any money. The easiest way to clear title is a lawsuit, in which a court definitively determines who owns what. Many such lawsuits are collusive in nature, that is, both parties want a determination, and are willing to let a third party—the judge—settle the matter. The Albemarle County Circuit Court of Law and Chancery held on May 8, 1836, that for $2,700 Levy would receive the house and 218 acres.[138] The necessary papers were then quickly drawn up; Uriah Levy reported "My heart leaped."[139]

There have been various interpretations given to Levy's motives—that he sought public approval, that he hoped for financial gain, or that he had social or political ambition—but none of them stand up to closer scrutiny. He got very little acclaim for his generosity in donating a statue of Jefferson to the country, and Americans at the time were not very enamored of old houses; significant public interest in historic preservation would not develop until after the Civil War. He certainly made no money on Monticello, and in fact poured tens of thousands of dollars into the estate. As for social ambitions, he did not live there for long enough periods of times to capitalize on his status as master of Monticello. Nor could he easily invite friends there, as his nephew would; the development of cheap and

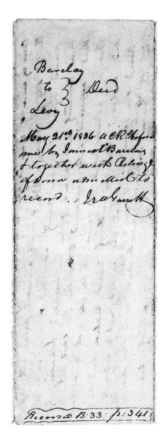

Deed of sale from Barclay to Levy (courtesy of Special Collections, University of Virginia Library).

reliable train networks would be a post-war phenomenon. Beyond that, he already enjoyed rather large social status as a wealthy bachelor in New York.

Charles Hosmer suggested that Levy's purchase of Monticello might well be viewed as an early manifestation of the historic preservation movement, the drive to save and maintain noteworthy historic buildings.[140] One might buttress this claim with a letter Levy wrote to John Coulter, noting that "The homes of great men should be protected and preserved as monuments to their glory."[141] We can never really be sure of any of these reasons, other than the fact that Levy held Jefferson in high regard. Even more than the colossal statue in the Capitol, the saving of Monticello was indeed an act of homage to the author of the Declaration of Independence and the Statute for Religious Freedom.

It is fortunate that Levy was doing well in the New York real estate market, because restoring and maintaining Monticello would be an expensive proposition. Although he lived there at most for a few months each summer, and then not every year, he stabilized the building, made necessary repairs, and also bought land to enlarge the estate. Unfortunately, there are no detailed records, such as Jefferson had kept, of Levy's expenditures and repairs; all we can go on are some scattered letters as well as the reminiscences of visitors to the estate during Uriah's tenure.

Various accounts agree that Levy immediately set to work on making the necessary repairs. He hired an overseer and superintendent, Joel Wheeler, who has been described as a dirt farmer and "a sour-looking man with a sharp voice."[142] But despite the great damage he did three decades later, in fact Joel Wheeler proved an ideal instrument for Levy's purposes, one who knew what had to be done and was capable of carrying out Levy's orders.[143]

First the place had to be cleaned up, inside and out.[144] Levy bought enough slaves to maintain an adequate cleaning, repair, and maintenance force on the grounds.[145] Levy probably owned about twenty slaves; when the Confederate government seized the house in 1862 or 1863, they sold off nineteen.

The work crews immediately began clearing up leaves and dead branches from the paths; they hauled away debris, trimmed the lawns and pulled out the half-dead mulberry trees Barclay had planted. Local craftsmen came in to repair the roof and walls, and replace the numerous broken windows with new glass. Levy had the ninety-six-foot well cleaned out so that Monticello once again had a supply of fresh water. Levy also began reconstructing the landscaping and garden designs. Inside the house workers cleaned and applied fresh coats of paint, and made repairs to the seven-day clock in the entrance hall.

Only a few of Jefferson's own possessions remained; most had been sold off at the auction after his death. Apparently Levy tried to buy some of these items back, but since he never made an inventory it is unclear how well, if at all, he succeeded. Most sources agree that he attempted to put Jefferson's bedroom with its sleeping alcove back pretty much as it had been during Jefferson's last years on the mountain.

Under one of the collapsed terrace roofs, Levy also found a phaeton of Jeffersonian design that supposedly had carried its owner to Philadelphia in 1776 to write the Declaration of Independence. Levy went to considerable effort to refurbish it and would later show it to visitors, claiming that it had indeed made that famous trip.

After giving Wheeler orders as to what he wanted done, Levy spent the winter of 1836-1837 in New York, looking after his real estate interests. In the spring he returned to Virginia, bringing with him his sixty-seven-year-old mother Rachel, whom he installed as the mistress of Monticello. She thought the place "terribly grand," and when she died on May 7, 1839, Levy buried her there, not far from the house.[146] After her death Levy's younger sister Amelia served as the mistress of the house until he married.

In addition to restoring the physical appearance of the building and buying what Jefferson artifacts he could, Levy also added significantly to the acreage, although he never built it up to the size it had been at Jefferson's death. In 1837, only one year after he received clear title, he quintupled the size of the estate by paying $1,742.04 for 960 acres that had at one time belonged to James Monroe.[147] Two years later he purchased another tract of 1,423 acres adjacent to Monticello from John and Jennetta Sampson, and at some time also purchased a working farm not too far from Charlottesville, which he called the Washington Farm, on which he grew tobacco and grains. At Monticello he raised horses and did some light gardening.

In the purchase of land from the Sampsons we get a small glimpse of how Levy related to at least some of his neighbors. Most studies of Monticello and of Levy indicate that the people of Charlottesville acted rather coolly to the Yankee who had come to buy Mr. Jefferson's house. In the standard biography of Levy by Fitzpatrick and Saphire, the authors write that "the new owner was neither welcomed nor accepted by the local people. They were affronted by his residence at Monticello—not, apparently, because he was a Jew but because he was a Yankee."[148] Some of them, however, resented his religion as well. George Blatterman, who as a boy had known Jefferson and as an old man would know Jefferson Monroe Levy, seems to have detested both uncle and nephew. In his memoirs Blatterman noted that Uriah Levy had "purchased Monticello at a very small price. He was a Jew of the Jews and very unpopular." His comments on both Levys are larded with anti-Semitism.[149]

Given the fact that Uriah Levy was only in the area two or at the most three months a year, one wonders how much contact he actually had with his neighbors. Certainly some disliked him, but not all. He apparently made friends with Louis Leschat and his wife Sophie. The couple lived in Charlottesville, and during Uriah's first two years spent considerable time at Monticello giving him technical advice on the restoration work.[150] He also seemed to have struck up a relationship with his neighbor John Sampson, from whom he purchased over 1,400 acres of land. We have a letter that Uriah wrote to Sampson indicating that at least between these two men, no ill will existed:[151]

Having been informed that you are anxious to get rid of the strip of land that adjoins me, and I feeling disposed to help an old neighbor along, and one whose departure I regret extremely so much so that had I been at home I should have pensioned you rather than we should have lost our dear Mrs. Sampson whose departure myself and Sister [Amelia] have actually grieved over.

Having learnt that yourself and Mr. Jefferson disagreed in the negotiation for your land, it can be no indelicacy on my part knowing as I do the amount about which you differed in my now offering myself as a purchaser. I therefore request that you will frankly come down to your lowest notch cash per acre and reply to me per return of post, directed to me at Washington City at Gadsby's hotel as I leave here tomorrow for that place and probably from there to Europe. With my own and sister's best regards to yourself and amiable lady and family, I am yours truly,

P.S. Your sons are both well. One of them past [sic] last night with us.

Uriah made one other friend, one who would serve him and his family for the next four decades, a local Charlottesville attorney named George Carr. In 1838, before the navy recalled him to active duty, Levy gave Carr full power of attorney to act for him as a general superintendent over Monticello during his absences,[152] and apparently relied on him for advice in running the estate. In 1858 he wrote Carr from overseas that "I am sorry I could not have the benefit of your personal inspection of affairs at my lower [Washington] farm." The supervisor of that farm, Mr. Garrison, is "faithful and attentive but he needs some one to advise and direct him. You must give him the benefit of your superior judgment and experience."[153] When naval duty prevented him from going to Monticello one summer, he offered the house to Carr and his family as a pleasant place to be in the hot months.[154]

Levy never seems to have been socially isolated during the months he stayed on the mountain, since the stream of visitors never ceased. Uriah apparently delighted in the fact that people came to pay homage to Mr. Jefferson, and he often took them on tours of the house and gardens. One day, however, a great surprise awaited him among the pilgrims coming up the mountain.

A familiar-looking young man engaged Levy in conversation, but did not tell him his name. Levy kept looking at him, trying to figure out if he knew the man, when the visitor could no longer contain himself. "I am your brother Jonas," he said, "and we have not seen each other for thirteen years, when I was only a lad of fifteen." The two men had both chosen sea-faring careers that had taken them to many ports but never to the same place at the same time. The two fell on each other, and Uriah insisted that Jonas stay with him for several weeks, during which the younger man, who had also become a sea captain, got to know Monticello intimately.[155] Years later this would prove a great advantage to Jonas when he tried to acquire the estate.

The stream of visitors never stopped, and although some complained that the owner of the house did not want them there, other accounts suggest that Uriah accepted the pilgrimages as an integral part of the estate. Mr. Jefferson's house had been saved, in part, so people could pay homage to his memory.

According to his wife, a young woman named Virginia Lopez whom he married in 1853,[156] Levy not only enjoyed the visitors, but often had fun with them. Levy, according to his wife's reminiscences, delighted in donning an old coat and, taking a pair of shears, would go around the property pruning the shrubbery. Occasionally the sightseers would come across him and, mistaking him for a gardener, would ask for Captain Levy so they could get permission to see the house and gardens. He would reply that the grounds were there for all to see, but that the captain had gone to town. However, if they knocked at the front door someone would show them through.[157]

If he were inside the house he would sometimes make things up about the furnishings. The portrait of his aunt, Madame Noel (a tutor to Princess Charlotte of England), had been painted in court costume with a number of feathers adorning her hair. Levy told visitors that this was actually a painting of the great Pocahontas herself. When his wife remonstrated with him for deceiving the tourists, he said "they had come a long distance to hear and see something, and he had sent then home happy, as they always seemed to be very pleased with his dissertations."[158]

❦

How well did Uriah Levy do as guardian of Monticello? In general he gets high marks from scholars of historic preservation, but there are conflicting contemporary accounts. A letter reprinted in *The New York Mirror* in November 1839, from "M.S." claimed the exterior had "the appearance of utter dilapidation," although the interior was still in a fair state of preservation.[159] An English visitor in the early 1840s wrote that one would not believe Monticello to be the property of a man rich in money or taste. At the time of Levy's purchase, the house and grounds had become as dilapidated as the tomb, and the roads broken up and destroyed; so they remained, "for nothing had been done apparently to improve either." The interior was slightly better, and "we thought we had not seen any interior of an American residence in the South, better finished, or in more harmonious proportions than this." But he lamented Levy's additions, such as a full-length oil portrait of himself.[160] In 1851 John Walters reported the exterior to still be in "terrible condition."[161] A visitor to Monticello in 1853, however, reported the mansion to be in good condition, and a few of Jefferson's belongings could be found inside the house. Benson Lossing had first visited Monticello during the Barclay interregnum, and recalled that at that time the interior of the house appeared barren, with all the great artifacts of natural history gone. Captain Levy showed Lossing around, and he found the exterior of the building and grounds about the same as when Jefferson left it.

While the interior furnishings had changed, the basic architectural design had been preserved. Lossing found a plaster bust made from the David statue, as well as a stone model of a capital, designed by Benjamin Henry Latrobe, and featuring the leaves and blossoms of the tobacco plant. Nearby stood a model of the *Vandalia*, which had been one of Levy's commands. There were a number

Uriah Levy (courtesy of U.S. Naval Academy Museum).

of oil portraits on the walls, including one by Sir Joshua Reynolds of Madame Noel, Uriah's aunt. The great clock still hung in the entrance hall in working order. In the parlor nothing of Jefferson's remained except two large mirrors, four-and-a-half feet wide and twelve feet high.[162] A few years later, two young men, presumably students at the University of Virginia, left an account of their visit, and they too indicated that the interior of the house was in good condition, although the graveyard, its fence, and the stele over Jefferson's grave had fallen into disrepair.[163]

Even the Rev. Stephen H. Tyng, who despised Jefferson's ideas on religion, found the house in good order, although not attractive to his eyes. He visited Monticello in May 1840, and reported that Captain Levy "has been so troubled with the frequency of visits to his dwelling, that he has the reputation of being averse to receiving company to his house." He had no trouble gaining entry, however, because he was with a member of Jefferson's family, "to whom it is understood that the doors are always open." He found the beauty of the outdoors, created by God, breath-taking, and then rejoiced in the desolation of the grave site, which he took as emblematic of the triumph of Jesus over "all his opposition."[164]

Whose word shall we take? Did Levy welcome sightseers or did he make it difficult for them to make the trek up the little mountain? Levy apparently did little to discourage pilgrims; his wife, like Mrs. Barclay before her, reported that "we were overrun with sightseers."[165] Levy would have been perfectly within his rights had he closed the road and barred all, but he didn't. Even the people who complained that he did not welcome them went on to relate their experiences walking through the house and gardens. It appears that Levy, in maintaining the house in memory of Thomas Jefferson, accepted the fact that a shrine attracts visitors.

Was Monticello "in good condition" or was it "desolate"? One can dismiss the notion of desolate. Jefferson had failed to maintain the house and grounds properly in his declining years, and much of the description of ruin that visitors noted in the 1820s and during Barclay's ownership related to surface conditions. Paint wears out, floors need to be cleaned and waxed; exterior wooden trim, especially in humid areas, needs to be replaced periodically; glass gets broken. But the house itself, with its thick walls and firm foundation, was never at this time in danger of collapse or disintegration; Jefferson had built too well for that. In fact, the house would not get a major structural renovation until the middle of the twentieth century.

Uriah Levy had purchased a house that badly needed some paint and roof repairs as well as a good cleaning. The grounds were in worse shape, because not only had Barclay neglected the gardens and lawns, but had destroyed some of the fine trees that Jefferson had planted. But here again some devoted gardening could do wonders. Nearly everyone agrees that Uriah Levy did in fact bring the house, if not the entire landscaped area, back to a better condition than it had been at Jefferson's death. But the house had not been in great condition even then, and would not be put back into pristine form until the Thomas Jefferson Memorial Foundation purchased it in 1923 and turned it into a house museum.[166]

Beyond that, as William Howard Adams notes, at least some of the criticism that attached to Uriah Levy's stewardship resulted from his absentee ownership and the indifference of caretakers who lived at the house in his absence. But perhaps more important were the expectations pilgrims had of the site. Today visitors to Monticello view a house that probably never existed in Jefferson's time. It is well maintained, and loving care has been given to recreating what scholars believe to be the furnishings of the different rooms or the treatment of the grounds. It is what Jefferson visualized but did not actually accomplish; it is an idealized Monticello.[167]

In the Jacksonian era visitors saw a house that constantly needed attention, grounds that often went untended during the master's absence; they did not see the idealized Monticello they associated in their minds with Thomas Jefferson. But were it not for the work of Uriah Levy and his nephew, there might not be a Monticello for pilgrims to visit today.

☙

In 1967 James Bear, then director of Monticello, asked "what a naval officer expected to do with a place so remote from the scene of duty."[168] In fact, Uriah Levy did not spend great amounts of time at the estate, but he clearly loved the house and land in the Blue Ridge. In 1842 he wrote to his friend David Caddington: "When I walked out to my favorite spot a little elevated above the

Lawn, then I cast my Eye on My Fields, My Woods, My Hills, My Silver River, My Hounds, My servants my friends and peaceful home, then there my heart swells with joy & only sighs for her alone."[169] He buried his mother there along a walk approaching the main house, and when late in life he married, he took his bride up the mountain to be the chatelaine of Monticello.

But he remained an officer in his country's navy, and despite the problems he had had in his earlier tours of duty, he also had supporters in Washington who valued his skills. On September 7, 1838, Levy received orders from the Navy Department to report to Pensacola to take command of the U.S.S. *Vandalia*, part of the West Indies command. He commanded the ship for fourteen months, until late November 1839, when he was court-martialed once again.

By this time, Uriah Levy had become a firm opponent of flogging. He had first witnessed the brutality of corporal punishment during a sixteen-month tour of duty as a lieutenant aboard the U.S.S. *United States* in 1818-1819. Rules governing American naval conduct derived from the British Articles of War, which dated back to the time of the Restoration, when they had been formulated by the Lord High Admiral, the Duke of York, who later became James II. Use of the lash to maintain discipline and enforce rules of conduct had thus been a common practice of the British and later the American navies for close to two centuries. Supporters justified the practice on the grounds that common sailors were the dregs of the earth, and only harsh discipline would keep "the collected filth of jails" in order.[170]

A gunner's mate had returned drunk and abusive from shore leave. He had been tied to a rack, flogged into unconsciousness, and then spread-eagled on the deck where pails of salt water were poured over his bleeding back. The spectacle had sickened Uriah, and in the ensuing weeks he could speak of little else, complaining that such brutality did not belong in the navy of a democracy. His fellow officers, already suspicious of him as a Jew, now also considered him subversive for questioning the common practices of the time.

When he took command of the *Vandalia*, he determined to do away with flogging, and from all reports he turned the ship into an efficient and effective command with minimal use of the lash. However, in one incident he tried to use shaming rather than corporal punishment, and it backfired on him. For a relatively minor infraction, rather than have a young sailor whipped, Levy ordered that his trousers be pulled down and a spot of tar and some feathers put on his buttock. His fellow officers considered such action scandalous, and this led to Levy's sixth court martial. The naval board found him guilty, and sentenced him to be dismissed from the navy, but its findings were reversed by President John Tyler. He would not be given another assignment at sea for eighteen years. But he remained on the navy's active list, and in May 1844 received a promotion to the rank of captain.[171] What makes this promotion all the more interesting is not only did Captain Levy not have a ship, but he was nine years younger than most naval officers promoted to that rank.

During the 1840s, while the navy refused to give him an assignment, Levy wrote letters to newspapers and articles condemning the continued use of the whip in American ships, and in 1849 supposedly published a number of them as a pamphlet, *An Essay on Flogging in the Navy; containing Strictures upon Existing naval Laws, and Suggesting Substitutes for the Discipline of the Lash.*[172] It is not surprising that the navy remained cool toward his request for a ship when he managed to focus the harsh light of public and congressional criticism on one of its time-hallowed traditions. Senator John P. Hale of New Hampshire took up the cause, and soon became the leading opponent of the lash in Congress. Naturally the navy opposed Hale and Levy, and declared that "it would be utterly impracticable to have an efficient Navy without this form of punishment."[173] But in September 1850, Hale attached an anti-flogging rider to the Naval Appropriations Act, and two years later Congress finally put an end to the discipline of the lash.[174] While Uriah Levy reveled in the title of "the father of the abolition of flogging," at the least he shares this honor with Hale. Moreover, the surge of Jacksonian reform that stretched from the 1820s through the 1850s provided a context in which flogging appeared a barbarous relic of an older era, one unfit for the new American empire. Certainly, as far as the growing number of men and women opposed to slavery were concerned, if it was a terrible act to keep a human being in bonds and to whip him, then it could be no less terrible to whip a supposedly free man.[175]

During all this time the official navy record lists Uriah Levy as waiting orders. Then in 1855 Congress enacted a law to "Promote the Efficiency of the Navy," and set up a board to review personnel who, "in the judgment of the board, shall be incapable of performing promptly and efficiently all their duty both ashore and afloat."[176] The board met in secret, and in September 1855 notified Uriah that he was being stricken from the rolls; this was salt in the wound, since the law provided that those who had been incapacitated for ill health or old age should be placed on the reserve list. Those stricken from the rolls had only "themselves to blame for their incompetency." "The traveler, moving forward under a clear sky," he wrote, "who is suddenly stricken down by a thunderbolt" could not have been more astounded. "My capacity to perform all the duties of my grade … were matters of public notoriety, and officers thus competent were not within the operations of the law."[177] Although sixty-four years old at the time, he decided to fight, but the 1855 act made no provision for appeal. Levy hired one of New York's leading lawyers, former United States Attorney General Benjamin F. Butler,[178] and petitioned Congress to amend the law to allow for review.[179] A number of the other two hundred officers dropped by the secret panel, emboldened by Levy's determination, also demanded a review. Senator John J. Crittenden of Kentucky, appalled at the actions of the panel, had already requested the reinstatement of Levy, and in January 1857, Congress passed an amendment to provide for appeal.[180]

Levy took advantage of the new law, and in November of that year he, his wife, Butler, and their aides installed themselves in a series of suites in Gadsby's Hotel. Each day they went to the Navy Department on a route down Pennsylvania Avenue past the White House, where Levy could point out the monumental statue of Thomas Jefferson that he had given to the country. The navy thought it could make easy work of Levy's appeal by bringing up the six courts martial, and it spent several days going over them. When Butler wanted to rebut these charges, the chairman of the review panel ruled the request out of order. So Levy sat patiently for several days while naval officers read the findings of those trials into the record, followed by the testimony of one serving officer after another that Uriah Levy was unfit to hold command in the navy.[181] When the last witness for the navy sat down, they must have felt quite confident that they had heard the last of Levy.

But Benjamin Butler deserved his reputation as a great lawyer. First he lined up thirteen naval officers on active duty, as well as six retired officers, to testify to

Levy's fitness; three others sent in depositions. The chief of the Philadelphia Navy Yard, Senior Commodore Charles Stewart, testified that "when Captain Levy served under me, he performed his professional duties to my perfect satisfaction. I thought he was competent in 1818 and I think he is competent now. I'd be glad to have him on my ship under my command." Witness after witness made the point, one that the navy understandably had tried to ignore, that nearly all of Uriah's troubles stemmed from the fact that he was Jewish, and that anti-Semitism infected the ranks of naval officers.

When the naval witnesses had finished testifying, the court must have assumed that Butler had finished; in fact he still had two surprises left for the inquiry. He now called fifty-three additional witnesses, men who were leaders in their chosen professions, to testify to Uriah Levy's character. Bank presidents, doctors, government officials, newspaper editors and merchants paraded to the witness stand. Former senator John A. Dix of New York, Representative Aaron Vanderpoel of New York, former mayor James H. Blake of Washington and others all testified to their high regard for Uriah Levy and their belief in his ability and integrity. What started out as a minor appeals board hearing in a small room in Washington had grown into a national new story, as reporters crowded in each day to see who else would testify.[182]

After they had finished, Butler called one more witness to the stand—Uriah Phillips Levy. On December 19, 1857, Uriah began his statement, and in it he gave not only a clear statement as to his own religious beliefs, but also to the need to eradicate religious prejudice in the navy and in American life. The one word that most aptly describes this part of his testimony is "Jeffersonian," and it is worth quoting at length:[183]

> My parents were Israelites, and I was nurtured in the faith of my ancestors. In deciding to adhere to it, I have but exercised a right guaranteed to me by the Constitution of my native state and of the United States, a right given to all men by their Maker, a right more precious to each of us than life itself. But, while claiming and exercising this freedom of conscience, I have never failed to acknowledge

and respect the like freedom in others. I might safely defy the citation of a single act, in the whole course of my official career, injurious to the religious rights of any other person.

Remembering always that the great mass of my fellow-citizens were Christians, profoundly grateful to the Christian founders of our republic for their justice and liberality to my long-persecuted race, I have earnestly endeavored, in all places and circumstances, to act up to the wise and tolerant spirit of our political institutions. I have therefore been careful to treat every Christian, and especially every Christian under my command, with exemplary justice and ungrudging liberality ....

I have to complain—more in sorrow than in anger do I say it—that in my official experience I have met with little to encourage, though with much to frustrate, these conciliatory efforts. At an early day, and especially from the time when it became known to the officers of my age and grade that I aspired to a lieutenancy, and still more after I had gained it, I was forced to encounter a large share of the prejudice and hostility by which, for so many ages, the Jew has been pursued. I need not speak to you of the incompatibility of these sentiments with the genius of Christianity or the precepts of its Author. You should know this better than I, but I may ask you to unite with the wisest and best men of our own country and of Europe in denouncing them, not only as injurious to the peace and welfare of the community, but as repugnant to every dictate of reason, humanity, and justice.

Levy went on to deliver a bravura performance that lasted three days. According to one Washington newspaper, "It was one of the most glorious, if not brilliant, pleas ever made in the history of the United States Navy: a plea that 'right should be done!'"[184] He refuted each and every charge against him, pointed out the pervasive anti-Semitism that infected the navy and that he had faced for more than four decades. On December 22, he finished his appeal with these words:[185]

What is my case today, if you yield to this injustice, may tomorrow be that of the Roman Catholic or the Unitarian, the Presbyterian or the Methodist, the Episcopalian or the Baptist. There is but one safeguard: that is to be found in an honest, wholehearted, inflexible support of the wise, the just, the impartial guarantee of the Constitution. I have the fullest confidence that you will faithfully adhere to this guarantee, and therefore, with like confidence I leave my destiny in your hands.

Levy's faith proved justified. On January 29, 1858, the panel restored him to the active list with his previous rank of captain, and three months later the navy offered him the command of the U.S.S. *Macedonian*, then fitting out in Boston to join the Mediterranean Squadron. Levy accepted, but perhaps realizing that he had the navy in a bind, he made a very unusual request—he wanted to take his wife along to a port in the Mediterranean. She was an orphan, he said, not a native of the United States, and would be left without any protection once he sailed. The navy brass must have fumed over this, but they allowed him to take Virginia with him from Boston to the first port in Italy touched at by the *Macedonian*.[186] He also took along his favorite nephew, Asahel, as a clerk.

Levy commanded the ship for nearly two years. During that time, he was given command of the Mediterranean Squadron, and as flag officer enjoyed the courtesy title of commodore. (He used the title the rest of his life, although technically he remained a captain. Congress did not establish the rank of commodore as the grade above captain until July 2, 1862, more than three months after Levy's death.) He apparently maintained discipline and efficiency without resort to the lash, and the presence of a woman on board proved to be a great tonic for morale. She later noted that since she could not bring a maid with her, she took along a young boy named Jack in the hope that he might be trained to take the maid's place. The plan failed, since "the sailors spoiled him so that he was of little use to me. [Moreover,] they put him up to all sorts of pranks on the officers."[187] The Levys proved to be a popular couple at the various social functions he had to attend as senior American officer in the Mediterranean.

We have an interesting description of Levy while on this tour of duty. The *Macedonian* as part of its tour stopped in Beirut, where Levy dined with James Finn, the British consul to Jerusalem. In his diary Finn described Levy as "a fine looking rosy old fellow aged 69 [sic], with strong Jewish features which looked curious with cocked hat, epaulettes & cape buttons, with abundance of jewelry." Levy told Finn that before sailing, he had gone to the Boston Repository for Bibles and Tracts, and bought a good many which he had distributed in the various countries around the Mediterranean. Finn wondered why a Jew should do this, and Levy told him the same question had been asked in Boston. He had answered that he knew the religion of Christ had civilized the world, and therefore he wished to recommend it every where.[188]

Nor did Levy forget Monticello. Before sailing from Boston he wrote to George Carr, summing up what he expected during his absence. Apparently he had no concern about Joel Wheeler's management of Monticello, but worried about the man he had hired as supervisor of the Washington Farm, a Mr. Garrison. You know, he told Carr, "how much a farm requires the eye of the master and how much it suffers from his absence. Mr. Garrison is an excellent man but he will need your counsel and advice and I hope you will give him the benefit of your superior knowledge." He had just had a letter regarding the "miserable" tobacco crop, and Carr must urge Garrison "to try and do better."[189]

When the *Macedonian* arrived in Spezia, Sardinia, Levy found mail from Carr about business matters as well as other news. Apparently the crops had not done well again. "Shall I ever hear that our part of Virginia has produced good crops?" Levy replied. "'The wheat has turned out badly,' 'the tobacco crop will or has failed,' 'the oats are all straw,' 'we have had too much or too little rain' has been the dolorous burden of the song for many years."[190]

Carr had also enclosed a copy of a local newspaper account of July Fourth celebrations at Monticello, and in his reply we get what is the most sustained statement we have of Uriah Levy's feelings about Thomas Jefferson:[191]

> It must have been a spirited affair and I am rejoiced that Virginians
> more and more appreciate the nation's birth day and honor the mem-
> ory of the man who was among the first if not the first to call the

nation into being, who guided its infant steps aright, and taught its infant tongue to lisp no other sentiment than those which were truly Republican.

Let every year add to our love and veneration for Thomas Jefferson. There is no fear of his being made an idol. His life, his writings, his acts and example forbid that, but the most grateful emotions of our hearts can not inspire our lips to utter language which will more than express the just mode of praise we owe him. There is something appropriate in solemnizing the nation's natal day at the tomb of Jefferson and although I was many miles from Monticello I was full of thought of what might be happening there.

☙

Uriah served on the *Macedonian* and as flag officer of the Mediterranean Squadron until July 14, 1860, when he returned to New York; in the ship's hold he carried a wagonload of earth from Palestine as a gift to Shearith Israel, for use in the traditional Jewish burial service. Virginia had returned a little earlier aboard a commercial ship, and they now made their home in the house he owned at 107 St. Mark's Place; they spent the rest of the summer of 1860 at Monticello, his last stay at the house. By then sixty-eight years old, he could have retired from service, since it appeared unlikely he would ever get another assignment at sea. But he chose to remain on the active list, partially out of pride and perhaps sensing that if the South seceded, the Union would have need of all the experienced naval officers it could get. When war did break out in April 1861 he went to Washington to see Abraham Lincoln. Although he owned property in Virginia, Uriah announced his loyalty to the Union and reportedly offered the president not only his sword but his entire fortune for the Union cause. He wrote to Secretary of the Navy Gideon Welles that "I am ready for service, for any service which in my rank I can be useful. I have served ever since 1812 under the flag of the Union and I am not one to abandon it in the day of peril."[192] Although Levy talked excitedly about a commission, neither Lincoln nor Welles saw any way to send the elderly warrior back to sea. The president, however, did have a sense of irony, and later on in 1861

Lincoln named Levy to the court martial board in Washington, the same body that had heard charges against him six times in the past.[193]

Levy's health, however, began to fail. He complained of abdominal pain, and in the late winter of 1862 he came down with a bad cold that developed into pneumonia. He died at home on March 22, 1862, one month shy of his seventieth birthday. He received an impressive military funeral, and was buried in the cemetery of Shearith Israel, the Spanish and Portuguese Synagogue of New York, in Cyprus Hills, Brooklyn. On the tombstone is inscribed the epitaph he himself had chosen: "In memory of Uriah P. Levy, Father of the Law for the abolition of the barbarous practices of corporal punishment in the Navy of the United States."

But Uriah Levy had one more surprise in his bag, for he had determined to leave Monticello, which he had surely saved from ruin, to the people of the United States.

Chapter Three

WHERE THERE'S A WILL ...

"I give, devise and bequeath my Farm and Estate at Monticello, in Virginia, formerly belonging to President Thomas Jefferson, together with all the rest and residue of my Estate, real personal or mixed not hereby disposed of wherever or however situated for the People of the United States ..."
—URIAH PHILLIPS LEVY[194]

Uriah Levy last saw Monticello in the summer of 1860, little knowing that Mr. Jefferson's house would soon endure nearly two decades of adversity that would bring it to the brink of total ruin. First, the outbreak of the Civil War led the Confederacy to seize Monticello as the property of an enemy alien. Then his widow and younger brother led a fight to overturn his will and take control of his considerable estate. The ensuing court battles left Monticello without a legal owner until 1879, when Uriah's nephew, Jefferson Monroe Levy, finally gained full ownership. During this period Joel Wheeler lived atop the little mountain, but took no care of it; the man who had worked so well with Uriah to preserve Monticello now seemed hell-bent on ruining it.

❦

Levy had written his last will and testament on May 13, 1858, just before he left New York for Boston, where he took command of the *Macedonian*, and the will was entered for probate on June 9, 1862.[195] He made a number of bequests to family and friends, the largest being the Washington Farm and $5,000 to his favorite nephew, Asahel, the son of his brother Isaac. Several other relatives received bequests of $1,000, and a number of relatives and family members received amounts ranging from $25 to $100 to purchase mourning rings "in testimony of my regard for them."[196] He ordered his executors to erect over his grave either a bronze or iron statue of him, "the size of life at least," at a cost of not less than $6,000. His wife Virginia received a widow's dower of the income of one-third of his estate, which he considered "adequate for her full support," as well as the use of all household furniture, plate, and plated ware for as long as she remained unmarried. Upon her remarriage or death the furniture would go to Asahel.

The most interesting part of the will concerned Monticello, and it is quoted here in full:[197]

> I give, devise and bequeath my Farm and Estate at Monticello in Virginia, formerly belonging to President Thomas Jefferson, together with all the rest and residue of my Estate, real personal or mixed not hereby disposed of wherever or however situated to the People of the United States or such persons as Congress shall appoint to receive it, and especially all my Real Estate in the City of New York. In trust for the sole and only purpose of establishing and maintaining at said Farm of Monticello in Virginia an Agricultural School for the purpose of educating as practical farmers children of the warrant office of the United States Navy whose Fathers are dead. Said children are to be educated in a plain way in the ordinary elementary branches to fit them for agricultural life and to be supported entirely by this fund from the age of Twelve to Sixteen and each of them to be brought up to do all the usual work on a farm, the said Farm to be so cultivated by the said Boys and their Instructors, as to raise all they may require to feed themselves, and the Schoolmaster and one other Teacher and one Superintendant of the said Farm. I also give and bequeath for the purpose of giving such fuel and fencing for the said Monticello Farm School two hundred acres of wood land of my Washington Farm called the Bank Farm in Virginia, the said two hundred acres to be taken off from said Farm hereby devised to my nephew Asahel and to be designated by said Asahel.

Excerpts from Uriah Levy's will (courtesy of the American Jewish Archives on the Cincinnati Campus of the Hebrew Union College—Jewish Institute of Religion).

In establishing said Farm School I especially require that no professorship be established in said School or professors employed in the Institution. My intention in establishing this School is charity and usefulness and not for the purpose of pomp. In proportion to the smallness in number of the Teachers so will industry prevail. The institution may be kept within the revenue derived from this endowment and under no circumstances can any part of the real or personal estate hereby devised be disposed of, but the rent and income of all said Estate real and personal is to be held forever inviolate for the purpose of sustaining this Institution. The Estate and Lands in New York can be leased to great advantage for that purpose.

Should the Congress of the United States refuse to accept of this bequest or refuse to take the necessary steps to carry out this intention, I then devise and bequeath all the property hereby devised to the People of the State of Virginia instead of The people of the

United States Provided they by acts of their Legislature accept it and carry it out as herein directed and should the people of Virginia by the neglect of the Legislature decline to accept this said bequest, I then devise and bequeath all of my said property to the Portugese Hebrew Congregation of the City of New York whose Synagogue is in Crosby street New York [Shearith Israel], and the old Portugese Hebrew Congregation whose Synagogue is in Cherry Street Philadelphia [Mikveh Israel], and the Portuguese Hebrew Congregation of Richmond Virginia [Beth Shalome], provided they procure the necessary Legislation to entitle them to hold said Estate and to establish an Agricultural School at said Monticello for the Children of said Societies who are between the ages of Twelve and Sixteen years and whose Fathers are dead, and also similar Children of any other denomination of Hebrew or Christian. In order to enable said Hebrew Congregations to hold said Estate and carry on said Farm School a charter will probably have to be obtained upon the application of said Congregations to the Legislature of Virginia and New York.

Should the fund arising from said Estate be more than sufficient to support and educate the said Children of warrant officers of the United States Navy, the directors of the said School are then next to select the Children of Sergeant Majors of the United States Army as the beneficiaries, and if a surplus is still remaining they are then to select from the Children of Seaman in the United States Navy whose Fathers are dead.

Item. I direct my Executors herein after named or such of them as shall qualify to invest the funds arising from said Estate in some safe paying Stocks as fast as they accumulate and to hold the whole of the property and Estate hereby devised and bequeathed for said School and in their hands until the proper steps have been taken by Congress or the Legislature of Virginia or the said Hebrew Benevolent Congregations to receive the same and discharge said Executors.

As his executors, Levy named eight men, an unusually large number. In New York he chose four attorneys: Benjamin F. Butler, the man who had defended him in the last review case; his friend David V.S. Coddington; his favorite nephew Asahel, to whom he had left the largest personal bequest after his wife's dower; and another friend, Joseph H. Patten. Butler died shortly after the will had been written in 1858, and the other three would carry the burden of its defense. In Baltimore he named his friend Dr. Joshua Cohen and Cohen's brother Jacob. Dr. John B. Blake would represent the estate in Washington, D.C., while George Carr of Charlottesville would continue in his role as Levy's attorney in Virginia. One can understand the selection of the four New Yorkers; the bulk of the estate could be found there and would need the closest supervision. In addition, if Congress and Virginia passed on the offer, one of the residual legatees, Congregation Shearith Israel was located in New York. Blake would be useful in representing the estate to Congress, while Carr could do the same to the Virginia legislature, or in dealing with Congregation Beth Shalome. It is unclear why he chose the Cohen brothers of Baltimore, yet did not choose at least one executor in Philadelphia, the home of the third residual congregation, Mikveh Israel.

The will is also confusing in terms of the order of inheritance. Congress, clearly, was Uriah Levy's first choice, followed by Virginia. But did he mean the congregations to go in order, i.e., first refusal to Shearith Israel, then to Mikvah Israel and then to Beth Shalome, or were they to act in concert? No provision was made should all refuse, and although Levy lived nearly a year after the start of the Civil War, he made no amendments recognizing that Monticello now stood behind enemy lines and in the *de facto* control of the Confederacy.

The will is silent on exactly what use was to be made of the house. Levy probably knew that the Mount Vernon Ladies' Association had purchased George Washington's plantation on the banks of the Potomac intending to turn it into a memorial to the first president.[198] The suggestion that Uriah Levy pioneered in historic preservation does not stand up to a fair reading of the will. It is clear that he intended the three thousand or so acres he owned to be farmed, but what did he intend for the house itself? He probably meant that it should continue to be a shrine of some sort to Jefferson, but from the will one could legitimately infer that it would be utilized as a dormitory for the boy farmers-in-training or perhaps a house for the three men chosen to supervise their work, hardly an effort to create an historic museum-house. And, it should be noted, while the will clearly implies that by working the farm the school could be self-sufficient, there is no mention of the twenty or so slaves that Levy owned at the time, and certainly no provision for their manumission.

There is an unverified story that had Levy lived one day more, he would have written a new will.[199] This theory is based on the assumption that Uriah's marriage to his young niece nearly a decade before his death had angered certain members of his family, especially his youngest brother Jonas, and there had been strained relations ever since. But Uriah did not die suddenly, and had he wanted to change his will certainly had the time to do so. Given the elaborate nature of his instructions, the inevitable conclusion is that Uriah Levy really did want Monticello to go to the people of the United States.

☙

One needs to remember that Monticello constituted but a small portion of Uriah Levy's wealth. As the chief executor of his uncle's will, Asahel Levy had an outside appraiser inventory and value Uriah's assets. The personal goods, including paintings, plate, silver and other non-property items, came to $131,606.15.[200] In October 1862, Asahel, on behalf of the estate, paid taxes to New York City and County of $1,204.05 on twenty-four separate properties; an inventory on May 1, 1863, listed twenty-five properties.[201] A New York Court described Uriah's real estate holdings, exclusive of Monticello and the Washington Farm, as over $200,000.[202] In modern dollars, his total New York estate of $331,000 would be valued at between $3.3 and $5.3 million. Even after deducting the various cash bequests, the cost of his monument, and the paintings he gave to the Historical Society of the City of New York, the residual amount to be used for the support of the agricultural school at Monticello came to about $300,000.

Such a sum proved irresistible, and the Levy clan quickly fell to squabbling over who should get what. Uriah's widow Virginia and his youngest brother Jonas—whom Uriah did not even mention in the will—led the legal attack to break the will.

Sometime around 1852 or 1853 Uriah's niece Virginia Lopez, the daughter of his sister Fanny, had come to Monticello to live with him and Amelia, his unmarried sister. Virginia, who had been born on September 25, 1835, would have been around seventeen at the time, and from all reports attractive and outgoing. In 1853 the sixty-one year old captain married her, much to everyone's surprise, but the two of them seemed quite happy in the decade they had together.

Why did Levy, for so many years a confirmed bachelor, marry a woman young enough to have been a granddaughter? Moreover, she was not just his sister's daughter. Fanny had married a West Indian banker named Abraham Lopez, whose family was related to that of the Phillipses and Levys; in fact, there

Inventory of the Personal Estate of Uriah P. Levy (Thomas Jefferson Foundation).

were at least fourteen different lines on a genealogical chart connecting Uriah to Virginia. Uriah at one point claimed that he married her to "protect" her. Her father had made a number of unwise investments, and had died leaving his wife and child penniless. Jewish tradition calls for the nearest unmarried male relative to marry and care for a widowed or orphaned female member of the family.[203]

Nonetheless, eyebrows were raised both within and without the family. George Blatterman charged that the marriage violated Virginia's constitutional prohibition against such close consanguineous marriages, and that every year Uriah had to leave Monticello and go to New York in order to avoid a grand jury indictment.[204] Jonas Levy apparently heard this tale, possibly from Blatterman himself, and later in the litigation wondered if he might disqualify Virginia by having her marriage to Uriah declared invalid under Virginia state law.[205] He was no doubt disappointed to learn that although a grand jury had looked into the matter, the marriage did not violate any of the Commonwealth's laws.[206]

Calling cards for Captain and Mrs. Uriah P. Levy (courtesy of Special Collections, University of Virginia Library).

Whatever his reason for marrying her, Uriah seemed to be happy with Virginia, and as noted in the previous chapter, took her with him when he assumed command of the *Macedonian*. At times, however, he must have wondered at his action. A proud, reserved man, he now had a child bride who often acted like a teenager. In her memoirs she tells the story of a time when rowdy college students rode up to Monticello. She apparently joined in their games for a while, and then went to get a pistol to force them to leave. Unfortunately, she forgot to unwrap the gun, much to the amusement of the visitors, but after a while they went back to the University, and as she put it, they parted friends.[207] An inveterate flirt, she charmed the sailors on the *Macedonian* as well as most men she met at this time of her life. One poet spoke of "the infinite variety of your charm" and "the bubbling effervescence of your youth." This may have made it difficult for her older husband to keep up with her, but he tried, dying his graying hair and mustache jet black so he looked more youthful.[208]

His young wife also proved to be expensive, as Virginia took full advantage of Uriah's wealth and generosity to buy clothes and more clothes. On board the *Macedonian* one of the junior officers wrote that "she seemed determined to show off her dresses for every time she came on deck she had a different one." On another occasion the same officer entered the captain's cabin to find "the tables and chairs covered with ladies' apparel, hoops and skirts, bonnets and shoes, etc., etc."[209] But Uriah clearly indulged her and found her to be a delightful and attractive companion at all the different social events they attended during his command of the *Macedonian*.

With such expensive tastes, Virginia may have found the traditional widow's dower insufficient to continue the lifestyle she had become accustomed to as Uriah's wife. Although the income from a third of his estate would have been a considerable sum, she in effect would have had only a life interest and would have been unable to touch the principal, which would have reverted to the fund to support Monticello on her death. If she broke the will, however, she would have complete control and ownership of over $100,000.[210] It is possible that Jonas, aware of her extravagant habits, may have encouraged her to join in a suit to break the will. In any event, the widow Levy did not remain so for very long. Not yet twenty-seven years old at the time of Uriah's death, in 1866 she married a Danish Jew, William Rée, by whom she had at least one child. She lived almost to her ninetieth birthday, and her memoirs, recorded in a journalistic interview only a few months before her death, vividly reflect the high spirits of the young naval wife she had been seven decades earlier.

٭

For Uriah running away at ten as a cabin boy, the sea must have seemed a great venture, but as he matured he saw it as an honorable career, first as a master of a merchant ship and then as an officer in his country's navy. For Jonas, the youngest brother, the allure of the sea seems to have taken a more adventuresome turn, and while he never became a pirate, a touch of the buccaneer informed many of his business dealings. In the late 1830s and early 1840s, he lived in St. Juan Batista in Mexico, and when the United States declared war in 1846, the Mexican government gave him only twenty-four hours to leave St. Juan. He claimed that he and his family escaped by floating down the river in an open canoe. He then used a ship he owned to ferry American troops to Vera Cruz, after which he talked General Winfield Scott into appointing him the captain of the port of Vera Cruz.[211]

After the Mexican War Jonas put in a claim for goods he said had been lost or confiscated during the hostilities, and after several years of negotiation the Treasury in 1854 agreed that his losses amounted to $54,669.40. He would never collect, however, because auditors could never validate the records that he presented, and when he applied to the Court of Claims in 1858, the judge ruled against him because he lacked the evidence to substantiate his loss.[212] For the rest of his life Jonas petitioned Congress to pay him what he claimed the government owed him, and after his death his son Jefferson continued the battle. As late as 1921 Rep. Henry M. Goldfogle put in a bill to pay Jonas's heirs the amount he claimed plus nearly seventy-five years of accrued interest, but it failed to pass.[213]

Had Jonas received the money, he intended to set up a packet line that would carry mail from New York to San Francisco in twenty days, as well as make rapid connections between New Orleans and Latin American ports. He asked Congress to advance him $287,500 as well as award him a mail contract for $575,000 a year to effectuate his scheme. As an added inducement, he offered to build at private expense a railroad across the Isthmus to further reduce travel time between the coasts.

Uriah always remained loyal to the Union, even though he owned slaves and an estate south of Mason and Dixon's line, but Jonas appears to have been so pro-South as to come perilously close to treason. He was involved in the Baltimore anti-Union riots of 1861, and played a role in a rebellious volunteer militia unit until Union forces took over Fort McHenry and the city waterfront. He also communicated frequently with the Confederate government, and in November 1861 wrote to the Confederate Secretary of War, his old friend Judah P. Benjamin, proposing a plan to use a new iron steamship, the *North Carolina*, to carry cotton and other southern goods to Europe and to return with military stores. Benjamin approved the plan but could not, as Levy requested, advance any funds for the venture.[214]

In terms of Monticello, there is evidence that early on Jonas attempted to gain control of the estate. One version has it that Uriah asked Jonas to go to Virginia to check the property. In the early days of the war travel between North and South remained fairly open, and even later on visitors could, with appropriate papers, pass between the lines. Jonas reportedly got as far as Richmond, where he may—or may not—have been temporarily detained.[215] We do know that he wrote to George Carr in June that since "all communications are cut off from my brother and may not be open again until the close of the war, I will be pleased to have some information in relation to the [estate] on the mountain and the welfare of the Negroes."[216] There is no copy of a reply from Carr, and in fact, no record of any further communication until after the war.

However, in August 1861 Jonas apparently took up residence in Monticello, and wrote to Judah Benjamin asking for the arrest of Joel Wheeler, who had remained at his post as overseer and caretaker of the estate. Jonas had raised the Confederate flag over the house, despite the fact that he knew his brother to be loyal to the Union, and Wheeler had pulled down the Stars and Bars and "spoken disrespectfully" of the Confederacy. Jonas signed his letter "Captain of the late Maryland Navy," and Benjamin promised to refer the matter to the governor of Virginia who would investigate, and if justified, would issue a warrant for Wheeler's arrest.[217]

In 1862, shortly after his brother died, Jonas made another effort to gain possession of Monticello. He wrote to Benjamin H. Hill of Georgia, chairman of the Confederate Senate Committee on the Judiciary, requesting an amendment to the Sequestration Act allowing him to seize the estate of his brother, an enemy alien. Jonas described himself as the only relative of Uriah in the Confederacy, and declared "I am a loyal citizen of this Confederacy and donated all my energies to the success of its cause."[218] In July Jonas informed Carr that he intended to contest the legality of his brother's will, and although he had absolutely no legal basis for such a claim, he declared that "independent of the invalidity of said will, I have a preferred claim against all late Brother's property, both real and personal, within the Commonwealth of Virginia."[219] When the Confederacy put Monticello on the block in 1864, Jonas attempted to enter a bid, but it is unknown whether he succeeded in doing so.[220]

It is unclear just where Jonas spent the war years. According to Samuel Rezneck, he had business interests in Wilmington, North Carolina, which he used as a base to help the Confederate cause. The official records of the Confederacy "reveal a continuous and substantial series of transactions between Levy and the military authorities for the supply of goods, principally ironmongery and building materials."[221] He may also have played both sides of the fence, especially after it became clear that the South would not prevail. When the war ended he complained to the federal government that he had not been reimbursed for materials he had supplied to Union forces.[222] And somehow or other he, or his agents, led the attack on his brother's will.

Before we turn to the legal labyrinth involving the will, we need to note what happened to Monticello. In June 1861 Uriah Levy offered his sword to the Union, well aware that Monticello now lay behind enemy lines. Although the dates are not clear, it appears that sometime between August 1861 and February 1862 the Confederacy labeled Monticello the property of an "enemy alien," and took possession of it under the Sequestration Act passed in 1861.[223] Levy died on March 22, 1862, and Carr, still acting as his attorney (and probably aware that he had been named as one of the executors of Levy's estate) tried unsuccessfully to block the seizure. He brought suit in the District Court of the Confederate States of America for the Eastern District of Virginia, but the presiding judge ordered a sale

Jonas Phillips Levy (courtesy of the American Jewish Archives on the Cincinnati Campus of the Hebrew Union College—Jewish Institute of Religion).

by public action "for cash in Confederate treasury notes." The auction was advertised for November 1863 by Henry L. Brooke, the receiver for the district, "and immediately after the sale of the house and land, there will be a sale of 19 Negro slaves, a variety of household furniture, etc." The event, however, did not take place until November 1864, when Benjamin F. Ficklin became the new owner with a bid of $80,500.[224] As soon as the war ended in April 1865, all such sales were declared invalid and the properties reverted to their former rightful owners. By then, however, Uriah Levy had died, and a bitter legal battle had commenced that would tie up title to Monticello for another fourteen years.

Everything hinged on the disposition of Monticello. If the federal government accepted the gift, it would effectively put an end to any suit by the disgruntled family members. If, however, Congress declined or failed to act on the donation, then the suit would continue. It seemed clear that the contingent beneficiaries did not count. Virginia had seceded from the Union, and while it might have physical dominion over the house and land, it would never, so long as the war continued, gain control of the more than $300,000 in real and personal property in New York. The three synagogues, whose charters would have to be amended in order to receive the bequest, had absolutely no interest in Levy's gift, and the smallest of them, Beth Shalome in Richmond, also sat behind enemy lines.

Asahel duly informed Congress of Captain Levy's bequest, and on the last day of the session the Thirty-seventh Congress debated accepting the gift. The members of the Senate found themselves clearly uncomfortable about doing so. To begin with, the Republican majority—actively prosecuting a war against slavery (the Emancipation Proclamation had been issued earlier in the year)—had little interest in the home of the founder of the Democratic Party and a slaveholder to boot. Even if inclined to accept, it would certainly be embarrassing to claim property behind enemy lines already confiscated by the Confederacy.

Beyond that, Congress had practically no experience in receiving gifts. James Smithson, a British chemist, had left his fortune of $550,000 to the "United States of America, to found at Washington, under the name of the Smithsonian Institution, an Establishment for the increase and diffusion of knowledge among men." Smithson had died in 1829, and Congress had debated and delayed until 1846 before it accepted the bequest and chartered the Smithsonian.[225] But that had been a straight bequest, unencumbered by the problems of a civil war and a family lawsuit and, as Senator Ira Harris of New York noted, if Congress accepted Monticello, "we must accept a law suit with it." Mr. James R. Doolittle of Wisconsin was even more explicit, when he suggested delaying any decision until they had more information:[226]

> For we, by accepting the devise, especially if the whole property is in litigation, may be worse off than the person who bought the elephant. We may be as bad off as the man who supposed his father-in-law gave him a large donation on his wedding day of certain stocks in a railroad corporation. He felt himself rich, but when he began to inquire into the value of the stocks, he found that they were perfectly good for nothing, and more than all, that the stockholders were liable to assessments.

In the end the Senate tabled the motion to accept and joined in a House resolution that the attorney general be authorized to ascertain the facts, and report his evaluation of the situation and recommendations to the next Congress.[227]

The attorney general, Edward Bates, asked Patten for information, and he and Asahel Levy drew up a memorandum that they forwarded to T.J. Coffey, the acting attorney general in February 1864.[228] Bates also asked the United States Attorney for New York, E. Delafield Smith, to investigate. A week before the Court of Appeals would hear the case, Smith advised Bates that if the government had any interest in receiving the bequest, it ought to be represented at the hearing. "The trust appears so onerous, however, that it has occurred to me the authorities might conclude to decline availing themselves of the provisions of the will."[229]

Bates decided to have the government represented at the hearing, and Smith appeared on behalf of the United States at both appeals court hearings. This appears to have been a precaution, in case by some stretch of the imagination the courts upheld the will. His true feelings regarding the bequest he conveyed in a letter to Vice President Hannibal Hamlin saying that, inasmuch as the bequest was under litigation, he was not ready "to advise the government to assume a trust which, beginning in troublesome and expensive controversies, may end in complete failure." Even if the courts sustained the will, he questioned "whether it is sound policy for the government to assume the execution of purely charitable trusts, however laudable their purpose and ample the funds provided for them."[230] With this letter, all interest by the government of the United States in Mr. Jefferson's house ended for nearly fifty years.[231]

Multitudes of charitable and educational foundations abound in the United States today, controlling billions of dollars donated to them, often in the form of a charitable bequest. Moreover, the control that a donor can exercise is practically limitless, and if a man or woman is of sound mind, he or she can elect to leave money to support stray cats or maintain a water fountain in a park. But the law of charitable bequests at the time Uriah Levy wrote his will differed considerably from that of today, and in fact was then going through a period of radical transition. While no impediment blocked a donor from leaving part or even all of an estate to recognized charitable institutions such as schools, churches or hospitals, the manner in which Levy tried to settle his lands ran against strong legal currents.

To understand the legal complexities that surrounded Levy's will and the litigation it triggered, we must start, as did all American and English courts at the time, with 43 Eliz. c.4, commonly called the Statute of Charitable Uses. Parliament passed the law in 1601 in an effort to impose some order on charitable giving, which had been in turmoil since Henry VIII had overthrown the Church of Rome and confiscated the property of the monasteries.[232] The Act of Elizabeth directed donors to endow secular rather than religious beneficiaries. It did this in large part by relaxing the rules that voided vague or uncertain bequests when the gift went to a charity. The law needs to be seen as part of a broader effort by the Tudor government to take care of the poor through secular rather than religious agencies. Instead of giving land and money to churches, the Act of Elizabeth encouraged bequests to take care of the poor, orphans, and other unfortunates, and to provide schooling for them. It also gave the Chancellor and the courts of equity broad power to ensure the effectiveness of the gifts.

The Statute of Elizabeth and related laws traveled across the Atlantic with the colonists as part of their common law baggage. But the Church of England, although established in the middle and southern colonies, never developed the extensive institutional network of schools and charities that it operated in England. Moreover, the colonists did not appear to be as "religious" in the New World as their kinfolk in the Mother Country, and proved less inclined to leave their property to charity. Exceptions can, of course, be found, such as the gifts of John Harvard and Elihu Yale to the colleges that now bear their names. But the colonies had no monasteries, the plenitude of land made it available to all, and American law from the beginning favored a dynamic rather than a static view of property.[238] Most states disestablished churches after the Revolution, and in any event the congregational form of governance that predominated in the states gave power over church holdings to the local laity rather than to a central church office or prelate.

New York, where Uriah's will would be interpreted, accepted the English law of charities, but prior to the Revolution there were so few organized charities that the law had little practical application.[239] Following independence the New York legislature, like that of most other states, continued a great part of English common and statutory law in effect, although with the express provision that the new state assembly had the power to amend or even abolish it. Within a short period, some New York courts began interpreting the law regarding charitable bequests in a manner hostile to the continuation of permanent, indefinite charitable trusts, and also to bequests to the poor at large or uncertain groups or persons.[240] In the process the courts transmuted the idea of mortmain: the dead hand now described not the recipient but the donor. The law disfavored efforts to tie up property for an indefinite future.

In 1853, in what clearly was an idiosyncratic decision, New York's highest court unexpectedly—and against all historical evidence—affirmed that state law incorporated the English rules. "The law of charitable uses as it existed in England, at the time of the Revolution … has not been repealed and the existing Courts of the State having equity jurisdiction are bound to administer that law." In the case of *Williams v. Williams*, the Court of Appeals held that two legacies, one to a church and the other to trustees of a fund for the education of poor children, both met the condition of the English law, and that the donees had the necessary authority to receive and use these funds.[241] Had the *Williams* doctrine—which certainly gave the most liberal interpretation possible to the law and the greatest leeway to the intent of the donor—continued, the courts might well have sanctioned Uriah's plans. But the *Williams* case marked a quirk in jurisprudential development and it would soon be overthrown, in part by the disposition of the Levy will.

At about the same time, the Supreme Court handed down a decision that seemed to indicate a liberal attitude toward charitable bequests. The Marshall Court had, for reasons that are unclear, accepted a clearly wrong interpretation of the Statute of Charitable Uses in *Baptist Association v. Hart* (1819),[242] and had struck down a bequest to an unincorporated association to be held in trust for the education of ministers. Much criticism followed, and in *Vidal v. Girard* (1844), the high court upheld a bequest of nearly $6.7 million to the mayor and aldermen of the city of Philadelphia for the funding of an orphans' home. In his opinion, Justice Joseph Story noted that common law doctrine governing charitable uses had existed before the Statute of Elizabeth, and so if a state repealed that law then the old common law doctrines would govern unless the state statutorily modified them. Pennsylvania had no legal prohibition against the type of bequest made by Girard, and therefore the will should be considered valid.[243]

A related legal development that would also affect the outcome of the will dispute involved the developing law of corporations. Today corporate charters, whether to private businesses, educational or charitable institutions, are often worded in broad, permissive language, and courts tend to interpret them liberally. Now one applies for a charter to an administrative agency whose main job is to confirm that the application reflects the general purpose of the organizers and comports with the appropriate laws. In the early nineteenth century legislatures issued charters, which they worded very carefully, giving the corporation exact and limited powers. A company chartered to build a turnpike, for example, could not build a canal or, in fact, do anything but construct the road. A school chartered to teach young men could not run a hospital, nor could a hospital exceed its charter to run an asylum. A corporation could not act *ultra vires*, beyond the limits of its chartered powers.[244]

The person who drafted Uriah Levy's will (most likely Coddington or Patten) understood that chartered charitable institutions, including religious congregations, could only act within the powers granted them by the charter. While each could be the beneficiary of a devise that supported the congregation, provided for a building to house it, or generated an income for rabbis or teachers, they could not under the laws of the time accept bequests or use income for purposes beyond what they were permitted to do under their charter. So if Congress or Virginia declined the bequest, the synagogues—whether they chose to act individually or jointly—would need new charters or charter amendments granted by their respective states to allow them to do so.

By the late 1850s, however, New York and other states began radically revising their laws on charitable trusts. The growing wealth of the country gave more people the wherewithal to endow charitable agencies. At the same time, disgruntled heirs and would-be heirs wanted to gain the wealth for themselves. New York did not specifically address the issue in its code revisions of 1827 and 1828, but language in passing abolished all uses and trusts "except as authorized and modified in this article."[245] The legislature did not act specifically on this matter until April 1860, when it enacted a law prohibiting any person with a spouse, parent, or child from leaving more than one-half of his or her estate in trust to a charitable, religious or educational institution.[246] Following *Williams* the courts began to move away from a generous allowance of charitable bequests to an out-and-out attack on them as subversive of republican values. The dead hand of the deceased would not be allowed to frustrate the needs and desires of the living. The result, that charitable trusts had been in large measure abolished, may have, as Carl Zollman claimed, rested on bad law. But this was the law under which Uriah Levy's will and the challenges to it would be adjudicated.[247]

❧

The records of the period do not tell us much as we would like to know about the case of *Levy v. Levy*. It is clear that the executors defended the provisions of the will, but they also may have agreed to the suit, and perhaps may even have been instigators of it, in order to clarify their responsibilities.[248] Given the changing nature of charitable gifts law, and the fact that the main object of Uriah's plan lay in the South behind enemy lines, the executors appear to have gone into court to find out what the law required them to do under the circumstances, while the family, led by Virginia and Jonas, sued to gain control of a considerable amount of property.

If nothing else, it appears that Virginia and Jonas managed to unite practically the whole of the Levy clan in behalf of their suit. While the formal title of the law suit lists the family simply as "Virginia Levy and others," the others involved were: Amelia Levy and Eliza Levy, formerly Eliza Hendricks, Uriah's sisters; Joseph M. Levy, Isaac M. Levy, and Jonas P. Levy, Uriah's brothers; George Washington Lopes and Abigail Peixotto, the children of Uriah's deceased sister Fanny; Morton Phillips, Rachel Murphy, Mary Ann Scooler, Fanny Liebschutz, Benjamin Levy, Uriah Levy and Amelia Levy, the children of Uriah's deceased brother Morton.[249] Neither in this nor in any of the other cases did the name Jefferson Monroe Levy appear; under the laws of both New York and Virginia, the heirs at law included only the widow, the parents if still alive, living brothers or sisters, and the children of deceased siblings. The distribution would be one-third to the widow, and then one-seventh of the remainder to each surviving sibling, and one seventh to each of the families of deceased brothers or sisters, to be divided equally among their children.

The trial court, unfortunately, was not a court of record at the time, so we do not have a full account of arguments and conclusions. We do know that Judge William F. Allen tried the case without a jury at the Special Term of the Supreme Court in February 1863, and reached the following conclusions of law:[250]

> That the bequest of $1,000 to the Jewish hospital was valid.
>
> That the devise to give the "rest and residue of the estate" to the people of the United States, or to the state of Virginia, or to the congregations, was void.
>
> Because the gift of the "rest and residue of the estate" was void, it must pass as if there were no will, that is, to Levy's intestate heirs, including his widow, as defined under the state's statutes of descent, i.e., according to well-established formulas for the distribution of an estate.
>
> That the devise of Monticello to the government was also void.

There is no elaboration of these findings, but we can assume that the trial judge acted on two basic premises—the growing antipathy toward such open-ended bequests, and the belief that the government of the United States ought not be the beneficiary of charitable gifts.

Both sides entered elaborate briefs on appeal, and while we need not go into all of the details, we should note their main points. The brief for the executors, drafted by Joseph Patten, had forty-one separate paragraphs attempting to rebut the trial court ruling.[251] Patten argued that the bequest to the *people* of the United States was perfectly valid, since that clearly meant to the *government* of the United States, which could not only receive the bequest but serve as its administrator as well, and to prove his point he used the Smithson gift. As for the holding that the accumulation of income violated the mortmain statute, Patten argued that it did not, since the executors were to accumulate the income only until the Congress or one of the residual legatees took over the property and began to administer the trust. As for charges that the trust either violated existing statutes or ran against the public policy, Patten went to great lengths to draw a line, often a very weak one, to show how the Levy bequest did not run against existing law. As for public policy, "this bequest is good to the United States."[252] Perhaps Patten's most important claim, although a point that the court refused to discuss, involved the "real" beneficiaries of the will. According to Patten, this was neither the government of the United States, nor the Commonwealth of Virginia, nor the three Hebrew congregations, but the orphaned children who had a legal right to come into court to enforce their claims. Finally, even if technical problems existed with the wording of the will, Uriah Levy's intention "must be carried out."[253]

Alexander W. Bradford argued the case for the family, and interestingly, he lists Joseph Levy (a brother) rather than the widow as his chief client. He had only seventeen points to make, all designed to affirm the rightness of the trial court's decision and to refute Patten's brief.[254] He naturally stressed the inability of the government of the United States to inherit, but went on to claim that the residual legatees—the state of Virginia and the three Hebrew congregations—also lacked capacity. He attacked the will for its vagueness as to whom it benefited and how it should be administered, claiming that New York laws required a clearer statement of a testator's wishes. But even if a clearer meaning had been put into the will, he claimed New York laws prohibited putting lands into a trust. If a bequest is not valid by the law of the domiciliary state (New York) or by the law of the state in which property is located (Virginia), then it cannot be valid at all. Perhaps his most powerful argument concerned United States Supreme Court cases that held devises to persons incompetent to take, such as an unincorporated association, to be void.[255] Even if the definition of those devises could be somehow fitted into the definition of charitable gifts in the Statute of Elizabeth, he argued, it did not matter because, he claimed, the Statute of Elizabeth had never been and was not at the time the law of New York.[256] The will should be defeated and the property distributed among the rightful heirs.

A three-judge panel of the General Term of the Superior Court (the intermediate court of appeals), consisting of Josiah Sutherland, Thomas W. Clerke, and Joseph Mullin heard the case and handed down its decision on November 30, 1863. Sutherland wrote the opinion of the court, joined by Clerke, but we start with the minority opinion, because to some extent all three judges agreed on some of its major conclusions.

The minority opinion, written by Judge Joseph Mullin, began with a sorrowful note that "it would be to me a source of profound regret if the benevolent intentions of Commodore Levy, as manifested by his last will and testament, should be defeated by some rule of law which we are bound to recognize and enforce."[257] Mullin seemed to disregard the 1860 law, perhaps because he had what to him appeared a more important issue to deal with, namely, that the United States could not be the recipient of such a bequest. The devise is to the people of the United States, and while there existed no corporate body by that name, "it is too clear to require argument to show that the testator intended the government of the United States as the trustee to execute the trust."[258] Mullin then went into an extended discussion of why trusts should be interpreted as much as possible to reflect the wishes of the donor (the *cy pres* doctrine), and why small technical deficiencies, such as misnaming the executor, should not be allowed to frustrate the intention of the giver.

He then moved to the issue of whether the United States could receive property in the form of either a grant or a trust. The main argument raised by the heirs against the United States receiving rested on the legal rule that corporations cannot accept property beyond the strict rules of their charters. Since the charter of the United States—the Constitution—did not provide for accepting property, the family claimed that the will had to be defeated. Mullin rejected this argument, and claimed that the Constitution, through the implied powers it gave to the government, clearly permitted it to accept grants of property; moreover, it did so on a regular basis by taking land through grants for forts, lighthouses and other public buildings. "If then the rule is a general one that those who can take by grant are capable of taking by devise, it would seem to follow necessarily that the United States may take by devise." If the government can take by devise, then it also follows that the government may act as a trustee for that devise.[259] As an example, Mullin pointed to James Smithson's bequest to the United States, and the government's action in that case, as far as he was concerned, settled the matter: "the estate vested at once in the government, subject to be divested by its refusal to accept the trust or neglect to discharge its duties."

But what if the government did so refuse, and the contingent trustee, the Commonwealth of Virginia, stood disqualified because of the rebellion? Then a court of equity would appoint some person to discharge the duties required, because the rule of equity is that "when a valid trust is created, it shall not fail for want of a trustee."[260] Clearly Mullin considered Uriah Levy's bequest a noble idea, and wanted to see it implemented. He even dismissed recent cases that had held against such trusts, and said he considered the rule in *Williams v. Williams* the better one. While certain parts of Levy's will went against the technical rules of charitable bequests, these he believed could easily be corrected so that the larger purpose could be effected. He would have reversed the trial court on the main points, upheld the bequest, and had the defects corrected.

In the majority opinion Judge Sutherland, joined by Judge Clerke, agreed that the government of the United States, acting for the people as a whole, had the power to take by devise and so serve as a trustee—but only in the District of Columbia, which it governed directly. This accounted for the legitimacy of the Smithson bequest. But, Sutherland went on, the federal government had no power to take and administer a bequest to be carried out in Virginia, or in any other sovereign state. Congress might have the power to incorporate a bank, but under the Constitution it had no power, express or implied, to charter a corporation for the purpose of administering or carrying on a private charity in a state. Therefore, the government could not accept the devise, had no power to take under it, and this made it void.[261]

This states-rights argument might sound strange coming from a northern state in the midst of a civil war that pitted the federal union against the states. But it is really not so strange. In New York a significant part of the population adhered to the Democratic Party, and in the early years of the war actually favored allowing the southern states to secede. But more important, even the staunchest pro-union Republican believed in a federal system of government in which state sovereignty played a very important role.[262] While the war nationalized a number of rights, certain areas remained firmly within the control of the states. Although black men and women would no longer be considered property, the law of property and of the passing on of that property remained within the purview of state law. Until and if the federal government passed a law specifically enabling itself to receive property in trust and to serve as the administrator of that property, then as far as New York law went, Congress had no authority to act.

The state of Virginia, on the other hand, could receive Levy's bequest and act upon it, because Monticello was located within its domain. Moreover, in normal times it could receive the residual estate and establish a corporation for its management. But these were not normal times, and because Virginia could not act in a manner in which it could receive the New York property, then it too failed to qualify under the will.

But the most important point to Judge Sutherland seemed to be the clause that the executors should "*hold the whole of the property ... until* the proper steps have been taken."[263] The word "until" apparently made this a conditional devise, that is, one that depended upon certain conditions being met. In addition, the executors were to accumulate the income on the residual estate until those conditions had been met, something Sutherland held violated state law.

Finally, as if all of these barriers were not enough, the final nail in the coffin of the will was the fact that New York law prevented a testator from setting up more than 50 percent of an estate if survived by a spouse, parent or child. Had Uriah given the dower third to Virginia and disposed of an additional 18 to 20 percent through smaller bequests to individuals or charities, then leaving the rest in a single trust would have passed muster. But this combination of problems left little room for the executors to maneuver, and so they asked for review by the Court of Appeals, New York's highest tribunal. That court accepted the appeal.

❧

The Court of Appeals, consisting of eight members, handed down its decision eighteen months later, and gave the heirs all that they had sought. Justice William B. Wright wrote for a highly divided bench, and held that the disposition that Uriah had wanted to make could not be done under the laws of New York. The dedication of the residual estate for the support of the farm school "according to the ordinary rules of law, and the general rule in chancery as to trusts, is void" because of the vagueness of the beneficiary.[264] Wright maintained that there had to be a particular donee, grantee, or devisee who could come into court to claim and defend the bequest. A group of unnamed orphans of such a general class as the children of warrant officers, or alternatively children of any religious denomination, failed to meet that definition. "Nothing could be more indefinite in a legal sense."[265] He did not challenge Uriah's purpose, but rather noted that the purpose had been defeated by the failure to meet the necessary legal definitions of who would benefit. A charitable trust, he wrote, "is simply an indefinite or uncertain trust—a trust without a beneficiary; and certainly a trust of that description is void by the rules of the common law as it existed at the time of adoption by us, and now exists."[266]

This ruling, of course, ran contrary to a long string of cases, especially *Williams*, and Wright then proceeded to either distinguish the Levy will from the earlier decisions or simply to rule them as out-and-out wrong. Henceforth the dead hand of the donor would not be allowed to govern the disposition of such a large fortune for the benefit of an indefinite group. The fact that the gift had been for charity made no difference, and those who relied on English precedent, especially 43 Elizabeth, rested their case on false premises. Despite the clear history that New York courts had, in fact, followed English case law in regard to charitable gifts, Wright argued that the English law had been "forced" upon New York.

New York law, Wright emphasized, did not discourage charity; to the contrary, it welcomed it, but only through the medium of corporate bodies created by the legislative power for that purpose. The charters of charitable organizations must clearly state their responsibilities and powers, and this had been the clear intent of the state ever since independence. Time and again the legislature had enacted statutes designed to encourage philanthropic giving, but had required that the corporations receiving this beneficence have the necessary authority and structure to do so. As recently as 1848, 1849, 1860, and 1862 the legislature had refined the laws of charitable giving in New York. This had made, Wright noted, a system totally different from the British; New York did not tolerate trusts for indefinite objects. "We have," he emphasized, "repealed all statutes that support, maintain, and restrict indefinite uses."[267]

Wright then turned to the question of whether the United States or Virginia could be the proper legatees of a will naming them to direct a charitable trust, and he concluded that they could not. Of course, he had to somehow explain away the Smithson bequest, and he did so in a most clever way. The Smithson gift was "an English charity," and as such, was governed by the domicil of the donor. Since English law allowed such a bequest, then the government of the United States could accept it! But under American law governments are limited by their constitution, and political bodies could not act as trustees for charity. If "the devises and bequests were intended to be made to the United States, and to the State of Virginia, as political bodies, I think they are void, because neither the United States or the State is capable of taking as a trustee for the management of the special charity." As for the religious organizations, only one—Shearith Israel in New York—had a corporate charter, and none of them had the authority to act as a trustee.[268]

The learned judge could have stopped there, but he not only wanted to make sure the Levy bequest could never be effected, he wanted to make sure that no similar bequest in the future would have any hope of withstanding judicial scrutiny. And so he piled on additional arguments: the will ran against the statute of perpetuities, and deprived property of its most important attribute, the ability to be alienated (sold or transferred) in every generation;[269] the trust is void under the state's law governing uses and trusts;[270] and since the devise required the use of both the land (located in Virginia) and the residual property (located in New York), the laws of either state being against the devise the whole bequest must fail.[271]

Where some of the judges involved expressed sympathy with the purpose of Uriah's will, Wright declared that "I cannot say that I regret this result. The purpose may be, in a general sense, charitable, but the plan for carrying it out is manifestly impracticable, not to say impossible. Aside from incapacity, there is a manifest unfitness in the government of the United States, or the State of Virginia, becoming the trustee or the administrator of a fund donated by an individual for the furtherance of an object in no way pertaining to the administration of these governments."[272] Civil War experience to the contrary, people in 1865 still saw government, at both the state and federal level, as instruments of limited authority.

The national government could prosecute one of the bloodiest wars in history, but it lacked the simple authority to administer a charitable trust.

Despite the vigor of his opinion, Wright only enjoyed the full agreement of two of his seven brethren, Henry Davies and John K. Porter. Noah Davis and John Brown declined to rule as to whether the will failed under New York law but concurred in the result, on the grounds that the trust failed under the laws of Virginia, the location of the real property involved. Brown also thought the United States incompetent to take as a devisee of a charitable bequest. Judge Platt Potter concurred with Davis and Brown that the device failed under Virginia law, but dissented from Wright's conclusion holding the trust void under New York law. Chief Judge Hiram Denio and Judge William W. Campbell dissented completely, and would have upheld the will.[273] None of these men, unfortunately, chose to file a written opinion explaining their views, but the force of Wright's opinion clearly carried the day. Uriah's will was now void so far as the courts of New York were concerned, and his heirs could now divide up his wealth.

Levy v. Levy enunciated a rule that remained the law of New York State for many years. Robert Fowler, in his then definitive treatise in 1896, cited the case as authority nearly thirty times.[274] The absurdity of the holding became manifest a quarter-century later, however, in the saga of the Tilden will. Samuel J. Tilden, a wealthy railroad lawyer, governor of New York, and presidential candidate, died in 1886, and left the bulk of his five-million-dollar estate "to establish and maintain a free library and reading room in the city of New York." When the New York Court of Appeals ruled the bequest invalid,[275] the resulting public uproar led the state legislature to enact the so-called Tilden Law, which restored the law of charitable bequests to the status of the *Williams* case.

༥

The decision of the Court of Appeals came down in June 1865, and the justices refused the usual certificate needed to appeal to the United States Supreme Court, on the ground that the case had been decided on local law and had not involved any constitutional issues. The executors now had to liquidate the estate and divide it up among the heirs. David Caddington was spared this task, dying in September, and the burden initially fell on Asahel's shoulders. He also had to deal with the fact that his co-executor, Joseph Patten, took possession of a large part of the personal estate, and Asahel feared that Patten intended to abscond with it. Asahel then went into court to have Patten removed as an executor. Within a short time all of the surviving named executors had renounced their roles. Patten's misbehavior led the court to require him and Asahel to each post a surety of $260,000, a very large and costly bond, or resign as executors; they chose the latter course.[276] Eventually Virginia Rée qualified as administrator, and the estate appears to have been distributed by the end of August 1869.[277]

As this saga unfolded, Asahel had urged George Carr to "take some interest" in Monticello, and told him that he need not wait for the final probate, but could exercise authority without it. Asahel apparently assumed that with the will declared invalid, all Carr had to do was sell Monticello, and then the proceeds could be divided along with the rest of the estate. In fact, it would be over a dozen years before such a sale would occur.

The story now shifts to the activities of Jonas Levy and his efforts to gain control of Jefferson's house. At first it seems that all Jonas wanted was to have the will declared invalid in Virginia as well as in New York, have the estate sold and garner the proceeds. He seems to have acted apart from the other heirs in this, as well as in his efforts to track down assets that he suspected Uriah of owning but that had not been accounted for in the estate. For example, in the summer of 1867 he pestered the Treasury Department to search its records for any government bonds that Uriah had owned, since he had heard that prior to his death Uriah had deposited $10,000 in a Washington bank for the sole purpose of buying such bonds.[278]

As for Monticello, the story is considerably more complicated. From the available documentation, it appears that initially Jonas simply wanted to see the estate liquidated, and to do so he needed to have a Virginia court declare his brother's will invalid under local law. The estate would then be sold and the proceeds distributed. But somewhere along the line Jonas came up with another idea, namely, that either he or his son Jefferson should become the new owner of Monticello. As early as May 1868, he tried to secure a summer rental on Monticello, so he would

Jonas P. Levy to George Carr, July 5, 1862 (courtesy of George Carr papers, University of Virginia Library).

be in physical possession, but Joel Wheeler objected, claiming he had a year-to-year lease on the farm and was then living in the house.[279]

Jonas hired a local attorney to act on his behalf, since he probably suspected George Carr of loyalty to his late brother's wishes. He retained William J. Robertson of Charlottesville, a former member of the Virginia Supreme Court and one of the state's leading attorneys. Robertson notified him in early 1868 that the decision of the New York Court of Appeals would not be binding in Virginia, although he had no doubt that the local courts would reach the same conclusion. He suggested the tactic of a simple partition suit, in which the court could declare the will invalid and order the distribution of the estate according to Virginia law. Apparently Jonas had worried that the Commonwealth might try to claim Monticello as the secondary legatee, and Robertson assured him that this issue would not even arise if they took the tactic of a partition suit rather than suing Virginia. Although he did not say so in his letter, Robertson could not have been unaware of the seriously depressed economy in Reconstruction Virginia, and that a cash-strapped state government would not be eager to defend a questionable claim to a property it could not afford to maintain.[280]

Levy agreed with this strategy, although he made it clear that he wanted the issue of possible state ownership resolved. He had no doubt that Virginia courts would declare the will void as to the gift to the United States, but he did not want to take any chances that it might uphold the bequest to the state. It was at this time that Jonas raised the question of the validity of Virginia and Uriah's marriage, hoping to prevent his sister-in-law from receiving her one-third of the estate.[281] It appears that the widow and the youngest brother, close allies in the New York suit, had become somewhat estranged by this point.

Robertson agreed to prosecute the case, but he needed to know whom he represented. Jonas had sent him a list of names, but the lawyer wanted to be sure of the relationships.[282] Although partition suits are in general collusive, and this one certainly was, it is important to get all of the names listed. In addition, non-family members were now involved because of the problems of Uriah's widow. She had remarried in 1866, and in the summer of 1868 she seems to have run through much of what she had received from the distribution of Uriah's New York properties. In addition, her new husband, William Rée, had been arrested for various crimes and had to post a heavy bond to stay out of jail. To raise more money she apparently pledged her interest in Monticello, and her creditors insisted on representation in the suit.[283]

By June Robertson had prepared the bill for partition, and was asking Jonas to forward the necessary security costs, about $100. In September 1868, Robertson brought suit in the Circuit Court for the City of Richmond on behalf of Jonas

Levy, his wife Fanny, and his sister Eliza Herricks against other members of the family and their lawyers. In November the court handed down its decision, declaring Uriah's will void and ordering Monticello (the house and 218 acres) sold and the proceeds divided among the heirs. To effectuate its decision, the court named George Carr of Charlottesville as commissioner for this purpose.[284]

The division followed somewhat the same pattern as in New York. Virginia Levy Rée would receive one-third as dower, and the seven siblings would divide the rest equally. But because some of them were dead, their shares would go to their children, if living, or to the surviving siblings. Notes by George Carr as he attempted to understand the family ties tell us how the monies from the sale would be distributed:[285]

- Virginia Levy Rée, widow: $\frac{1}{3}$ as dower, and $\frac{1}{3}$ of $\frac{1}{7}$ as daughter of Fanny Lopez
- Amelia Levy, sister: $\frac{1}{7}$, but since deceased after Uriah, her share distributed
- Eliza Herricks, sister: $\frac{1}{7}$ and $\frac{1}{6}$ of Amelia's part
- Joseph Levy, brother: $\frac{1}{7}$ and $\frac{1}{6}$ of Amelia's part (not sure if alive)
- Isaac M. Levy, brother: $\frac{1}{7}$ and $\frac{1}{6}$ of Amelia's part
- Three children of Fanny Lopez (deceased sister) $\frac{1}{7}$ and $\frac{1}{6}$ of Amelia's part
- Jonas P. Levy, brother: $\frac{1}{7}$ and $\frac{1}{6}$ of Amelia's part
- Seven children of Martin Levy (deceased brother): $\frac{1}{7}$ and $\frac{1}{6}$ of Amelia's part

But what would Monticello fetch? In fact, could it bring in very much at all given the lack of hard currency in post-war Virginia? Recall the difficulty that Martha Jefferson Randolph had in selling the estate after her father's death. The family had hoped to realize $70,000 on the house and had gotten less than a tenth of that amount. When Barclay tried to sell it a few years later he too found very few people interested. In addition, the house was in far more wretched condition than it had ever been. Joel Wheeler had been living at Monticello, but had not been taking very good care of it, details of which will be discussed in the next chapter. One need merely note here that in March 1869, Judge Robertson wrote to Jonas that "the place is very much neglected, and in a most dilapidated condition."[286] Jonas tried to get Wheeler removed, but for some unknown reason George Carr came to the old man's defense, and repeatedly assured Jonas that the house and grounds were well cared for.[287]

Normally, court-ordered sales take place within forty days of the decree, unless there are extenuating circumstances or appeals. Apparently Asahel announced that he intended to file an appeal, although on what legal grounds he planned to proceed is unknown. This would have held up the sale, but the court required a bond of $1,000, payable in cash, for the appeal to proceed, and we can surmise that by this point Asahel had no great desire to lay out even more money trying to defend his uncle's will.[288]

Carr informed Jonas that he would try to arrange the auction in the latter part of February 1869, but from the beginning he had his doubts. "The prospect of selling Monticello at a fair price to any person living in Virginia at this time is rather gloomy," he wrote. "Can't you find some person in the North where money is more plentiful who would be willing to purchase."[289] In late January, Carr suggested to Levy that the sale be put off. "The winter is a bad time to sell land. Everything in the country looks dreary. Land buyers from the North come South in the spring or summer. Particularly the view from Monticello and the appearance of everything about it, is much better in the spring and summer than in winter."[290] Levy agreed and Carr scheduled the sale for May.

News that Monticello would be on the block did, in fact, attract the interest of several buyers. Edwin Blair Smith wrote to Carr on behalf of members of the Jefferson and Randolph families living in the North, wanting to know what the Levy family wanted (a figure that Carr himself never learned) and what legal encumbrances clouded title to Monticello.[291] Then in early April Carr put advertisements in Virginia papers, and sent copies to Jonas suggesting that he place similar ads in northern papers. The auction would be held on Thursday, May 13, on the premises, and the sale would be of the house and 218 adjoining acres. Terms would be one-third of the purchase price paid in cash, another third on twelve months' credit, and the last third on two years' credit. Bonds would have to be posted for the amount deferred on credit, with full title passing only when the last installment had been paid; possession would be given on the day of sale.[292]

Jonas had no sooner learned of the scheduled sale when he received a letter from Judge Robertson with disturbing news of a little-known provision of Virginia law, a provision so obscure as "to have been entirely overlooked by the members of the bar and bench, so completely so that a case ... that would have been ruled by it was recently decided ... as if no such law were in existence." Because the State of Virginia had been named in Uriah's will, it could appeal the decision of the circuit court even though it had not been a party to the case. The only bright note that Robertson could offer was that if the state did not appeal within two years, it forfeited its rights to do so, and the decree of the circuit court would be final. This information had been discovered by Egbert R. Watson, like Robertson, a judge who had been ousted from the bench by the Reconstruction government and who now planned to return to private practice. Robertson feared that should a potential buyer of Monticello retain Watson, he would be honorbound to inform him that no clear title existed while the state had the option of appealing the circuit court decision. He suggested that Jonas retain Watson, since so far no one else seemed aware of this law.[293]

Ten days later Robertson wrote that his partner, Mr. Southall, who represented a potential buyer, had discovered the hitherto unknown provision, and that should the state appeal, it would probably win. The only thing to do was to postpone the sale of Monticello for at least two years. If the state failed to exercise its rights, and Robertson believed this would be the case, then the circuit court decree would become final and the sale could go ahead. Until then, no one would buy it with this cloud on the title. Having little choice, Jonas agreed to an indefinite postponement of the auction.[294]

The Commonwealth did file suit; Asahel Levy received a letter in mid-July to the effect that Robertson, acting as counsel for the state, had filed a petition in the Supreme Court of Appeals arguing that the New York high court as well as the Virginia circuit court had erred in finding Commodore Levy's will invalid, and that since the United States had not exercised its claim, then Monticello should go to the Commonwealth.[295] Robertson had not turned his coat, and in early August he informed Jonas that he had been out of town on business and on his return had discovered that the state had filed an appeal. That October he wrote that the court of appeals had put the case on its docket, but unless someone put in an appearance representing the defendants in the case, namely Jonas and the other heirs, it would probably not be argued in the coming term. Robertson had deliberately not gone forward, and he strongly urged Jonas to let matters lie for the present; the current court was staffed by appointees of the military Reconstruction, in which Virginia lawyers had little confidence. But, it might be that Jonas would get a better hearing now than when Reconstruction ended and the old elite reclaimed the bench. A few days later Robertson reported that the court of appeals had recessed until January without taking any action on the state's appeal.[296]

The court of appeals eventually did hear the case in November 1872, but before then trouble arose on another front. In May 1870 a joint committee of the Virginia General Assembly agreed to report a bill accepting Uriah Levy's bequest of Monticello. Robertson suggested immediate action, and implied that his contacts in the legislature would rally to the sides of the heirs. Apparently many members of the assembly assumed that not only would they get Monticello, but also the $300,000 to support it. Once they learned that there would be no endowment for Jefferson's home, the bill died a quiet death.[297] And then the last of the legal barriers melted away when the court of appeals confirmed the circuit court decision on January 29, 1873.

In an opinion largely devoted to rehearsing the terms of the will and the decisions of the New York courts, President (chief justice) Richard C.L. Moncure took an easy out to avoid grappling with the merits of the case. Since the United States government defended the devise in the New York suit, then the decree of the New York court bound Virginia as well even though the state had not been a party to the earlier litigation. Where the New York court had been vehement in its defense of states rights, the Virginia judges took a tack that even mild supporters of states rights must have found strange. The fact that the federal government had looked after its interests could, under no circumstances, be construed to mean that it had foreclosed Virginia's options.[298]

In what is clearly a secondary portion of the opinion, Moncure gave a much more defensible analysis of why the will should be voided. The trust, he declared, was by its nature indivisible. Even if the New York decree did not reach the question of who would own Monticello, the devolution of the Virginia property could not be separated from the residual estate meant to support the farm, and that part clearly came within the scope of New York law. Once the trust had been broken in part, he concluded, it failed completely, and the land must go to the heirs.[299]

In April 1873, George Carr prepared once again to put Monticello on the market, and he so informed Jonas in a very upbeat letter. "Now is a very good time for the sale," he wrote. "From the number of letters I received, when it was advertised before, and the enquiries made of me, since the decision of the Court of Appeals when it would be offered, I believe it would bring a high price." He planned to begin advertising at once, and to hold the sale in late May or early June.[300] Levy welcomed the news, but asked Carr to get together with William Robertson so that any remaining legal questions could be cleared away. "It is my wish and those who I represent that the whole hassle of the estate shall be closed." On the same day he informed Robertson that he believed his nephew Asahel wanted to purchase Monticello for a friend.[301]

Levy worried about just how much land actually went with Monticello. He knew the immediate house sat on a plot of 223 acres, but he believed that it should include another 138 acres that his brother had bought. In addition, the will had provided that 200 acres should be taken away from the Washington Farm and added to the Monticello holdings, so that there would be a total of 561 acres. Carr tried to dissuade Jonas from worrying about the two additional parcels; the title to them had still not been settled, and in any event they were not contiguous to Monticello, whose lot included 218 and not 223 acres. He believed the property would bring between $30 and $75 an acre, since the trustees of the estate of Judge Carlton had recently sold that land for $75 an acre. "I would not let the property go as Commissioner with my present impressions for less than $40 per acre." In other words, Jonas and his co-heirs could really expect at the most $16,000 for Monticello, and more realistically $8,700. The house itself he placed little value on, since it appeared to be going to waste rapidly, with no money available to maintain it. In addition, no one was carrying insurance, and fire could devastate the building at any time.[302]

Clearly Jonas and others had expected far more from the sale of Monticello. At one time they believed the estate to be worth at least $70,000, and even with the building in disrepair he declared he would not be willing to let it go at less than $200 an acre. This demand led Carr to threaten to resign as commissioner, a step he apparently did not take because Judge Robertson talked him out of doing so. As late as November 1875 Carr attempted to resign again, only the court would not accept the resignation. But the dispute between Levy and Carr led to still further delay in selling the last part of Uriah's estate.[303]

A variety of factors would keep Monticello off the market, including a continuous squabble between Carr and Jonas over, among other things, Wheeler's continuous occupancy of the house;[304] a slump in real estate prices in Virginia; disputes among the heirs; and the death of Joseph Levy, which further confused the distribution.[305] By this point there were forty-nine parties to the dispute, each of whom could expect to realize only a small portion of the proceeds. So in July 1876 Jonas attempted to liquidate Monticello through another avenue, by offering it for sale to the United States.

In July 1876 Jonas wrote to Senator Justin Morrill of Vermont, informing him that Representative R. Milton Speer of Pennsylvania had introduced a bill in the House of Representatives, authorizing the President of the United States to enter into a contract with the heirs of Monticello to purchase the estate. The family had had repeated offers for its purchase, which had been declined, "in consequence of our desire to keep the same in our Family as our ever lamented mother is buried on that mountain." But, even so, in order to honor those great men, Thomas Jefferson and Uriah P. Levy, "we will meet the government on fair and reasonable terms as to its purchase."[306] Congress had not wanted the estate fourteen years earlier for free, and had no interest in buying it now.

It is believed that at this point Jonas gave up the idea of selling Monticello, and instead began making arrangements so it would pass into the hands of his son, Jefferson Monroe Levy. The son, with the help of his father, began buying out the interests of other heirs, and so was unhindered when he finally bid upon and won Monticello. There is scant documentation on this matter, but what there is makes this scenario not only possible but likely. We do know that the twenty-five-year old Jefferson Levy visited Charlottesville, probably for the first time, on behalf of his father in the late summer of 1877. In June of that year he had written to George Carr that "we think the place had better not be sold at present," and in September he arrived with a letter of introduction from his father that Jefferson "visits Charlottesville & Monticello on business which he will explain to you."[307] By the following spring Jefferson apparently wanted to rent Monticello for his own use during the summer, although his efforts came to naught when Wheeler refused to vacate.[308]

By this point Jefferson had more than a simple pecuniary interest in Monticello. After all, he was not one of the heirs at law, and his immediate family's one-seventh share of the proceeds would be small. He began to complain about Wheeler's care of the house, his refusal to vacate, his failure to make repairs with the money Jefferson supplied for the purpose. "I desire possession now," he told Carr in June 1878, "to save the place from ruin."[309] By November he was trying to get Carr to cooperate in ejecting Wheeler, and he proposed to put his own man in place to take care of the house, but Carr kept avoiding the matter.[310] The poor man had dealt with Monticello, Wheeler, and various Levys for more than four decades, and had probably had enough of all of them.

How many of the heirs Jefferson Levy bought out is unclear. One source suggests that by April 1877 he had bought out about half.[311] On December 16, 1878, Jefferson informed Carr that "I have bought other interests out since I visited you." It is possible that by the time of the auction, Jefferson Levy owned nearly all the outstanding claims by his family against Monticello. If he already owned all the claims, then why did he have to bid at the auction? The claims were against the proceeds of a court ordered sale; even if Jefferson Levy had owned all of the

Monticello West Front, c. 1870 (courtesy of Special Collections, University of Virginia Library).

outstanding claims, under terms of the court order there had to be an auction, and anyone could enter a bid. If someone else had bid higher, then Levy would have gotten all or nearly all of the proceeds. But when Monticello finally went on the block at public auction at eleven o'clock on the morning of March 20, 1879, Jefferson Monroe Levy did in fact enter the high bid of $10,050, one third-down and other two-thirds payable within two years.[312]

On July 7, 1881, the Circuit Court of the City of Richmond entered a final decree in the suit Jonas Levy had bought thirteen years earlier, confirming Jefferson Levy as the new owner of Monticello. The house and 218 acres of land were valued at only $4,360, with state taxes listed at $27 a year, and county and school taxes at $20.89. The property he received was exactly that which his uncle had taken nearly fifty years earlier, and the court decree referred to the same survey that had been used then.[313] But the house was in far worse shape than it had been when his uncle had gone up the little mountain, and a real question existed whether Jefferson Monroe Levy could save Monticello from total ruin.

Chapter Four

THE SAVIOR OF MONTICELLO

"I hope you will not dwell on Mr. Jefferson's lottery or poverty, for he was
a great man and ought to be treated from the large and not the little points
of view. He was the providence of his household, and his estate almost came
out right; after he went his loss was manifest. Monticello was the seat of
political power for more than fifty years. In retirement he was less disput-
ed than in office. He combined the natures of Franklin, the philosopher,
with Washington, the explorer and executive."

—JEFFERSON MONROE LEVY[314]

Monticello now had a new owner, one who in the next quarter-century would
pour thousands of dollars into its restoration and maintenance. In doing so,
Jefferson Monroe Levy surely saved the house from extinction, because the property he purchased at auction literally stood on the brink of total ruin. It had not only
been neglected but abused in the two decades between Uriah Levy's last visit and
the sale that finally closed out the dispute over his will. But in saving Monticello,
Jefferson Levy had his own ideas of what he wanted the house to be, ideas that
shock modern historic preservationists, and that upset people in his own time.

❦

No major Civil War battles took place near Charlottesville, and so Monticello at least escaped the devastation that the war visited on other great houses
in the South. But what had once been a noble estate had fallen into complete disrepair. A young schoolgirl, Sarah Strickler, visited Monticello in 1864, and
declared that it had gone to ruin. "The parlour retains but little of its former ele-

gance, [and] the ballroom on the second floor has a thousand names scratched over its walls." Jefferson's tomb had also fallen into bad shape, as people broke off pieces of the gravestone; in fact, she took a piece herself as a souvenir.[315]

Jefferson Monroe Levy, 1852–1924. Undated photograph (courtesy of American Jewish Historical Society, Waltham, Massachusetts and New York, New York).

The war would have caused disruption in any event, especially with the title belonging to a Union Navy officer. The greater danger to Monticello, however, came from its nominal custodian, Joel Wheeler. When Uriah had been alive, Wheeler had been a trustworthy superintendent of the house and grounds, and even during the war had initially tried to keep up the place as he thought Captain Levy would have wanted. But the war went on, Uriah died, and the family fell to squabbling over the will. During this time no one thought to pay Wheeler, and so he decided that Monticello itself should provide an income for him and his family. He permitted the young people of Charlottesville and the students at the University of Virginia to use the mansion for balls and entertainments—for a fee. The grounds provided an ideal setting for a picnic—for a fee. The Monticello Guard would come up the hill for target practice, and would pay Wheeler so the men could be quartered in the house. Pilgrims still came to pay homage to Mr. Jefferson, and Wheeler charged them twenty cents apiece for admission into the decaying building.[316]

On the spacious west lawn that Jefferson had laid out with such care, Wheeler planted his vegetable garden and built a sty for his pigs at one end. He stabled cattle in the basement during the winter, and in the drawing room with its beautiful parquet floors he set up a hand-fanning mill to winnow his grain. As for maintenance of the house, he seems not to have done anything. The gutters fell away, the roofs rotted, rainwater flooded the basement, and the elements took their toll on every part of the great house.

Monticello East Front, c. 1870s (courtesy of Special Collections, University of Virginia Library).

As accumulating filth and decay made one room uninhabitable, Wheeler moved on to another, abandoning an ever-larger part of the house to bats, mice and other vermin. Had Monticello not been so well built it is doubtful if it could have survived Wheeler's occupancy. The terraces collapsed into the dependencies, and mere shells were all that were left of the North and South Pavilions across the lawn. The arches at the top of the pillars along the dependencies fell off, and the columns themselves stood forlorn and detached. When portions of the main roof gave way, Wheeler banged up some wooden shingles to cover the holes, and at the same time shingled over the third floor skylights. He even used the parlor as a makeshift granary. A photograph taken in the 1870s shows grass and weeds growing in the remaining gutters. Thomas Rhodes, who would later be Jefferson Levy's superintendent, charged that "Monticello was wantonly desecrated."[317]

Had Uriah's will been honored, even after the war, or had the Levy family stopped its squabbling long enough to look after the house, much of the damage might have been avoided, and for this Jonas especially, but also Jefferson, must bear some of the responsibility for the house's deterioration. But Joel Wheeler essentially had the run of the estate with no supervision for almost two decades. Jonas did try to oust Wheeler on more than one occasion, but with little success. In 1869 he came across a news clipping that "the mansion of Thomas Jefferson at Monticello … is sadly in need of repair, and has been stripped of many things of interest and value." The item, he told George Carr, fully confirmed his belief that Wheeler should be evicted as soon as possible.[318]

Ironically, George Carr not only refused to take action regarding Wheeler, he defended him and maintained, as he told Jonas, that "the property is well taken care of."[319] The record is silent during the early 1870s, as the family and the Virginia courts and legislature went through their pavanne of determining who should own the house, but in 1873 Jonas again heard reports about the sad shape of the property, and wrote to Carr with the plea "any information will oblige." Carr rode up to Monticello, and had to report that the house was indeed in bad repair. It needed painting and the windows new glass. But, "it is as well taken care of, by Mr. Wheeler as it would probably be, by any tenant." As for reports that Jonas had heard that the west portico had been made into a coach house, Carr had seen no evidence to support the rumor.[320]

In fact, Carr seems to have seen Wheeler's occupancy as a favor. "Mr. Wheeler agreed to occupy the property and take care of it, without charge and without paying any rent." He would be willing to stay on and take care of the dilapidated old house until a new owner came to take possession. When such a person did arrive, however, he would need Wheeler's permission since the man had a lease on the property that Carr renewed every twelve months.[321] A year later Judge Robertson reported that Wheeler still occupied Monticello, since Carr, in his capacity as commissioner, needed someone to take care of the house.[322] Because Carr did have legal powers and responsibilities as commissioner, his decision to keep Wheeler on could only be negated by the sale of the property, an event that did not take place until 1879.

Jonas P. Levy to George Carr, November 17, 1875 (courtesy of George Carr papers, University of Virginia Library).

Apparently Wheeler did pay some rent, or at least he did in some years. There are rental agreements in the Carr Papers giving Wheeler use of the house and 223 acres of surrounding land. Wheeler promised to take good care of the land and to return it in "as good order as it is now in." The documents, strangely enough, do not carry any comparable references to the condition of the house. Wheeler paid $75 a year rental in 1873, and then $150 a year in subsequent years, the agreements running from January first to the following January. If the sale took place during the year, Wheeler agreed to vacate the house, lawns and yards, retaining the use of a small house on the property, pasturage for his animals, and the right to finish his crops and harvest them.[323]

The provision about relinquishing the house quickly proved a sticking point between Wheeler and Jefferson Levy, even before the latter had bought the property and secured a clear title. When Jefferson planned on visiting Charlottesville in the spring of 1878, he informed Carr that he intended to take possession of Monticello, at least on a temporary basis.[324] When he got to town, he angrily discovered that Wheeler had no intention of allowing him even temporary use of Monticello. "He states he will not give up the place." Various accounts relate that Wheeler, by now an old man, had come to believe that he owned the place, and that he had lived there so long as to have squatter's rights to Monticello. It was Jefferson Levy's first encounter with Joel Wheeler, and it foreshadowed the difficulty he would have, even after purchasing Monticello, in dislodging him.

The visit must have been a shock to Levy in more ways than one. This seems to have been his second look at Monticello, whose rights he had been slowly buying from his relatives, and as he wrote to Carr:[325]

In my estimation the place is in worse condition than last fall the only repairs made is [sic] a small part of the roof and office the Ball Room [*] is nearly ruined the sashes & glass he agreed last fall to have put in before winter he has not touched & so remained open to the elements all the season and in repairing the roof they exposed part of the ball room so the brick work & wall is giving away also and off part of the copper roofing. Mr. Jefferson's office which was never occupied since Mr. Jefferson's time he has placed Colored people in and says he has a right to put Colored people in the house if he [*] in fact it seems to me he is trying to ruin the place he has not in my estimation expended any more than seventy-five dollars on the place and that for the part of the roof repaired though he shingled the part of the roof in such a manner as to close all the windows in the upper story I hope you will see him and come to an understanding as it is very important to the place that I obtain possession this spring or the whole place will be destroyed. I informed him I would not give up my rights and that I would send some one [*] about June to take possession.

A month later Levy reported to Carr that Wheeler had "defied" him again, and declared that he would never leave the house until it was sold at public auction. Levy felt he had to gain immediate possession in order to save Monticello. "Wheeler is destroying the place," he lamented, and "he seems to do it from spite." Although Levy had given him $300 and charged him to repair the portico, Wheeler had failed to do so. Beyond that, he was violating his rental agreement by cutting firewood beyond his need and selling it off the property.[326]

Apparently Carr had agreed not to renew Wheeler's lease and had told him that he would have to give up the property. Wheeler refused to do so, and Levy urged Carr to act forcefully. "He will remain there forever if you allow him to impose." Wheeler had been going around Charlottesville saying that he would not give up Monticello to anyone, including the heirs or a new purchaser.[327] By December 1878 Levy had made firm plans to oust Wheeler at the end of his rental year, and to install a man of his own choice as the temporary custodian of Monticello. "Mr. Wheeler can have no excuse to remain longer."[328] But as Levy soon learned, the fact that Wheeler had no legal right to remain at Monticello proved of little avail in dislodging him.

☙

Before examining his stewardship of Mr. Jefferson's house, we may well ask, "Who was Jefferson Monroe Levy?" Unlike his famous uncle, there have been no books written about him. His never wrote a memoir, or delivered a lengthy speech that could in any way be construed as autobiographical. The collection of his papers

Jefferson Monroe Levy (center) with brothers (courtesy Mrs. Richard C. Lewis).

is thin, and consists mainly of clippings scrapbooks, mostly devoted to his attempt to retain ownership of Monticello, a subject discussed in the next chapter. He never married, so there are no descendants with family stories. What we know must be pieced together from scraps here and there, and while that will give us a sketch of the man, it is by no means a full portrait.

Born in New York on April 15, 1852, Jefferson Monroe Michael Levy was the second of five children, two girls and three boys.[329] He always prided himself on his ancestry, which on his paternal grandmother's side he could trace back to 1660, and he belonged to and was active in both the Sons of the American Revolution and the Sons of the Revolution. He attended both public and private schools, and after graduation from New York University[330] read law in the offices of a prominent New York attorney, Clarkson N. Potter.[331] Levy apparently enjoyed a successful law practice, but he made his fortune speculating both in stocks and in real estate. In 1902 a newspaper article listed him as among the "Hebrew Millionaires in the United States," but given his expenses at Monticello, he certainly had become quite affluent long before then. He devoted at least part of each day to studying real estate conditions in the city, and like his uncle, seems to have had a knack for spotting where people would be moving, and buying up property ahead of the crowd.[332] His niece Frances (also known as Fanny), the daughter of his brother, Louis Napoleon Levy, recalled that he had a special ticker tape from London in his office. Frances has also given us a portrait of her uncle: [333]

> He was a very tall and big man. My father often brought us to visit his family who lived in a fine old house on East 34th Street, where his sister Amelia [Mayhoff] kept house for family and two brothers [Jefferson and his younger brother Mitchell both remained bachelors]. On Sunday morning we would be sent in to see Uncle Jeff, who would be lying on a big four poster bed, surrounded by the Sunday papers and there would be two big greyhounds stretched on the bed beside him. I don't think he was at all interested in greeting his nieces and although a very wealthy man in those days … we never received anything of value from him or any gifts on birthdays. He gambled very heavily in the stock market …. [H]e gave the impression of being a V.I.P. which he probably was. Especially in the Waldorf-Astoria, where he was well known and where he gave many lavish parties.

Levy cut quite a swath on the New York social circuit, and his scrapbooks include not just notices of his political activities, but of his social life as well. Tall, good-looking, well-connected, and quite wealthy, he had a full social calendar, both as a guest and as a host. He frequently went to Europe, and wore finely tailored clothes from Bond Street. Frederick Rhodes, the son of his superintendent, recalled Levy as "very elegant." He often wore a morning coat, a giant pearl scarf pin, European cuff links, bright cravats, and waistcoats with piqué edging.[334] Newspapers often mentioned Levy's name as a potential suitor for one woman or another, but he remained a confirmed bachelor all his life. As late as 1912, when he was sixty years old, he felt compelled to issue a denial to a rumor, current in both Washington and New York society circles, that he and Miss Flora Wilson, the daughter of the secretary of agriculture, would wed.[335] His domestic arrangements suited him well. In the winter he and his brother Mitchell were cosseted by their sister Amelia in New York, and in the summer she presided over Monticello and took care of him there as well.

Politically Levy aligned himself early on with the Democratic Party, when most well-to-do Jews voted Republican. He helped found the Manhattan Democratic Club, which had close ties to Tammany Hall, the powerful political machine that dominated New York City politics. With its support Levy ran for and won election to Congress three times, to the Fifty-sixth (1899-1901) and Sixty-second (1911-1913) Congresses from the Thirteenth New York District, and to the Sixty-third (1913-1915) from the Fourteenth District.[336] Levy exercised a great deal of influence within city and state Democratic politics, and in 1916 when he attended the state party convention, he was described as one of Tammany's "Big Four," the other three being Norman E. Mack, Boss Charles F. Murphy, and Sheriff (later governor) Alfred E. Smith.[337]

In general, Levy would be characterized as conservative, but one should not dismiss him as a hidebound mossback. Although he disagreed with much of the dominant progressive thought of the early twentieth century, he also opposed corruption in local government and campaigned relentlessly for municipal reform. One of his proudest claims remained that he forced a reform of the surrogate practice in New York, a court that had long been the bastion of corruption and cronyism. Levy took the lead in codifying the election laws, which in the 1890s were cumbersome and confusing, and wrote—or caused to be written—a handbook for citizens explaining their rights as well as electoral practices.[338] A fiscal conservative, he threatened a lawsuit when the city government exceeded its constitutional debt limit, and funded Bureau of Municipal Research publications on the matter.[339]

In Congress he joined with other conservatives. During his first term he was one of the leaders of the so-called "Gold Democrats," those who broke away from the party's nominal leader, William Jennings Bryan, and his call for the free coinage of silver. He also challenged the secretary of the treasury repeatedly on that official's failure to act in a prudent manner in responding to market downturns that in particular affected New York City. During his career in Congress he consistently opposed investigations into business, and especially two of the most publicized congressional hearings, one into the Steel Trust and the other Pujo Committee investigation of the Money Trust, claiming that such meddling in private business "would prove disastrous to the country and would bring on financial distress." Levy opposed the income tax, the revision of the antitrust laws during the Wilson administration, and the regulatory activities of the Interstate Commerce Commission.[340] Levy claimed to have written and introduced the bill that created the Federal Reserve System, but in this area he took credit for something over which he had little influence.

By 1913 nearly everyone agreed that the nation's banking system needed a drastic overhaul. There had been no central bank in the country since Andrew Jackson had killed the Bank of the United States in 1832, and the financial panic of 1907 had shown the system at its most rigid and ineffective form. Conservatives wanted a central banking system completely in private hands, which would have left control over the nation's money in the hands of the big New York bankers. The National Monetary Commission, headed by Senator Nelson W. Aldrich, proposed just such a bankers' bill, and Levy introduced it into Congress. But progressive Democrats, headed by Secretary of State William Jennings Bryan and Secretary of the Treasury William Gibbs McAdoo, wanted a central bank controlled by the federal government, and they also wanted the government to take over currency issue, which had hitherto been the province of private banks. Woodrow Wilson, although initially a supporter of the private scheme, came around to the more progressive view, and with his encouragement Congress adopted the Federal Reserve System in late 1913, a measure that bore practically no resemblance to the Levy bill.[341]

In a similar manner, he claimed that a speech he gave in opposition to a proposed isthmian canal across Nicaragua helped to defeat that proposal and make possible the building of the Panama Canal. Levy in fact consistently supported a strong navy, and after World War One began he often called for large increases in the military budget.[342] When he decided not to run for re-election in 1914, he probably realized that he was out of step with a majority of the country and of his own party.

One final aspect of Jefferson Levy's life that one should note is that although he was not an observant Jew, he nonetheless proudly identified with the Jewish people in much the same way as his uncle had done. He belonged to Shearith Israel, the Old New York Sephardic congregation, and like Uriah, would be buried in Cyprus Hills Cemetery. He also joined with other well-to-do Jews to protest the rash of pogroms in Russia in the early years of the twentieth century and to provide aid for the victims. The National Committee for Relief showed how effective the Jewish community could be when it organized, and in 1906 many of the members, but not Levy, joined to form the American Jewish Committee.[343] Levy neither flaunted his religion nor hid it; like his uncle, he admired Thomas Jefferson for making it possible for Jews in the United States to partake fully in civil affairs. And like his uncle, he too presented a statue.

In 1905 Levy had a copy of the Jefferson statue made and presented it to the village of Angers, the home of the sculptor who had made the original for Uriah. Levy traveled to France in the late summer and took part in an elaborate ceremony in which he gave a brief speech extolling Jefferson as well as Franco-American friendship. "We always have," he declared, "and always will look towards you as our friends .... It is more than appropriate that you in the heart of France should have a statue of the greatest statesman and philosopher of modern times."[344]

❦

To reclaim Monticello, Jefferson Levy needed someone on whom he could rely to get the work done and who shared his desire to restore Thomas Jefferson's home to its former elegance. First, however, he had to get rid of Joel Wheeler, and this proved harder than anticipated. By now the old man believed he owned Monticello, and it took a court order to finally evict him from the premises.[345] Having gotten rid of Wheeler, however, Levy found it nearly impossible to hire

Monticello East Front, c. 1870 (courtesy of Special Collections, University of Virginia Library).

a suitable replacement. He hired and fired a series of unsuitable men until Thomas Fortune Ryan, a New York financier who owned Oak Ridge, a nearby summer place south of Charlottesville, recommended Thomas L. Rhodes. A local man, Rhodes and his wife lived at Monticello for nearly a half-century, and while Levy owned the house Rhodes had complete control over the restoration. When the Thomas Jefferson Memorial Foundation bought Monticello in 1923, Rhodes stayed on as superintendent, but without the control over restoration he had enjoyed under Levy.

Much had to be done, and it is worth recalling the terrible state to which the house had descended. Congressman Augustus A. Hardenbergh of New Jersey visited Monticello in 1878 and reported back that:[346]

Desolation and ruin mark everything around the place. I went through the house in which Jefferson lived. There is scarcely a whole shingle upon it, except what have been placed there within the last few years. The windows are broken, everything is left to the mercy of the pitiless storm. The room in which Jefferson died is darkened; all around it are the evidences of desolation and decay—a standing monument to the ingratitude of the great republic.

The initial work, like that Uriah had faced, involved cleaning up the mess, this time the one left by Joel Wheeler, and making basic repairs to the house—fixing the roof, replacing the gutters, replacing broken windows and the like. Apparently the interim caretakers, whose names we do not know, did well enough so that by 1887 Frank Stockton could write that the "whole establishment has been put in excellent order by the present owner … and is now as sound and substantial a country mansion as it ever was."[347] Around this time, one of Thomas Jefferson's descendants visited the homestead and reported that "J.M. Levy is cleaning & repairing & painting & the place or house rather is looking well."[348] Levy, like his uncle, also began buying up neighboring property as it became available, and by 1905 had purchased 1,569 acres in addition to the 218 that came with the house at the auction.[349] The last acquisition came in 1905, when Levy purchased from the Metropolitan Museum of Art what had been known in Uriah's time as the Washington Farm. That land had gone by will to Asahel Levy, who had turned it over in 1866 to his good friend, Jacob S. Rogers, who left it in his will to the museum.[350] With this purchase Jefferson increased the Monticello estate to about the size it had been at Uriah's death.

In some ways the restoration of the exterior of the house proved the easiest task. Despite the years of neglect the basic structure had not changed; repairs, though extensive and expensive, followed a simple template. Broken windows needed new glass, not redesigned frames. Levy did not fix everything; when the Thomas Jefferson Memorial Foundation took over in 1923, the columns and arches of the terraces atop the dependencies had only been replaced in a few sections. But Levy did do a great deal in restoring the outside of the house, and no doubt made it possible for the Foundation to do more accurate historical restoration when it took over the property.

Years later Jefferson Levy declared that he had attempted to restore Monticello "to its original state," and he had maintained "as near as possible, the conditions which obtained at the time Jefferson had lived there."[351] The dean of the

University of Virginia Department of Engineering, William Thornton, told a congressional hearing that "I do not know of any one thing Mr. Levy has done to make Monticello different from what it was at the time of Jefferson, and I know of hundreds of things he has done to make it the same."[352] Levy once boasted that he and his family still used candles at Monticello, since that was how the house had been lit in Jefferson's day. "A great candelabrum with 40 or 50 candles is still the means of lighting the gallery. Every room has a separate candelabrum."[353]

Chandelier in Monticello Dining Room, c. 1912 (courtesy of Holsinger Collection, University of Virginia Library).

The truth, however, is that changes were made. While candles may have been used occasionally, the inventory of items in the house indicates that all rooms had lamps as well. Late Victorian families of comfortable means no longer used chamber pots, and Levy had a modern bathroom installed in the old house. He did some remodeling on the second floor to make the bedrooms more comfortable, and installed dormer windows where there had been skylights for the third-story bedrooms, and at the ends of the third floor hallway. The same engineering professor who claimed that Levy had done nothing to change the Jeffersonian nature of Monticello also reported that Levy had considered hiring the New York architectural firm of McKim, Mead & White to add some rooms to the house because he needed greater space for entertaining, something which surely would have distorted the Jeffersonian lines.[354] Levy and his family did not live the same way that Jefferson and his family had lived seven decades earlier; their tastes were different and although Levy would later claim that he had tried to make Monticello into a shrine to Jefferson, he nonetheless treated the house as his private property—which it was—and decorated it to suit his tastes. The same writer who praised the renovation of the house in 1887 also noted that "there is a modern air about its furnishings and fittings which is not Jeffersonian."[355]

Two different developments took place simultaneously, and the two did not always run in easy tandem. On the one hand the Levy family wanted to enjoy their summer home in the Virginia Piedmont, and this meant furnishing the house with comfortable Victorian furniture. On the other, Levy at least partially and Thomas Rhodes especially wanted to restore Monticello as much as possible to the condition it had been in during Jefferson's lifetime. The result can best be described as a hybrid, a unique house and landscape, developed at the end of the eighteenth and beginning of the nineteenth century, partially modernized and partially restored, with some items inside the house having belonged to Jefferson, others that dated from Jefferson's era, and still others that were the modern personal belongings and furniture of the current owner.

Was this historic preservation? Not by modern standards, which aims at recreating, as much as possible, the exact milieu that existed when the original owner lived in the house.[356] The Thomas Jefferson Foundation has carried on extensive historical research—and is still doing so—to ascertain the conditions that pertained at Monticello when Thomas Jefferson lived there. For example, its staff discovered a shadow of the original wallpaper in the North Octagonal room, identified the original paper, and commissioned an accurate copy. Jefferson's minute record-keeping and landscape archeology have allowed the restoration of the lawn and gardens to his designs, and archeological excavations have also informed our knowledge of the larger plantation life. Both Jefferson's records as well as the accounts of visitors have provided a good idea of the furnishings and what artifacts and decorations Jefferson had, and intensive searches have been carried on to locate either the originals or accurate facsimiles. The visitor to Monticello today does not enter the house as it was when Jefferson lived there; modern preservation requires temperature and humidity controls that just did not exist a century ago. But these are well hidden, and what the visitor does see is what our best historical knowledge tells us the house looked like nearly two hundred years ago, down to an open book on Jefferson's night table.

People who visited Monticello during Jefferson Levy's tenure saw many things that might have been Jeffersonian, and they also saw the heavy, bourgeois furniture favored by the late Victorian middle class. Apparently Levy did try to get some Jeffersonian items. He believed that his uncle had purchased some of the household furnishings that had been sold after Jefferson's death, and so he secured the bills of sale for the items sold at the Confederate auction. He managed to reclaim some of the items, and to anyone who brought back things voluntarily he refunded the purchase price. But Monticello had also been vandalized during the war, and many items could never be reclaimed. In some instances Levy managed to have copies made. The beautiful parquet floors that had elicited such praise from visitors shone once again.[357]

Levy went to Europe frequently, and apparently had one or more agents who kept an eye out for Jeffersonian artifacts, which he reportedly bought when they came on the market.[358] But it is impossible to determine the extent of these purchases. It is probably exaggerated, as Henry Ferguson suggested, that "Levy made repeated trips to Europe in search of the mansion's original furniture, wall-papers, and rugs, and when the originals were unobtainable he had costly copies made from whatever sketches he could find."[359]

We do know the following: most of Thomas Jefferson's household furnishings had been sold after his death, and although some papers and furnishings did remain, these apparently passed to Barclay and then to Uriah Levy upon the subsequent sales of the house. Uriah Levy made some effort to recover Jeffersonian originals, and while we have no record of his achievements on this point, it is fair to assume that he had limited success. During the nearly twenty years of war and mismanagement, practically everything in the house disappeared, either through sale, theft, or souvenir-taking sanctioned by Wheeler. Jefferson Levy was able to track some things down locally, and purchased other items outside of Albemarle County and in Europe.

An unsigned staff paper prepared for the Thomas Jefferson Foundation says that Jefferson Monroe Levy "is known to have gathered a relatively large collection of the authentic items that had been liberally scattered throughout Albemarle County by the 1827 dispersal sale & looting Confederate soldiers in 1862." These treasures found their way to two locations; most came to Monticello, while a few went to the Mayhoff residence in New York. Because an inventory exists of the furniture and other items that passed from Levy with the sale of Monticello in

Monticello Parlor, 1912 (courtesy of Holsinger Collection, University of Virginia Library).

1923, one can authenticate those items; difficulties arose, however, in trying to authenticate the half-dozen or so furnishings in New York.[360]

The inventory, reproduced in full as an appendix, is an excellent guide both to how successfully Levy acquired Jeffersonian items, as well as to how he furnished the house itself. Among the items confirmed as belonging to Thomas Jefferson when he lived at Monticello are the seven-day calendar-clock with its cannonball-like weights, the folding ladder to wind the clock, a music stand, two gate-leg Sheraton style card tables, and a brass hanging lamp. The parlor had two pier mirrors, the cabinet had two side shelves, and an upstairs bedroom had a mahogany table stand. On the third floor was the body of the gig in which Jefferson supposedly rode from Monticello to Philadelphia for the Continental

Congress.[361] Other items might possibly have been Jeffersonian, but could not be authenticated at the time. One might look at this list and see it as very limited, or one could say, given the difficulties he faced and the problems of authentication, Jefferson Levy did rather well.

❧

If the interior of the house no longer had a late eighteenth century appearance, then how did Jefferson Levy furnish it? For this we have numerous reports of family and visitors, as well as photographs; all confirm that, aside from the Jeffersonian items he sought, Levy filled Monticello with heavy late Victorian furniture and idiosyncratic things that caught his fancy. He apparently hired the New York furniture store Sloan's to oversee the decoration, and as one scholar has put it, Thomas

Jefferson's Bedroom, 1912 (courtesy of Holsinger Collection, University of Virginia Library).

Entrance Hall, 1912 (courtesy of Holsinger Collection, University of Virginia Library).

Jefferson's entertainment rooms "took on the over-stuffed appearance of a Parisian banker's country house during Napoleon III's Second Empire. Elaborate imported chandeliers, mirrors, sideboards, and a spectacularly bedizened bed à la Madame du Barry decorated the hall, parlor, dining room and Jefferson's bedroom."[362]

Levy, according to Frederick Rhodes, who grew up on the plantation, liked French furniture and collected it. Among the pieces he brought to Monticello were a $25,000 malachite and copper carbonite table, and another made of different stones ground together and polished. Just as in Jefferson's time, big pieces for the upstairs bedrooms had to be hauled up the outside of the house or over the entrance hall balcony.[363]

In the front hall on the right stood a full-length portrait of Thomas Jefferson as president in an ornate gold frame, showing him standing at a table on which lay the Declaration of Independence. On the other side of the hall stood an equivalent-sized portrait of Uriah Phillips Levy in full naval uniform, also next to a table on which lay a "Bill to Prevent Flogging in the United States Navy."[364] Nearby could be found a model of the ship *Vandalia*, which under Uriah's command had been the first vessel in the Navy to abolish flogging. After a while Uriah's portrait was moved, Jefferson's picture crossed over to the left side, and in its place stood a full size portrait of the new owner, Jefferson Levy, dressed in his London best with a large greyhound.[365]

The parlor now sported tasseled draperies, embroidered with a gold "L." Tapestries showing Spanish scenes hung over the entrance hall balcony; an oak dining table and Chippendale chairs overwhelmed the dining room, which also featured an oblong Rubenesque picture over the mantel. In Jefferson's bedroom, which Levy used for himself, there was a gold Louis XIV bed on a

Jefferson Monroe Levy by George Burroughs Torrey (photograph, Thomas Jefferson Foundation; location of original unknown).

dais, covered in a Nattier blue damask that also hung on the walls, and the floor was covered by a blue velvet carpet to match. Voluminous blue damask curtains draped to each side fell from a gold coronet above the bed. (Jefferson's own bed rails had been removed from the alcove and stored upstairs.) Next to the fireplace Levy had placed two large armchairs, also covered in blue damask, as well as a large table.[366]

In 1899 *Munsey's Magazine* sent Maud Howard Peterson to visit Monticello, and the piece she wrote is accompanied by invaluable pictures of the house. To one unfamiliar with Monticello, the photographs could have been of any well-to-do

Monticello Dining Room, 1912 (courtesy of Holsinger Collection, University of Virginia Library).

late-nineteenth-century businessman's house. A shot of the small tea room adjoining the dining room has Jefferson's music rack barely visible on the far left; the wicker furniture is clearly modern. The dining room photograph shows heavier pieces, and the caption notes that "none of Jefferson's furniture is in this room." Upstairs in the dome room, Levy had brought in a billiards table.

Miss Peterson had nothing but praise for the current owner. "Too much credit cannot be given Mr. Levy for his intelligent care of the home and grounds. While ample means have restored much of their original beauty, no modern innovation has come in. It is his policy and his pride to keep the old house, the green terraces, the wide lawns, and the ancient trees as they were in the hands of the first owner."[367] Peterson noted that whenever possible, Levy had secured original bits of statuary and furniture, but that it had been a difficult task since so much of Jefferson's household had been scattered following his death.

Outside the house Levy seems, for the most part, to have left the work to Thomas Rhodes, who while preserving the open spaces also turned Monticello back into a working farm, much as it had been in Jefferson's time, although with a somewhat different emphasis. The steep road up to the main house had always been difficult and at times dangerous. Rhodes extended the driveway around to the back, so that now one had a one-way path that led up the hill and came down on a different route. Visitors walking around the grounds encountered a pair of stone lions, each holding a shield with an "L" engraved on it, along the stairway from Mulberry Row to the main house, while another set of lions, each with a paw on a ball, stood along the southwest portico steps.[368] Rhodes also repaired the old retaining walls and built new ones where needed. He cleared the lawns, and nursed the trees and shrubbery back to health.

He planted a large vegetable patch, which grew, among other things, "gigantic" strawberries and table grapes. Horses, cattle and even for a short while hogs grazed in the surrounding pastures, and in other fields corn and oats grew to

Lions at West Front (right) and near South Dependencies at Monticello, 1912 (courtesy of Holsinger Collection, University of Virginia Library).

feed the animals. The horses won prizes at the local Charlottesville fairs, and later in New York. Levy kept one stallion, four mares, and a number of Shetland ponies that his nieces and nephews rode when they visited. A visitor might be startled to see two huge greyhounds, "Jack" and "Telemachus," racing around the lawn.[369] Rhodes did not try to recreate the flowerbeds and other ornaments that Jefferson had planned, and which one now sees at Monticello.

Levy refurbished the house because, unlike Uriah, he and his family did spend a fair amount of time there, nearly all of every summer from the early 1880s until he sold the house in 1923. His father Jonas died in 1883 at age seventy-six and was quite ill the last few years of his life, but he too came to Monticello in the summer. His mother Fanny, however, came with him every summer from 1881 until her own death in 1893. According to Jeannie Blackburn, Fanny Mitchell Levy "was widely known as the charming hostess of Monticello, and will always be remembered as a lovely woman, cordial in her manner, giving genuine, kind welcome to Monticello, [and] taking great pleasure in showing the beauties of the old home to all her guests."[370]

But the real chatelaine of Monticello during much of Jefferson Levy's occupancy was his sister, Amelia Mayhoff, the same woman who presided over the house he lived at in New York.[371] Each summer she and her family and servants, and often those of her brother Louis as well, packed up several dozen trunks and took the train from New York to Charlottesville, reversing the procedure in the fall.[372] When the party arrived at Charlottesville, they would be met by two horse-drawn broughams, and with all the people and luggage it often proved a hard pull up the mountain, even for the farm's big workhorses. We have a charming recital of the family's arrival by Jefferson's fifteen-year-old niece Frances Wolff Levy, Napoleon Levy's daughter, written for her school newspaper:[373]

It is the month of June …. We have crossed a little creek which now looks quiet and peaceful, but at times it is a roaring torrent, carrying great trees and small huts along with it. Now we have started up the

"Little Mountain," which is the meaning of the Italian name Monticello, given it by Thomas Jefferson. The road is better now but very steep and even to these strong Virginia horses it is a heavy pull. Up, up we go. Here comes a haycart drawn by a pair of oxen and driven by an old colored man, who smiles and tips his hat to us as we pass. Our horses are tired and thirsty, and we stop while they draw in deep draughts of the clear, cold water coming from a natural spring which is on the side of the mountain.

At last we come to the pretty brick Lodge, and Aunt Liza comes out and swings back the great gates for us to pass through. How curved and steep the road is! I am frightened as I look on one side and see down, down to a seemingly bottomless ravine. Great trees grow along its sides. Far down a deer runs swiftly away at the noise of the carriage.

What is that? Ah, it is the bell telling travelers on the top of the mountain not to go down, as it is very dangerous for two vehicles to pass on such a narrow road. How beautiful it sounds as it dies away! It is twilight now and a silence has dropped over everything. Indistinctly I see the Scotch broom growing up the bank on the other side, and roses, too, climbing upward. Silence. Never have I heard such a stillness. The echo of the horses' hoofs on the stony road and the occasional cry of a peacock are the only sounds. We are passing Jefferson's burial ground, and the stones look white and ghostly. A light wind blows through the dark woods, and they seem to moan. Hark! A cry. What is it? Old Loom tells us that it is a fox down in the valley.

At last we are nearing the top. The horses run quickly across the lawn. There in the distance stands the house. We are getting nearer and can make out the four great white pillars of the south piazza. Through the windows the soft light of the lamps seem to welcome us. We go on past the rustic fence, and the sweet scent of the honeysuckle which is twined around it, is blown gently towards us. We give a long whistle. They hear it. The dogs begin to bark and an answering whistle comes back. On we go around the large lawn. The carriage stops in front of the great mansion; we are quickly helped to alight and taken up the long lawn. The doors of the house are thrown open, showing the great hall inside, and we enter amid the barkings of the dogs and the hearty greetings of the family.

Life at Monticello, however bourgeois the furnishings, proved different and exciting. While some well-to-do New Yorkers had summer homes in the mountains or at the shore, how many of them owned the former house of President Thomas Jefferson? How many of them attracted dozens of visitors each day, and how many of them had visitors that included presidents of the United States? How many of them had a working farm where the children could watch or help milk the cows, and ride Shetland ponies around the grounds? How many of them had a small cemetery on the grounds where one could squeeze between the bars and play inside? And how many of them boasted old buildings (the dependencies) on whose roofs one could play hopscotch?[374]

Monticello suited Jefferson Levy, and he liked playing the lord of the manor. While a few Albemarle County residents resented the fact that an outsider—a "son of Abraham," as one matron wrote in disgust—now owned Monticello, Jefferson Levy seems to have been a good neighbor during his annual visits. Although only a part-time resident, Levy took an active role in Charlottesville life.[375] When he was in residence the American flag flew over the house, and on July Fourth each year many of the local residents were invited to a big reception on the mountain. There were fireworks, a band from Charlottesville would come to play, and from Jefferson's music stand he would read aloud the Declaration of Independence. He also paid for all or part of the costs in upgrading the road from the town to the little mountain.[376] He welcomed local and even national groups, and in October 1892, for example, he and his mother welcomed the Albemarle Chapter of the Daughters of the American Revolution to Monticello in what the chapter president later recalled as "one of the grandest society events in the history of Virginia."[377] For the occasion, Mrs. Levy, herself a member of the D.A.R., wore a colonial outfit of lavender in which she later had her portrait painted. Wilson Cary Nicholas

Randolph, Jefferson's great-grandson and rector of the University of Virginia, declared that the Levy family "have lived here nearly sixty years, and in all that time have been the most courteous and considerate neighbors."[378]

Levy also involved himself in Charlottesville in another way—financially. In 1880, about the same time he started work on Monticello, he bought the old City Hall, restored it, and renamed it the Levy Opera House, which he then rented out for theatrical productions as well as for office and school space.[379] He also began buying up properties and renting them out, including a commercial building on the south side of Main Street, a saddlery at the corner of Main and Fifth Streets,[380] the old People's National Bank building on East Market Street,[381] a commercial residence on Estes Street,[382] the building in which the Michie Printing Company began its long career,[383] and others. He bought and sold properties, and one interesting document indicates that although he intended

Levy Opera House (courtesy of Dalgliesh, Eichman, Gilpin, and Paxton, P.C.).

to make money, he also wanted to be a good neighbor. In 1916 he thought he had agreed with a neighbor, a Mr. Burke, to sell off a few very small plots of land Levy owned adjacent to Burke's farm. Apparently there was some confusion over the exact size of the plots as well as the price, with Levy believing he should receive $500 and Burke thinking the price to be $300. Levy wrote to his lawyer, former judge R.T.W. Duke, that Burke "is a hard-working man; not at home until late in the evening and leaves early in the morning." The misunderstanding was not Burke's fault, and Levy instructed Duke to complete the sale at the $300 price.[384]

Despite all the purchases and sales, despite his reputed wealth and the large amount of money he put into Monticello to refurbish and maintain it (one estimate is that it cost him $40,000 a year for the upkeep of the estate), Levy, like most speculators, had what we would now call "cash flow" problems. During the thirty-four years of their collaboration, Levy usually paid Thomas Rhodes, but at times when the vagaries of stock and real estate markets left Levy short of cash, Rhodes had to lay out money to pay the workers and then wait for Levy to reimburse him.[385] His legal papers include a number of notes of loans he made to other people, and loans other people made to him, as well as letters from his creditors wanting to know why they had not been paid.[386] For the most part Levy had the money to indulge Monticello as well as his speculations, but not always.

Whatever its owner's personal finances, Monticello flourished. For the first time since Jefferson had lived there, important political figures began to visit the house. In 1888 President Grover Cleveland and some of his cabinet came to pay homage to the founder of the Democratic Party, as did Vice President Adlai Stevenson and nearly the entire Senate. William McKinley had a visit scheduled for the week after he was shot. James G. Blaine, the most prominent Republican leader of the late nineteenth century, slept at Monticello, and on leaving told his host "I want you, Mr. Levy, to know that though a Republican, I am a follower of Jefferson."[387] The Jefferson Club of St. Louis, Missouri, asked if they could hold their annual meeting at Monticello in 1901, and Levy agreed. The group, 250 strong, arrived by special train in October, enjoyed a luncheon with the usual political speeches, and with Levy's permission erected a large memorial made of Missouri granite north of the house.[388]

In 1903 President Theodore Roosevelt upset his Secret Service escort when he insisted on riding a horse up the mountain rather than use the presidential car. The poor guards, unused to horses, hung on grimly as their mounts went up the steep incline. Although the Mayhoff and Levy children were rarely allowed into the formal reception rooms with their highly polished floors, Levy and Mrs. Mayhoff made an exception that day, and just before Roosevelt sat down to a luncheon in his honor, the children came in and bowed and curtsied to the president, who patted them on their heads. In honor of his visit, Mrs. Mayhoff sewed a small American flag on the back of the armchair where Roosevelt had sat.[389]

For all the great men who came, however, Monticello was a family residence for the extended Levy clan. Jefferson Levy slept in a large four-poster bed in

Thomas Jefferson's bedroom, and like the first owner, kept that entire wing on the first floor for his personal use. Upstairs the Mayhoffs—Amelia, her husband Charles, and their son Monroe—occupied one wing, while Louis Napoleon Levy, his wife Lillian, and their four daughters occupied the other. When Mitchell, Jefferson's brother, came to visit, he slept in one of the guest rooms. Levy named all of the upstairs bedrooms after Jefferson's contemporaries—John Adams, James Madison, James Monroe, and the Marquis de Lafayette. On the top floor the servants occupied the small rooms under the roof.

If Jefferson Levy enjoyed his role as lord of the manor, his sister enjoyed her position as its lady. On many afternoons she would go visiting the ladies of Charlottesville in a fine carriage drawn by a pair of horses, with a footman in the rear seat. Or she would serve as hostess for teas on the west lawn. His niece recalled her as "a smart woman and a gracious hostess," who gave many parties on her brother's behalf.[390]

The children spent happy days there, and even when it rained, they found many things to do in the house. They would race up the narrow stairways to play on the top floor, where all sorts of things had been stored away, including the famous gig that Jefferson had supposedly ridden to Philadelphia. There was a dumbwaiter that went down to the wine cellar, and all sorts of places to play outside; moreover, the working farm proved very attractive to city-bred youngsters. "This morning we racked the hay," young Fanny wrote to her mother, and in the afternoon "we are going to pile the hay in Monroe's wagon & bring it to the barn for the ponies & horses."[391] All of the children were excited when Amelia brought home a four-week-old fox terrier puppy "no bigger than your hand," and if they walked down to the lodge, the gatekeeper might let them ring the

Letter from Frances Wolf to Lillian Levy, May 31, 1902 (Thomas Jefferson Foundation; gift of Mrs. Richard C. Lewis).

Page from Levy family scrapbook (Thomas Jefferson Foundation; gift of Mrs. Richard E. Lewis).

Amelia Mayhoff with son Monroe on Monticello West Front, circa 1900 (Courtesy of Mrs. Richard C. Lewis).

bell.[392] Nearly all the children (Amelia's son Monroe was sickly and did not always play with his cousins) loved the small herd of Shetland ponies that Uncle Jeff kept on the farm, and would go riding around the big lawn on one of the little horses whenever they could.

For Amelia, and her mother before her, Monticello may have been a great house to which famous people would come, but there were always family matters demanding attention. There exist a few letters written by Fanny Mitchell Levy early in the 1880s, shortly after her son had bought Monticello, and they talk not about Thomas Jefferson or the beautiful architecture or the Blue Ridge Mountains, but about more down-to-earth matters, like getting and keeping a cook, the problems of keeping a country house clean, the health of her grand-children, the problems she had. On July 4, 1881, she wrote to Louis that "your dear father [Jonas] is happy. He takes a good hour to his meals and everything is plentiful." She also notes rather disapprovingly that Amelia "has nothing to do which suits her."[393] When her three-year-old grandson Clarkson became sick while visiting, she wrote to her son-in-law at his office, not wishing to upset the child's mother. "He has one of his sick turns. We were up with him all night and we have taken turns to sleep since he has been here as he is very wakeful at night and on the top of this mountain you cannot get a doctor when you need it."[394]

But for all the problems, and even the occasional tightness of money, Jefferson Levy maintained a fine country home for himself and for his family, one where he could entertain the great and the near-great of the day. Fortunately, that idyllic time lasted for nearly three decades. But during that time he had to endure hundreds, then thousands of visitors to Monticello, and then from a totally unexpected quarter came a threat to his very ownership of Thomas Jefferson's house.

Chapter Five

MAUD LITTLETON'S WISH

"When the White House is for sale, then I will consider an offer for the sale of Monticello, and not before."

— JEFFERSON MONROE LEVY[395]

When he gained control of Monticello, Jefferson Levy knew he had not just acquired a run-down country house that, with adequate money, he could convert into a pleasant summer home in the Virginia Piedmont. Monticello had been the home of Thomas Jefferson, and ever since his death pilgrims had made the trek up the little mountain. Levy recognized that he would have to find a way to deal with them tactfully, allowing some if not most access to the grounds, and at the same time putting some limits in place to ensure the privacy of his family and its enjoyment of the estate.

He surely did not anticipate that his pleasure in Monticello, indeed his very ownership of it, would be threatened by a young woman transplanted from Texas to Brooklyn, whose campaign to wrest Jefferson's house away from Levy would reach all the way to Congress and even to the White House, or that it would come within a whisker of success.

❧

Many of the visitors who came to Monticello wanted to pay homage at Jefferson's tomb, and over the years had taken home little mementos—pieces chipped from the obelisk marking his grave. Ironically, Jefferson in his will had directed that the marker be made of "the course stone of which my columns are made, that no one might be tempted hereafter to destroy it for the value of the materials."[396] The plaque

Thomas Jefferson's original gravestone at Monticello, c. 1871 (courtesy of Special Collections, University of Virginia Library).

engraved with the famous epitaph, in which Jefferson had listed the three things for which he wanted to be remembered—the Declaration of Independence, the Statute for Religious Freedom, and the University of Virginia—had been taken into the house years earlier by Uriah in order to prevent it being carried off as a souvenir. The deplorable condition of the little graveyard, made worse by negligence during Wheeler's occupancy, led to many complaints to Congress and calls that something be done to restore the final resting place of the third president.

On April 13, 1878, Jefferson's 135th birthday, Representative Samuel S. Cox of New York introduced a resolution appropriating $5,000 for the purchase of the graveyard and the restoration of the marker over Jefferson's grave. It was scandalous, Cox averred, that the nation had done nothing to preserve and cherish the final resting place of this "avatar of progress," the "incarnation of American Democratic Republicanism."[397] The resolution passed, and Congress directed Secretary of State William M. Evarts to secure the site and provide a new monument. Evarts had already let a contract for the work when he heard from Jefferson Levy that some members of his family who owned interests in Monticello "stubbornly refused and would strenuously oppose the erection of the monument," and they were "unwilling to cede any of their rights to the ground and the control of the place." Either ignorant of the facts or deliberately ignoring them, Levy wrote that "the grave and its surroundings belong to the owners of Monticello and not to the heirs of Jefferson."[398] Years later Levy said he would have been willing to give the government the right of way, but there were too many Jefferson heirs, a number of them minors, and so they could not agree among themselves.

This put an end to the first effort to renovate the gravesite, but on Jefferson's birthday in 1882, Representative George Washington Geddes of Ohio offered a new resolution appropriating $10,000 to restore the tomb and marker. Sarah Randolph, Jefferson's great-granddaughter, had in the meantime sent Evarts a certified copy of the deed showing clearly that the cemetery and its use had been reserved to the heirs of Thomas Jefferson, with free access to it. Levy, by now in full ownership of Monticello, agreed to the resolution since it took no rights away from him. Congress erected a marker twice the size of the original one, and a surplus of $2,000 remained from the appropriation. Levy suggested that it be used to build proper steps from the driveway up the embankment to the gate, and that an iron fence surround the cemetery, suggestions that the government accepted. Jefferson's descendants undertook to maintain the graveyard, but did so poorly that in 1913, under intense public criticism, they established the Monticello Association to oversee the maintenance.[399]

Congress, in recognition of Levy's ownership, had not attempted to insert a proviso allowing full public access to the cemetery, since that would have turned the main road to the house into a public thoroughfare. As it was, visitors kept trooping up to the house, and Levy felt that although he could not prevent people from making the pilgrimage, he and his family had a right to some privacy. There were sporadic acts of vandalism that elicited threats to close the property entirely.[400] Levy attempted to control the flow of visitors, and at least until the early part of the twentieth century the scheme seems to have worked. One needed to gain permission to enter from either Levy, or in his absence from his agent, probably Rhodes. Initially he charged a small admission fee that he turned over for the construction and support of a hospital in Charlottesville. Yet even with the required fee and permission, between twenty-five and seventy-five visitors a day came to Monticello, and many of them felt no compunction at pulling out flowers, cutting bark off trees, or even chipping away at the house to take home a relic of their visit.[401]

Improved transportation, including rail and especially the new automobile, made it relatively easy for people to reach Charlottesville, and by the early twentieth century the number of visitors had doubled, and some forty to fifty thousand

Visitors to Monticello, circa 1914 (Thomas Jefferson Foundation; gift of Mr. and Mrs. Earl C. Leake).

people a year came to pay homage.[402] A Jefferson Memorial Association was organized in Virginia for the purpose of building a properly engineered road that would accommodate automobiles up the little mountain. It and the Interstate Good Roads Convention met in Charlottesville in 1902, endorsed the proposal, and sought congressional funding. In the end state and local funds built the road, with a significant contribution from Monticello's owner.

Whatever his original intentions, Levy seemed unable or unwilling to impede the flow of visitors. As noted in the last chapter, he eagerly hosted groups, such as the Daughters of the American Revolution and the Jefferson Club of St. Louis, and University of Virginia faculty had a standing invitation to visit the estate. After all, much of the pleasure of being lord of Monticello lay in being able to play the grand host and to show the domain to visitors. Charlotte Crystal, an Albemarle native, believed that Jefferson Levy, like his uncle, held Monticello "as a trustee for the people Jefferson loved," that is, for the American people.[403]

Later on, when the controversy over access to Monticello became a national debate, people testified to how welcoming Levy had been, even if he had not received adequate notice of their arrival. Erroll Dunbar recalled how in 1897 he had come, uninvited, and had been welcomed into the house by the caretaker. He had been free to look around, and had found the house, the grounds and the gravesite well tended.[404] A New York Jewish matriarch, Annie Nathan Meyer, recalled that after visiting Hot Springs, on the train back to New York the porter pointed out Monticello from the window and told her that on her next trip she should surely stop off and see Mr. Jefferson's house. The owner, the porter declared, "welcomed all visitors and was most generous and hospitable to all strangers."[405] Levy himself declared that "I have always welcomed the public to Monticello and never has a guest entered the gates of the estate whose presence has not been announced by the ringing of a big brass bell at the gate-keeper's lodge, a custom that has survived a century and a half."[406] Levy may not have wanted all those people milling around his house,

Monticello Gatehouse, 1913 (courtesy of Holsinger Collection, University of Virginia Library).

but he realized that he had little choice. For the most part he made the best of it, and many of the people who visited him testified to his hospitality.

Not everyone, however, found their visit to Monticello so rewarding, and in 1902 former congressman Amos J. Cummings of New York found little to praise in Levy's hospitality and much to complain about. In an article he wrote entitled "A National Humiliation," Cummings described his recent visit to Monticello as a horrendous event. A black man stopped him at the gate and demanded payment of twenty-five cents. The gatekeeper then told him that no one could see the inside of the house; he gained entry anyway, but to his disgust he found nothing of Jefferson's in the building. Cummings exploded that Levy, supposedly a trustee of the house, had the effrontery to charge this fee of "patriotic Americans," and that beyond that, he valued the house at the highly inflated price of $100,000. "Possibly he imagines that he can eventually sell it to either the State or Federal

Government for this sum." Cummings believed the public ought to have control over Mr. Jefferson's house, both to save it from decay as well as to do away with the admission fee.[407]

The Cummings incident alarmed Levy, not because he cared much about Cummings, but because he had begun to fear that an effort would be made to wrest control of Monticello away from him. He responded by sponsoring publication of a book in 1902 purportedly written by George Alfred Townsend, although scholars believe much of it may have been written by Levy himself. In the form of two long letters from Townsend reporting on a pleasant weekend he had spent at Monticello, the book praised both Jefferson and Uriah for all they had done. The booklet clearly also served as an answer to people like Cummings, especially the introduction Levy wrote for the book, in which he defended his stewardship of Jefferson's home.[408]

In fact, one effort had already been made to secure Monticello. William Jennings Bryan, the perennial Democratic candidate for president, had written to Levy in 1897 asking at what price he would be willing to sell Monticello to the government. Levy had retorted that all of the money in the Treasury could not pay for the house.[409] Levy assumed that his reply had put an end to the matter, but Bryan would raise the matter again after he became secretary of state in the Wilson administration.

Cummings had fumed and ranted, but essentially nothing came of his diatribe. Bryan would bide his time. Another visitor to Monticello, however, went away so disturbed—so she claimed—that she launched a national campaign against Levy. Before we examine that effort to wrest Monticello from Levy's ownership, we need to examine the context in which the struggle for Mr. Jefferson's house took place.

❧

Thomas Jefferson is such an icon in American history, and has been so for such a long period of time, that we sometimes forget he went into eclipse for a good part of the nineteenth century. He was slaveholder, and many in the North could not forgive him for putting other human beings into bondage. He believed strongly in states rights and wrote the Kentucky Resolution protesting the Alien and Sedition Laws, which many people saw as a precursor to the secessionist ideology that triggered the Civil War. The symbolic founder of the Democratic Party, he suffered as the party suffered, especially when Americans blamed the Civil War on southern states and their Democratic leaders.

But in the latter part of the nineteenth century, Americans began to rediscover Thomas Jefferson. The editor of the *Chicago Tribune* wrote in 1880: "It somehow happens that now and then a man lives who seems to have in his head every important idea that all his countrymen together get into theirs for a century after he is dead." Many of the great ideas of recent years had been anticipated, and "likely enough the whole identical plan worked out in detail, somewhere in Jefferson's writings."[410]

This seemed especially true of Jefferson's ideas on education. In the debate over the refurbishing of the gravesite, Representative William P. Frye of Maine declared:[411]

Mr. Speaker, I revere the memory of Mr. Jefferson above that of almost any other man, especially because he was the earnest, constant friend of the common schools. He drafted the article in the constitution of Maine relating to education, under the influence of which my State stands to-day pre-eminent for the general intelligence of her people.

Jefferson had indeed anticipated a great general plan of popular education in the plan he submitted to the Virginia General Assembly in 1788, the Bill for the General Diffusion of Knowledge.[412] The philosophy of the common school had, of course, been born in New England, and dated back almost a century and a half before Jefferson had proposed his version in Virginia. The Puritans in seventeenth-century New England, however, had created schools for religious purposes, so their children could read the Bible and be reared in the true faith. Jefferson wanted all children schooled for civic purposes, so they could become good citizens of a democratic republic. Among the six hoped-for outcomes of education he articulated in 1818 when planning the University of Virginia he listed "To understand his duties to his neighbors and country, and to discharge with competence the functions confided to him by either; [and] to know his rights."[413] By the latter part of the nineteenth century, people credited Jefferson with envisioning a great public school system, one that the citizens of the United States believed had played a significant role in the nation's greatness, and on whose shoulders rested the hopes of the future. The renewed interest led to the publication of two separate collections of his writings, one underwritten by the newly created Thomas Jefferson Memorial Association.[414]

In 1896 the National Association of Democratic Clubs sponsored a celebration at Monticello on April 13, an event that led to the annual series of Jefferson Day dinners held by the party. The centennial of the Louisiana Purchase in 1903 led to further praise for Jefferson; his far-sightedness, the argument ran, had gained for the United States enough land to lay the foundation for an "empire of liberty." Many Americans had discovered, or to be more precise, re-discovered, Jeffersonian principles of democracy. William Sumner Appleton, a rock-ribbed New England Republican, declared himself an "an ardent Jeffersonian in my principles."[415]

For some people these principles involved not just paeans to Jefferson in the abstract, but a commitment to the revivified Democratic Party he had founded. When the 250-member Jefferson Club of St. Louis came to Monticello, Jefferson Levy told them: "I am sure pilgrimages of this character cannot fail to inspire and unite our party; for as attention is called to the platform of true Democracy, as laid down by Thomas Jefferson, the people will rally around our banners and restore the government to our administration."[416] The victory of the Democrats in the 1912 election, giving them control of both the White House and the Congress, would become one crucial part of the context in which the battle for Monticello would be fought.

The second part of the contextual puzzle was to some extent more complicated, and involves the growing popular interest in the nation's history and in historic preservation. Americans had always been interested in their forebears, although more as icons for veneration than as actual historical personages. Perhaps the best way to make this point is to cite Parson Weems' idolatrous biography of George Washington, the one with the famous albeit totally untrue story of little George and the cherry tree. By the time the Philadelphia Centennial of the nation's birth had been celebrated, Americans had taken Jefferson's admiring comment on the men who had framed the Constitution—"demigods," he called them—and had turned them and the document they wrote into objects of veneration as well.[417] The idea of preserving the actual dwelling places of these men, however, had not received much attention. In a nation where the wide frontier of inexhaustible free land beckoned to all, place, outside the South and some parts of New England, had little attraction.

That began to change very slowly in the second half of the nineteenth century, and many scholars date the beginning of the historic preservation movement with the campaign to save Mount Vernon, the home of George Washington. Bushrod Washington, a member of the U.S. Supreme Court and Washington's nephew, inherited the estate, and by 1822 had posted warning signs that Mount Vernon, being private property, was no longer open for picnics on the lawn. He did, however, welcome "respectable strangers and others" who came to pay homage to the nation's first president. Around the mid-1840s Congress began to receive petitions from different individuals and groups wanting the federal government to buy Mount Vernon, so as to save it and Washington's tomb from "the uncertainties and transfers of individual fortune."

Bushrod's son, John Augustine Washington, indicated his willingness to sell the house and 150 acres of land to the government for $100,000, but the government then, as later in the case with Uriah Levy, had little experience and even less interest in entering this field. A decade later John Washington wanted $200,000, and in 1853 Miss Ann Pamela Cunningham broadcast an appeal to the women of the South to save Mount Vernon. We need not go into all of the details here,[418] but in 1858 the Mount Vernon Ladies' Association of the Union purchased the site, which became the first historic house in the country that would be held in trust as an object of veneration for succeeding generations.

The Mount Vernon Ladies' Association set the pattern for historic preservation for the rest of the nineteenth century—by private organizations, most though not all created and managed by women, and independent of government

Maud Littleton (Culver Pictures).

financing. Other groups included the Society for the Preservation of Virginia Antiquities, which would be run by women until the 1990s, the Society for the Preservation of New England Antiquities, and the Louisa May Alcott Memorial Association (an offshoot of the Concord Woman's Club) that saved Orchard House, the home of the Alcott family in Concord, Massachusetts. The presence of women both as members and leaders greatly influenced how the organizations operated and how the public and government perceived them. In large part, this activity represented the nurturing nature ascribed to women, which allowed them to go out of the home and gave women opportunities for active and creative work that would have otherwise been denied to them. Thus when Maud Littleton began her campaign for Monticello, it had the imprimatur of six decades during which women worked to save historic homes. The fact that conditions had changed, that the public at large had grown more interested in historic preservation, and that Littleton took effective notice of those changes, made her a very formidable opponent.

A third piece of the puzzle involves the growing nativism gripping the country, and the increased anti-Semitism that accompanied it. As we have seen, Uriah Levy faced anti-Jewish prejudice in the navy, and Thomas Jefferson had his share of antipathy toward Judaism as well. But for the most part Jews faced little overt prejudice of the kind they had encountered in the Old World, and at least part of the reason for this is the small number of Jews who lived in the United States. There may have been no more than 15,000 Jews in America in the 1840s, and despite a significant immigration of Jews from Germany and central Europe between 1840 and 1870, by 1880 the Jewish community still counted no more than 250,000, about one-half of one percent of the total population. Then came the great migrations of 1880-1920, in which millions of immigrants, about one million of them Jewish, entered the United States from eastern and southern Europe, coinciding with the enormous social and economic upheaval caused by post-Civil War industrialization. Successful Jews aroused resentment, and as John Higham noted, "in an age of parvenus, the Jews provided an all too visible symbol of the parvenu spirit."[419]

Portions of society that had never exhibited the slightest hint of prejudice toward Jews suddenly became virulently anti-Semitic. In a notorious incident in 1877, the Grand Hotel in Saratoga turned away the eminent banker Joseph Seligman, a policy soon adopted by other fashionable hotels, resorts, clubs and schools. The *Social Register* closed its list to Jews in 1892, and at the nation's colleges anti-Semitism became a common feature of campus life. Before long the country's best schools either excluded Jews altogether or imposed subtle and none-too-subtle quotas, while in better residential neighborhoods residents posted signs that Jews would not be welcome.[420]

What particularly galled Jews like the Levys is that they had been in this country far longer than many of the bigots who now attacked them. Moreover, they resented the newer eastern European Jews whose arrival they believed had triggered this anti-Semitism. But whether one had been in the country since the 1600s or had just gotten off the boat, it made no difference to the bigot.

Jefferson Monroe Levy (Brown Brothers).

Despite being affluent, politically influential, and a member of Congress, Jefferson Monroe Levy found himself the target of vicious anti-Semitic slurs, thrown by those seeking to wrest Monticello away from him.

Finally, one has to note how little the government knew about historic preservation. Throughout the nineteenth century the federal government took virtually no active role in preservation, nor as the twentieth century opened did it show any inclination to do so. Even though government in the progressive era had grown stronger, and citizens expected it to do more in terms of protecting the health, safety, and welfare of the citizenry, areas such as art, culture, and historic preservation remained beyond the normally accepted responsibilities and powers of the national government, although greater leeway existed for the states. During the debate over Monticello, for example, it is clear that people would have been more comfortable had the Commonwealth of Virginia bought the estate, and Congress had stayed out of the business altogether.

The first significant federal endeavor involved the creation of national parks, beginning with Yellowstone National Park in 1872. It also began a program of acquiring Civil War battlefield sites to protect them from development. In the southwest, still open territory in the 1880s and 1890s, the government also took some interest in preserving the adobe buildings of early Indian tribes from predators seeking artifacts, and in 1889 Congress designated the Casa Grande ruin in Arizona as the nation's first National Monument. It also appropriated $2,000 to protect it, the first funding of any kind by the federal government for preservation. In 1888 two cowboys looking for lost cattle came across the spectacular Cliff Palace of the Mesa Verde in Arizona, and for the next sixteen years scavengers looted the caves and sold the artifacts on the open market. Finally Congress established Mesa Verde National Park and in 1906 passed an Antiquities Act that provided stiff penalties for destroying or stealing artifacts from federally owned land. The number of national parks increased significantly during the tenures of Theodore Roosevelt and William Howard Taft in the White House, and in 1916 Congress established the National Park Service within the Interior Department. Despite this growth in federal ownership and protection of land and Indian sites, Congress showed no interest in the houses of the great.[421]

This, then, is the context in which Maud Littleton began her campaign.

❧

Maud Littleton grew up in Texas, an attractive southern belle who married Martin Littleton, a Democratic congressman from Brooklyn. She claimed that she had always venerated Thomas Jefferson, and looked forward to the time she could visit Monticello. She did visit the house in 1909,[422] and at the time raised no objections to Levy's stewardship of the home. But in Washington she looked around and saw no memorial to her idol, and decided that there should be one. In late 1911 she sent out thousands of copies of an appeal, "One Wish," most of which dealt with Jefferson's role in securing the capital for the South, and how the beautiful city lacked any memorial to him. The greatest monument, however, would be his home; Monticello should be a national shrine. "I thought how much more in keeping with his sense of freedom, and love of nature, if instead of erecting a statue to him in Washington, the nation, whom he loved so well, were to purchase and preserve forever to his memory the house and grounds and graveyard at Monticello, now owned by Mr. Jefferson Levy of New York." Thomas Jefferson, she declared was not "one man's man," challenging the fact that Jefferson Levy was the only person who had legal access to both the house and the tomb. Jefferson, she said, belonged to all the people, and that the people had the same wish as she did, to "lay upon his grave a nation's tears."[423]

Perhaps because of the revived interest in Jefferson or the growing interest in historic preservation, she hit a nerve. Hundreds of famous and near-famous people answered her plea, and in the early months of 1912 she organized a group known as the Jefferson-Monticello Memorial Association, with a goal of making Monticello into a national shrine. She later claimed that she had tried to contact Levy personally, and even had a tablet designed by Tiffany to commemorate Levy's public spiritedness in giving Monticello to her association.[424] Levy did not seem interested.

Up until this point Littleton appeared to be following a well-known track, a women's association that would lay claim to a famous house, secure the promise of the owner to sell it to them, then raise the necessary funds to purchase, restore and maintain it. The book itself did not, unlike her later writings and statements, attack Levy personally, but when he refused to play her game, Maud Littleton went off on a new and quite different path—she appealed to Congress to buy the property or, if the owner would not sell, to take it under its power of condemnation.

Littleton understood intuitively that things had changed considerably since John Washington had sold his estate to Ann Cunningham and the Mount Vernon Ladies' Association. At that time women's voluntary groups had little or no contact with the government in the sense of seeking aid. Cunningham worked with the Virginia legislature, but never asked nor expected the General Assembly to fund the purchase of Mount Vernon; she expected that women working independently could get the job done, and events nearly rewarded her faith.

By the early twentieth century, however, the state played a larger role in many areas of life in which it had previously been absent. Women's organizations such as the National Consumers' League had worked closely with state governments to secure passage of legislation protecting women and children workers. The expansion of government during the Progressive Era also transformed many previously private and charitable functions into state activities. Women had been at the forefront of the movement to convert welfare from a private charity into public assistance, and the settlement house movement had been the training ground for what became the social work profession. Littleton, therefore, understood that if she could not get Levy to surrender through a private appeal, she could try to approach him through the government.[425] But even if Congress agreed and appropriated money, Levy could still refuse to sell, and so she planned to ask that if Levy refused, Congress exercise its power of eminent domain.

The Fifth Amendment gives Congress the power to take private property for public use provided it is done through due process of law and just compensation to the owner is made. Eminent domain had been a power of government for centuries, but the federal government had rarely used it. Congress had, however, begun to use this authority to take ownership of Civil War battlefields, and the Supreme Court had upheld this action in 1896. In an unusually expansive opinion by Justice Rufus Peckham, a highly conservative member of the bench, the Court had given its blessing to the federal government's power to condemn and seize property of historical interest. "Any act of Congress," Peckham wrote, "which plainly and directly tends to enhance the respect and love of the citizen for the institutions of his country" must be valid.[426]

Levy took the challenge seriously, and as a lawyer himself knew exactly what the government could and could not do. If it chose to offer him money, he could accept or decline, but if it chose to condemn the property, he would have no choice except to try to fight in court the valuation that had been placed on his property. But he also lived in a time when, even if women were entering the public sphere more and more, a gentleman did not attack a lady openly. In this arena

Mrs. Littleton had a definite advantage; she could say almost anything she want-ed and Mr. Levy would be hard-pressed to respond to her. It mattered not if she had been accurate; he could at best answer quietly, perhaps point out her errors, and all had to be done "more in sorrow than anger."

He first tried the familial approach, contacting Martin Littleton, his col-league in the House of Representatives. When Littleton announced that he would not run again but would return to his law practice, Levy asked if he would take him on as a client, since his attention had recently been drawn to "a very entertaining sketch by a charming and accomplished lady." He only regretted that she had not consulted him so she could have avoided so many errors. He concluded that "under the circumstances and knowing you so well ... I need not point out what should be done."[427] If Levy hoped that Littleton would be able to silence his wife, he hoped in vain.

Without attacking Mrs. Littleton personally, Levy did try to get the facts straight, and in an interview with the *New York Times* listed the errors and inconsistencies in "One Wish" without ever mentioning its author's name—he had never been a party to the suit contesting his uncle's will (he had only been ten years old at the time Uriah died); there was no mystery surrounding Jefferson's grave, since it clearly belonged to the presi-dent's heirs; all visitors were freely admitted upon application for a card, and every year thousands of people had availed themselves of

One Wish by Maud Littleton (courtesy of Special Collections, University of Virginia Library).

this privilege; the house had not been neglected. "I have been frequently told that the property had been kept in as good if not better condition than it would be if owned by the government. These conditions have been maintained by me and my uncle for over eighty years."[428]

The resolution Mrs. Littleton sought would have established a committee of ten, five members from each house, who would "inquire into the wisdom and ascer-tain the cost of acquiring" Monticello so that it might be preserved for all

Americans.[429] On July 9, 1912, she took the witness chair before the Senate Committee on the Library, and after protesting that she was not an experienced speaker and hoped the committee would bear with her, launched into her testimony that ran, with attachments, almost fifty pages.[430] In the course of her remarks she paid abundant praise to her hero, Thomas Jefferson, and attempted to shame Jefferson Levy into selling Monticello in order to carry out his uncle's wishes: "No doubt, Mr. Levy would do his part toward the public ownership of Monticello, thereby honoring his ancestor who believed it should belong to the people." She failed to mention the purposes to which Uriah had intended to put the house. Monticello "can never be known except wholly and solely as the home of Thomas Jefferson," and no one really cared to have it as a memorial to Commodore Levy.[431]

She then launched into an attack on Jefferson Levy, citing a reference in the *National Cyclopedia of American Biography* that might have misled a reader to believe that Levy was Jefferson's grandson; the article also failed the test of truth in claiming that Jefferson had inherited Monticello from his uncle. But above all, Littleton criticized Levy for his alleged neglect of Monticello, and offered pictures of the house and the roads leading to it, implying that Levy had allowed the estate to go to ruin, and claiming that he denied people access to Monticello. The committee chair then turned to R.T.W. Duke, Levy's attorney. After stating that he was there as a private citizen and not as a representative for Levy, Duke denied Mrs. Littleton's charges about the condition of the house and grounds, declaring that Levy kept up Monticello "as well as I keep up my own home," and averred that Levy had always permitted free access by visitors. An indignant Maud Littleton declared she could never agree with that statement.[432]

The very fact that a Senate committee held hearings, which turned out to be a platform from which Maud Littleton could further expound her plan, is testimony in part to the groundswell of support she had already generated. She presented the committee with scrapbooks containing hundreds of letters from people endorsing her plan; the list of names alone runs four pages, and sample letters another three. All of this support, she declared, ought to lead Mr. Levy to do the patriotic thing, and sell Monticello to the government. Duke told the committee that Levy would not sell. "I think he would just as soon sell the kingdom of heaven as to sell Monticello. If properly approached, I think he might take the patriotic view and sell it to the United States Government," but he would never do that so long as Mrs. Littleton's association would play a major part in the estate's future. "He looks at the place as the apple of his eye."[433]

Mrs. Littleton had expected that, and she then pulled her trump card, a letter from former Assistant Attorney General James M. Beck, explaining that the federal government had the power of eminent domain to take Monticello, and that the Supreme Court had upheld this power in relation to historic sites.[434] This may have proved too much for some members of the committee, especially the Republicans, who loathed the idea that government could go in and take the home of a private citizen, simply because that house had once belonged to Thomas Jefferson. In the long run the tactic worked against Mrs. Littleton, but although Judge Duke did not respond, he knew that Levy feared condemnation more than anything, since he would have so little control of the proceedings and no legal way to stop it.

The resolution passed the Senate on July 17, and a week later the House Committee on Rules held its hearings. Since Mrs. Littleton's husband and Jefferson Levy both sat as Democratic representatives from New York, the hearings generated no little tension among the members. Once again Mrs. Littleton came supplied with the stacks of letters from people who had responded to "One Wish," and once again she confronted Levy, this time for turning Monticello into a monument to his uncle. She recalled when she and her husband had been guests of Levy in 1909, and how she had waited all her life to see the second Mount Vernon, the "treasure house" that had been Jefferson's:[435]

> We drove through the black night and deep mud up that steep road to the top of the little mountain. Nothing could be seen. Only above our heads a thick mass of bare limbs of trees, like serpents coiled above us. I can remember nothing now of the house and my visit, except that I have a vivid impression of portraits—big, oil portraits of the Levys—and ships—models of ships in which Uriah Levy was supposed to have sailed …. Everything was disappointing. I had a

heavy-hearted feeling. There was nothing of Jefferson to me in Monticello. He had dropped out and the Levys had come. One could hear and see only the Levys and the Levy family, their deeds of valor, their accomplishments, their lives.

She went on to denounce Levy for standing in the way of those who wished to pay homage to one of America's greatest sons. She charged that she had seen these pilgrims pause at the entrance, humiliated by the sense that they were intruding and not welcome. "Does he wish to keep this up?" she asked:[436]

> Is it not as humiliating to him as to them? And by what right must the people ask Mr. Levy's permission to visit the home and grave of Thomas Jefferson? ... Is he insensible to all emotions of patriotism and unselfishness? Does he want a whole Nation crawling at his feet forever for permission to worship at this shrine of our independence? Could he submit his feelings to the mortification of saying no? Would not the world cry out shame upon him, and where could he hide his head?

Mrs. Littleton concluded her appeal by painting a flattering portrait of John Washington, the Lees, and the Jacksons as people who cared about the public. The fact that the Washington and Jackson families had sold their homes, and the Lee Mansion in Arlington had been confiscated by the Union, did not matter. Her point was clear—these people were patriots and Jefferson Levy should emulate their example.

The committee held a second day of hearings on August 7, and gave Levy the chance to defend himself against Mrs. Littleton's accusation. While refusing to engage her directly, he defended his care of Mr. Jefferson's home, and reiterated his opposition to selling it. He held everything at Monticello—the house, the land, the artifacts—sacred, and he would never "listen to any suggestion for disposing of it, whether coming from a private or a public source."[437] He reviewed his stewardship of Monticello and how he had always welcomed members of the Jefferson family. "At Monticello—and I have it on the word of the leading men in public life for the last thirty years, Cleveland, Blaine, Reed, Hoar, Bryan, Hill—you will find there the atmosphere of the home of Jefferson. Did you find at Mt. Vernon an atmosphere befitting the home of Washington?"[438]

At the end of the hearings Mrs. Littleton took the stand again and urged the committee to support her project. Although the official transcript is silent, newspapers reported that she burst into tears at the end of her testimony.[439] The columnist Flora Wilson, who backed Levy in the matter, scoffed at Mrs. Littleton for this theatrical gesture. The real woman heroes, she wrote, "did not weep in battling for their causes: Clara Barton, Florence Nightingale, Jane Addams, Catherine de Medici, and Mary, Queen of Scots."[440]

During the fall both Mrs. Littleton and Levy marshaled their forces. She put out a second booklet, an expanded version of "One Wish" entitled "Monticello," and her committee continued to collect endorsements. She sent out thousands of letters urging individuals and groups interested in preserving

Monticello West Front, circa 1910 (courtesy of Holsinger Collection, University of Virginia Library).

Monticello to write to their senators and congressmen; to pass state and local resolutions calling upon Congress to act; to secure the support of their local newspapers; to join the Jefferson-Monticello Memorial Association and to form local branches; and to send contributions to her daughter, Miss Laura Littleton, the treasurer of the Association. She needed as many petitions to Congress as she could get, and would gladly send blanks to anyone interested in collecting signatures.[441]

Levy also marshaled his forces. In September he arranged for the noted photographer Rufus Holsinger to take pictures of the interior and exterior of the house, which Levy then used as an exhibit of the fine condition of Monticello under his care. He gave interviews to newspapers to correct what he saw as the inaccuracies in Mrs. Littleton's charges, and he pointed out correctly, that many of the people who had endorsed her plan when it involved the purchase of Monticello had backed away when they learned she wanted the government to confiscate his house. How he knew this is unknown, although it is probable that people wrote to him saying they had changed their minds. Above all, he lobbied effectively where it counted, among his colleagues in the House of Representatives.

One of those who now opposed Mrs. Littleton had once been among her biggest supporters, the influential preservation leader, William Sumner Appleton of the Society for the Preservation of New England Antiquities. Appleton had never been completely comfortable with the idea of Congress buying the house, and had urged Mrs. Littleton to follow the lead of the Mount Vernon Ladies' Association—raise money, and then buy the estate.[442] She wrote back that she would have willingly done that but Levy refused to sell. When she presented Assistant Attorney General Beck's letter and called for condemnation, this proved too much for Appleton:[443]

> I am a tremendous believer in buying Jefferson's home for preservation, but as luck will have it, I am also an ardent Jeffersonian in my principles, and can't help feeling that Jefferson would turn in his grave at the mere suggestion that the Federal Government should buy his home by right of eminent domain .... Frankly, I don't like the method

or the result, and am not at all clear in my own mind that it might not be better for the preservation of the house if its acquisition were post-poned until such time as the owner or his descendants might make a reasonable proposition to a voluntary association.

This notion that Jefferson would not have wanted the government to impose its will in such a forceful way, that he would not have wanted a private home—even if it had once belonged to him—snatched away against the wishes of its owner, and that he would not have wanted public monies used in such a way became a recurrent—and powerful—theme in the ensuing debate. As Levy put it in a public statement: "I think it will come as a keen surprise to the ordinary lay-man to hear that the Government can step in and take property away from a fam-ily that has had it for this long period."[444]

In the months and weeks leading up to the House vote, a lively debate took place in the nation's newspapers and magazines, and despite Mrs. Littleton's efforts, much of it ran against her. *Harper's Weekly* accepted her argument fully, and noted that "after a century of neglect the American people seem ready to pay prop-er honor to the memory of Thomas Jefferson by acquiring Monticello."[445] A big ad appeared in many of the country's papers on the day Congress would begin debate entitled "An Expression of a Nation's Gratitude to Thomas Jefferson." Signed by Samuel Gompers of the American Federation of Labor, William J. McGinley, Supreme Commander of the Knights of Columbus, and other notables, it urged support of Mrs. Littleton's plan to have Congress buy the Jefferson house.[446]

On Levy's side came one testimonial after another to the care he had lav-ished on Monticello, including one from Frank M. Randolph, a great-grandson of Thomas Jefferson who "abhorred" the movement begun by Mrs. Littleton. He and all his family, to whom Levy had always been so kind and courteous, felt that Littleton's efforts were "a travesty on justice."[447] Levy's hospitality now brought him a rich harvest. People who had visited Monticello wrote of how well Levy had maintained the place and how they had had no trouble gaining entry.[448] The Albemarle (Va.) Chapter of the Daughters of the American Revolution passed a resolution praising his stewardship of Jefferson's home and making clear that its members had no sympathy with either the goals or the methods used by Mrs. Littleton. The chapter then sent copies of the resolution to all the leading papers in the state, and Levy made sure that it received even wider distribution.[449] The *Richmond Journal* found the DAR action convincing: "Here is not only a home endorsement of Mr. Levy's proper care of Monticello, but one from the highest authority …. We would rather take the opinion of these patriotic women" than that of outsiders.[450] In a similar vein, Mrs. F.A. Walke of the Daughters of the Confederacy told Mrs. Littleton that the women of Virginia did not need her or the government's money to take care of their own.[451]

In one of the more interesting comments, a "Patriot" commented on Mrs. Littleton's constant references to Mount Vernon, and declared that if Monticello were to be managed in the same way as Washington's home, then:[452]

> it had better remain in the possession of its present owner. I visited Mount Vernon recently and was not greatly impressed with the way it had been commercialized. On the journey from Washington there was a continuous yelling of wares, postal cards, albums, etc. On arriving at Mount Vernon there was a din of dinner bells and cries, "Chicken dinner now ready, only 50 cents!" "This way to the dining room!" etc. And then a charge of 25 cents for admission, a small matter, probably, but very depressing.

Debate began in the House of Representatives on December 9, 1912. Robert Lee Henry of Texas, chair of the Rules Committee, tried to get a special rule that would allow the House to consider the Senate resolution immediately, and it immediately became clear that Jefferson Levy had some potent allies. John Dalzell of Pennsylvania attacked the resolution, saying that a ten-member committee would be a waste of time, since no committee could tell Congress how "wise" it would be to purchase Jefferson's home; each member would have to decide that issue himself. As for looking into the cost, what purpose would that serve? Congressman Levy, then sitting in the chamber with his colleagues, had repeatedly said he would not sell.[453]

Other members worried about the precedent this would set. "All over the eastern coast," worried Joseph Moore of Pennsylvania, "we have sites hallowed by the lives of distinguished men ... and every one of them would have an equal claim upon this body." The costs to the taxpayer would be staggering, and not just in the purchase prices. Each house would require staff to take care of it, and so "thousands of caretakers at salaries ... would have to be provided by the people of the United States." Similar bills had been defeated in the House in past years, Moore concluded, and he believed such good work should be left to voluntary bodies like the Daughters of the American Revolution.[454]

If Mrs. Littleton had expected to get support from Virginia, she soon found those hopes dashed. Edward W. Saunders of Virginia, who represented the Albemarle area, deflated the lady's claims of huge popular support based on the letters and petitions she had presented. He reported that many well-known people who had originally supported her cause had done so when they believed she only wanted Congress to purchase Monticello; they withdrew their support when they learned she wanted to confiscate it.[455] (In fact, Mrs. Littleton had little support in Virginia. The leading historical preservation society, the Association for the Preservation of Virginia Antiquities [founded in 1889], had no interest in Monticello or even in Jefferson, whom many conservative Virginians still considered a radical.[456]) Perhaps the cruelest blow came when at the end of the debate Scott Ferris of Oklahoma dismissed Mrs. Littleton and her group as "well-meaning persons, wrought up by emotion and commotion."[457]

When the vote came, the Rules Committee resolution went down by a vote of 101 for and 141 against, with many abstaining, including Martin Littleton. While Levy appeared jubilant over his victory, Maud Littleton, who had watched the debate from the gallery, refused to comment. She also refused to accept the vote as final, and immediately telegraphed Governor William Hodges Mann of Virginia that a prominent citizen of that state had authorized her to offer Levy four times the assessed value of the estate, which she had put in her testimony at $25,403. Moreover, title of the estate would then be donated to the Commonwealth. When reporters asked Levy if he would sell, he immediately put an end to Mrs. Littleton's gambit:[458]

I will sell Monticello under no circumstances. I have repeatedly refused $1,500,000 for the property. My answer to any proposition seeking the property of Monticello is: When the White House is for sale, then I will consider an offer for the sale of Monticello, and not before.

In a separate telegram to Governor Mann, who had apparently sounded him out on the offer, Levy expressed his appreciation of the offer, but "I cannot now commercialize the sentiment of years by putting a price upon this noble property." He defended his care of Monticello and he saw the house not only as a home he loved, but as a trust he carried in the memory of Mr. Jefferson. "I am not prepared to make or accept any offer depriving me of this cherished right."[459]

Mrs. Littleton had failed in her attempt for several reasons. Unlike other historic preservation groups, such as the Mount Vernon Ladies' Association, who raised private funds for their work, she wanted Congress to pay for Monticello at a time when Congress had little interest in preserving anything other than Indian sites on federal property. The notion of using the public purse for what many people saw as a private purpose offended their sense of propriety; time and again one would read that Jefferson would have been appalled at the idea. One should recall that when in office, with the exception of the purchase of Louisiana, Jefferson was a notorious tightwad with the public purse. Even in his declining years when he desperately needed money to save Monticello, he would not accept a gift from the state, believing it would be an imposition on the taxpayer. Littleton's call for condemnation through eminent domain offended even more people, who saw it as a threat to individual liberty and private property rights.

The Jefferson-Monticello Memorial Society never intended to raise the money needed to purchase Monticello, even if the owner had been willing. Right from the start Mrs. Littleton believed Congress should pay, and she used the donations coming in to her group to pay for a very clever and extensive public relations campaign to force Jefferson Levy to bow to her interpretation of the will of the people. Charles Hosmer suggested that if she had gone about it differently, she might have induced Levy to sell, but by attacking him, his care of Monticello, and his family, she completely alienated him. Ann Cunningham had gone to John

Washington and convinced him of the rightness of turning Mount Vernon into a public shrine. Maud Littleton assumed that Jefferson Levy shared not only her veneration of Jefferson (which he did), but that he also shared her view of what Monticello should be. When she learned that he did not, instead of trying to convince him and win him over as an ally, she publicly challenged him, thus ensuring that no matter what she did, Levy would not voluntarily agree to sell Monticello.[460]

If Jefferson Levy thought his troubles had ended with the vote in the House, he was sorely mistaken, for Mrs. Littleton immediately resumed her efforts. As soon as the House vote had been taken, she sent out a broadside of ten thousand letters to drum up support for forcing Levy to sell Monticello to the government.[461] Then she learned that a year earlier, during one of his periodic bouts of cash shortage, Levy had executed two mortgages on Monticello, one for $40,000 payable to John Uppleby, and the other to his attorney, Judge Duke, acting as a trustee for the Disney children, for $5,000, each to be paid with interest in three years.[462] In a scathing statement issued on December 27, she recalled that Levy had said he would never "commercialize the sentiment of years by putting a price on this noble property." At the very time that he said this, she charged, he already had commercialized it by taking the mortgage. She appealed to the "men and women of the United States" to make Mr. Levy listen to reason, to do the right thing and sell Monticello to the government. "If Mr. Levy is embarrassed to such an extent to be forced to put a mortgage on Monticello and thus make it a commercial pawn instead of a national shrine will he not permit the American people to sweep away this encumbrance."[463]

Levy responded that there was no mortgage on Monticello, but rather that it was on the Monroe place (what had been Uriah's Washington Farm) near Monticello. This may have been technically accurate, but records of the mortgage clearly indicate Monticello. Levy tried to end the matter by repeating that he had been offered fabulous sums for Monticello and had always refused, and that he could not get into a controversy with a woman. Mrs. Littleton's comment to that was "Oh, fudge!" She would return again and again to the issue of the mortgage, and in one way it clearly indicated the difference in their views. She saw Monticello as a shrine, one that should not be sullied by such crass considerations as mortgages, where Levy saw it as his home, his property, and as a property owner he had rights, including the right to borrow against its value.

Mrs. Littleton, and Levy as well, knew that with the election of Woodrow Wilson as the first Democratic president in sixteen years, there would be renewed interest in Monticello by the Democratic Party. Although some Republicans belonged to her organization, most of its members supported the Democrats. Both Wilson and his secretary of state, William Jennings Bryan, intended to do all they could to heal the fractures in the party and consolidate its power, and Monticello, the home of the party's founder, might well serve as a symbol means to do so. Beyond that, the Virginia-born Wilson was the first southerner elected to the White House since Zachary Taylor (another Virginian) in 1848; his election in many ways marked the end of Reconstruction and the return of the South to full participation in national life. Littleton, born in Texas, took full advantage of the fact that a Northerner owned the home of one of the South's greatest statesmen, a home that had become more Yankee than Virginian, more Levy than Jeffersonian.[464]

In 1913 Wilson and the Congress had little time to spare on Monticello. Starting with his special session of Congress in April to reform the tariff, and ending with the passage of the Federal Reserve Act in December, enacting the agenda of the New Freedom took up all of the administration's time. Mrs. Littleton spent her time trying to get 10,000 signatures on new petitions to Congress, and claimed that President Wilson backed her plan.[465] She went on a national lecture tour with the title of "The True Story of Monticello," but newspaper reports indicated only minimal interest. At the 350-seat Little Theatre in New York, only forty-two persons, plus two reporters, attended her talk.[466]

Levy for his part did not engage her in debate, directly or indirectly, although he defended his care of Monticello in an address to the Empire State Society of the Sons of the American Revolution. A rather uninspired speech, it consisted mostly of lengthy quotes from Judge Duke and others attesting to how well he had managed and preserved the home. He repeated what he had told the House Rules Committee the previous year, that "every stick and every brick in the

East Front, circa 1910 (courtesy of Holsinger Collection, University of Virginia Library).

home of Jefferson, every tree, every nook and corner, every foot of Monticello, is dear and sacred to me." The most interesting part of his speech, however, was his appeal to Jeffersonian principles and his implied charge that Maud Littleton would not know what to do with Monticello:[467]

> To those who say that this movement is really founded on reverence for Jefferson I can confidently turn and say, without possibility of contradiction, that all of the institutions which Jefferson did so much to establish, all upon which his fame rests, depend for their perpetuity on the sacredness of the right of private property. What is done at Mount Vernon for hire is done at Monticello from affection. If the Government itself should not assume the care of the property, but should commit to some quasi-public corporation or association, with a managing directress and a staff of paid assistants, I ask, is it likely

that a generation from today the home of Jefferson will be found standing in its present condition?

Although throughout the fight Levy continued to have many defenders, in 1914 the roof seemingly caved in on him. Maud Littleton's campaign, far from abating, picked up steam as thousands of people signed her petitions. She managed to get the Virginia General Assembly to pass a resolution declaring that Levy's ownership impeded public access, and then her backers in legislature refused to give Levy an opportunity to respond.[468] The debate in the press, which until now had been fairly civilized in temperament, took on a decidedly anti-Semitic tone among those opposed to Levy.

Dorothea Dix, the columnist famous for her advice to the lovelorn, published an article entitled "Monticello—Shrine or Bachelor's Hall?" in the nation's leading women's magazine. A Southerner by birth, Dix bemoaned the lack of true shrines to which an American could go for "a pious pilgrimage to the holy places where lived and died those who have made America great." But, "an alien now sits at the fireside," and no one could miss the point that by "alien" Dix meant Levy the Jew. Less explicit but still clear was the implication that the unmarried Levy had debauched Monticello, with whatever debased activities one normally associated with unmarried men.[469]

Dix further condemned Levy by resurrecting the old stories that his uncle Uriah had somehow cheated Jefferson's children out of their inheritance, by beating the messenger of the philanthropists to Charlottesville and buying Monticello from Barclay.[470] The story had been used in Cummings' earlier attack on Levy, and then picked up and given wide circulation in Littleton's 1912 pamphlet, "Monticello." Dix elaborated on it, claiming that the rider whom Levy had gotten drunk had appealed to him to take the money that had been raised and to give Monticello back to the Jefferson family, but Levy had heartlessly refused. She quoted a newspaper article that had fifth-generation "Judah" [Jefferson] Levy responding in a heavy eastern European accent "Mein frien,' you are a glever feller, but you talk too much. I will take a huntret thousand dollars." Surely the Democratic Party, Dix concluded "will do its duty to the great founder."[471]

Maud Littleton apparently had no qualms in exploiting the rampant nativist prejudice of the time, and consistently portrayed Levy, if not in openly anti-Semitic terms, then in code words the meaning of which her listeners surely understood. She referred to him as an "Oriental potentate" who, if he had true feelings for this country, would agree to sell Monticello. Frederic A. Delano wrote to his good friend in Richmond, Fairfax Harrison, asking him about the to-do over Monticello. Harrison, a descendent of Thomas Jefferson, wrote back a scathing indictment of Maud Littleton, and charged that "in aid of her campaign, [she] has not neglected any opportunity to create prejudice in her favor by reason of Mr. Levy's ancestors." People with whom he talked in Virginia, "conservative people," resented Mrs. Littleton's tactics and believed Levy had maintained Monticello adequately.[472]

In February 1914 Mrs. Littleton not only got the resolution she wanted from the Virginia assembly, but got Congress to pass a joint resolution declaring Monticello "the Mecca of all lovers of liberty." The Senate Lands Committee then took up the proposal for purchasing Monticello, and despite Levy's statement that he would not agree to sell, reported the proposal favorably.[473] The momentum seemed to be picking up, and the final straw came in September when Secretary of State William Jennings Bryan called on Levy to sell Monticello to the government.

Bryan recalled how he had suggested this a number of years earlier. "I have never relinquished the hope that you would some day yield to the popular desire that the government should own Monticello, and keep it in memory of the author of the Declaration of Independence, whose residence and tomb there make the spot sacred." Now that another bill had been introduced into Congress, Bryan pleaded, would this not be a good time to sell, and the secretary held out the implied stick that he spoke for the Wilson administration, which could easily push this measure through a Democratic Congress. But Bryan also held out a carrot as well. As for Levy's "very natural desire to occupy" it, Bryan pointed out a neat solution—the contract could reserve a life interest, so that Levy and his family could continue to use Monticello until his death, when full control as well as title would revert to the government.[474]

Levy knew he had lost. He might have held out against Maud Littleton and her association, because enough members of Congress supported him and did not care to spend the taxpayers' money on the purchase. But with the administration involved, Levy believed it only a matter of time before Wilson imposed party discipline in the name of saving Jefferson's home. In early October he capitulated, and in a letter to Bryan declared, "I bow to your wishes and those of the American people." He claimed that he had expended a million dollars on Monticello, a figure that is not unreasonable, and he offered it to the country for $500,000, "which will make me more than half-donor of Monticello, and thus consummate the people's will."[475] He suggested that the estate might well serve as the summer home of the presidents, an idea that Bryan heartily approved of but that received a cool reception from Wilson.[476]

Mrs. Littleton, of course, welcomed the offer, and did not question Levy's asking price. In fact, henceforth her attacks on Levy ceased, since she had gotten what she had wanted from him—an agreement to sell Monticello to the government. After all the enthusiasm she had generated, she fully expected that Congress would appropriate the money and the battle would have been won.

❦

While some people cheered Levy's decision, almost immediately voices of protest arose over the actual price. The county had assessed the house at $28,971, which the tax commissioners said represented between one-third to one-fifth of its actual value, that is, a number someplace between $86,913 and $144,855. One paper editorialized that Mr. Levy obviously would have a hard time justifying his $500,000 asking price, as well as his wish to be commemorated as half-donor of the estate.[477] A Michigan paper ran a headline that read, "Asks Fat Price for Monticello," then in smaller type, "Assessed at Less than $29,000, Congressman Levy Asks Half Million."[478] The *Louisville Post* ran an editorial, "What Would Jefferson Say?" and concluded that he would not have approved; the editors expressed their sympathy for Levy, but went on to note that if the American people really were consulted on this, "they would drop the whole matter and be done with it. Certainly this is not time to embark upon an expenditure of this character."[479] Stories in other papers reported much opposition to the selling price, and urged the government to thoroughly investigate the value of the property before spending any money.[480]

Maud Littleton had led her fight, and Jefferson Levy had opposed her, not because of the dollar value of Monticello but because of its sentimental worth. Both of them, whatever their other differences, saw the place as a shrine to one of the great men of the country. But Congress had no experience in sentimental value attached to property. In 1896 when Congress voted to buy the house where Lincoln had died, the legislators refused to pay one penny more than the assessed commercial value of the building.[481] Now Levy claimed the estate to be worth one million, and had he asked $150,000 or even $200,000, the sale probably would have gone through quickly; but even strong supporters of purchasing Monticello hesitated at the half-million dollar price. In many ways, Levy had his foes over a barrel. Congress had made it clear that it would not take the property through condemnation, so either they would meet his price or they wouldn't, in which case he would still have Monticello.

Starting in early 1915, bills were introduced into every Congress to appropriate the necessary money to purchase Monticello. Mrs. Littleton sustained her campaign to keep pressure on Congress. Jefferson Levy remained willing to sell. The President of the United States, one of the most astute political leaders since Lincoln in terms of dealing with Congress, time and again said he favored the bill—and yet it never passed.

On February 23, 1915, former congressman Jefferson M. Levy himself led off the witnesses at hearings before House Rules Committee. In a very short statement he declared that it had never been his wish or intention to sell Monticello, "but from a sense of patriotic duty, urged to do so by the call of the administration ... and at a great personal sacrifice, both from a sentimental and monetary standpoint, I have yielded to what appears to be the wishes of the country."[482] Mrs. Littleton followed, and gave a very lengthy statement reiterating all of her previous arguments about why Monticello should be purchased, although refraining from any criticism of Levy. In fact she went out of her way to praise him and to assure the committee that the asking price was not too high:[483]

At first sight the sum of $500,000 for 700 acres of land, with only a brick home and office, a few ancient and crumbling buildings upon it, and a simple and humble tombstone nearby, may appear to be an exorbitant price. But no real American who takes into consideration the patriotic memories that must be forever associated with the property ... can regard it so ....

And it is but fair to say that during the number of years it has been in Mr. Levy's possession he has gratuitously entertained many of the visitors to the place, has guarded the property, and watched over the remains of Mr. Jefferson probably as well as such an exacting public task could be done by an individual.

The only other witness, Congressman James Hay from the Albemarle district, briefly endorsed Mrs. Littleton's statement.

The committee knew, and Mrs. Littleton reminded them, of the fact that President Wilson favored the bill, which would have provided an immediate cash payment of $100,000 and eight additional payments of $50,000 each in government bonds. The White House had released a copy of Wilson's letter to Representative Oscar W. Underwood of Alabama, the powerful chairman of the House Ways and Means Committee as well as the Democratic leader in the House. Wilson had not only expressed interest in the bill, but "I most earnestly hope that there will be some interval in the business of the House which can be used for the passage of this most interesting piece of legislation, which I think will meet the approval of the whole nation."[484] But nothing happened. The war raging in Europe had caused considerable dislocations in the economy, and fear that the United States might be dragged into the war had led to increased appropriations for the Navy. But even so, one wonders why, in a budget that ran into the hundreds of millions of dollars such a small sum could not have been found and appropriated, or why the endorsement of the president and party chiefs should have had so little effect.

The story repeated itself in 1916. Sponsors introduced bills in Congress, committees held hearings, the president endorsed the measure, Mrs. Littleton brought her letters and petitions, and nothing happened, other than the Daughters of the American Revolution volunteered to be the custodians of the property, thus relieving the government of the actual maintenance although the group expected the government to provide the funds.[485] And nothing happened.

Hosmer believed that much of the blame for Congress failing to act rests on Levy's inability to give the money committees any help in arriving at an exact value for Monticello. When Mrs. Story, the head of the DAR, asked Levy to estimate what Monticello had actually cost him and how much it would cost the government to operate it on an annual basis, Levy evaded giving her any hard numbers, declaring it would be impossible to do so:[486]

> I ask, Is the same rule of thumb to be applied here as when the Government buys a site for a post office or a customshouse? Certainly not, after my long stewardship, without my consent. I ask again, If an appraisal be asked, where is the appraisal to stop? What limit be put on a place with such a founder, with such associations, with such a history? … I have gone into these matters at, perhaps, unpardonable length, so that I will not seem to be lacking in courtesy if I decline to be drawn into an examination as to who made me offers for the purchase of Monticello, how much offered, the amount of the yearly taxes, etc. The idea of selling Monticello was always abhorrent to me; I never could bear to consider its sale. If my statement be not sufficient that I was offered and refused $1,000,000 for the property, then it would be useless after this lapse of years to offer in corroboration further testimony on that point. If my statement on that point be not accepted without further evidence, I am content to abide by the consequences.

One might well conclude that Levy had outsmarted Littleton, Bryan, and Wilson. Aware of the reluctance of his former colleagues in the House to spend money on sentiment, or on projects new to their thinking, he realized that if he quoted a high enough price, one of two things would happen: either they would vote it, in which case he would at least get the money had had asked as well as a life estate in Monticello; or they would founder and refuse to vote the money, and he would be where he said he had always wanted to be, the owner of Thomas Jefferson's house. Once he had agreed to sell, the threat of condemnation had evaporated, and no one even mentioned resurrecting that idea.

This might well be true. But there is an undated, barely legible note from Levy, possibly to his attorney, written sometime in 1916 or early 1917:[487]

> Please try to have the note underlineextended without any payment except [*] .... If Senator Martin would only take a hand and help the Monticello bill it would go through. The President states that he is determined to pass the bill as he informed Mrs. Story. The Senator could add it to one of the appropriation bills as the secretary of state letter of acceptance is an agreement to purchase and it is bad faith of the [government?] not to pass the appropriation. Frank Clark of Florida states that he will report the Bill out soon as he obtains a quorum of his committee. I expect to be in Washington Monday [evening]. Try and see what you can do with Martin.

It would appear that whether he wanted to part with Monticello or not, he needed money, and rather than trying to slow down the legislature, actually wanted the bill to go through. Unfortunately we will not know which of these two scenarios, if either, Jefferson Levy actually had in mind.

The last hearings on the Monticello purchase took place just three months before the United States entered World War One, and the same situation applied. The proponents gave their testimony, but the committee could not agree on what constituted a fair price.[488] The only difference was that this time the House committee, led by Representative Frank Clark of Florida, decided to go see the house for itself, and on January 6, 1917, what the local paper termed a "Gay Party" arrived at Monticello to be greeted by Jefferson Levy and shown around the place. What should have been a simple junket actually turned into a farce of sorts. In the afternoon some of the congressional members got "awfully dry" and wanted Levy to open up the Thomas Jefferson wine cellar for them. He refused, claiming that he had left the key in New York, whereupon some of the members offered to break the cellar door open. Levy adamantly refused, and according to the reporter, Levy might now well have to reduce his price if he wanted to sell the house.[489]

This may have been the last chance to have put through the Monticello purchase, and in fact Wilson asked his chief political operative, Postmaster General Burleson, to try to get Frank Clark, the chairman of the House Public Buildings and Grounds Committee, to report out the bill, while in the Senate he asked Claude Swanson of Virginia to see if anything could be done.[490] But it was not to be. Within a few weeks of declaring his support, Wilson found his attention and that of the Congress captured by the German renewal of submarine warfare. On March 2, he had to tell the head of the DAR that "the objects in the way of the Monticello purchase have come to seem insuperable."[491] As Mrs. Littleton later told a friend, she had been very close to success in 1917 but the war finally defeated her.

Although he did not go broke, the First World War greatly reduced Levy's fortune, to the point that he could no longer afford to maintain Monticello. In early 1919 Levy listed Monticello with H.W. Hilleary of Washington, D.C., a real estate broker who specialized in large Virginia estates. Hilleary sent out a form letter to a list of wealthy individuals, noting that "the present owner, for sentimental and other reasons, has never before consented to part with it. I am allowed now to bring it to the attention of those who can appreciate and are able to own a property of such distinction and merit." If any of those who received this letter had responded, they would have learned that Monticello had been listed at $400,000 and that the owner would entertain any reasonable offer.[492]

Historic Monticello For Sale

This Virginia Colonial home, the artistic creation of the great statesman, Thomas Jefferson, with a freehold of 650 acres, is for sale.

An eminent Frenchman said of Monticello: "It is infinitely superior to any of the houses in America from point of taste and convenience, and deserves to be ranked with the most pleasant mansions of France and England."

Mr. Jefferson, after his return from an extended trip in France and Italy, said of his own immediate section: "How grand, how magnificent, how entrancing! Nowhere have I seen anything to excel the beauty of this country."

For price and further information, apply

Ad for sale of Monticello in 1922 appearing in Richmond Leader *(Library of Virginia).*

There would be one more desultory attempt to have Congress buy Monticello. In May 1921 the House received two different proposals. One from John Kindred of New York directed the secretary of the treasury to purchase the tombsites of both Washington and Jefferson,[493] while the other, sponsored by Thomas W. Harrison of Virginia tried to resuscitate the older proposal of paying Levy $500,000 for the property.[494] Neither one ever got out of committee.

Over the next few years several private organizations came together in an effort to purchase the Jefferson estate. In Richmond, women organized the Thomas Jefferson National Memorial Association, clearly modeled on the Mount Vernon Ladies' Association, and headed by Ruth Cunningham, who claimed to be a descendent of the MVLA founder, a rather spurious claim since Ann Cunningham had no children. After garnering a fair amount of publicity, Levy told them they had to raise $50,000 in actual cash to bind a contract that, the women claimed, would be underwritten by wealthy men from New York. They could not raise even a small amount of the sum.[495] About this time Marietta Minnigerode Andrews and Rose Gouverneur Hoes, two socialites prominent in Democratic affairs, formed the National Monticello Association, announcing that "women would make [Monticello] second only to Mount Vernon." Both groups received letters of encouragement from ex-president Wilson, but both soon failed.[496] Richmond newspapers appealed to Virginia's historic pride in its founders, but their plea fell on deaf ears.[497]

As several scholars have noted, the historic preservation movement, although started by women, moved in large measure under the control of men in the twentieth century, and Monticello is often given as the clearest example of this development. In February 1923 Stuart Gibboney and Henry Alan Johnston, two native Virginians who now practiced law in New York City, hosted a private dinner of lawyers and financiers to discuss Monticello. The group selected Gibboney and Moses H. Grossman (a leading New York attorney) to meet with Levy or his representatives to see if he would be willing to sell to them. By this point Levy had said yes to every organization that had approached him, and he agreed that this group should have a chance as well. Encouraged by the response, the men secured a charter in New York on Jefferson's 180th birthday, April 13, 1923, and on the same day held an organizational banquet at the University of Virginia. Unlike the earlier women's groups, the members of the Thomas Jefferson Memorial Foundation (TJMF) had influence and access to money. Eventually they succeeded in purchasing Monticello, and have run it ever since. But they, too, found Jefferson Levy, eager as he was to sell, very difficult to work with.[498]

Levy, even though he remained reluctant to give up Monticello, nonetheless needed the money, although he may have been less strapped for cash at some times than at others. According to Theodore Fred Kuper, to some extent Levy had fixated on having the federal government pay for Monticello. He considered Secretary of State William Jennings Bryan's letter to him as a contractual offer, which he had accepted, and he waited for the government to fulfill its obligation to him. Levy apparently had some offers, and claimed that both Andrew Carnegie and Jacob Henry Schiff had at one time offered to buy Monticello from him and to present it to the government as a shrine to Jefferson.[499] Then in the early 1920s Jewish leaders became concerned about the rise of the Ku Klux Klan. They saw Levy's obstinacy over selling Monticello as a red flag to the Klan and other anti-Semitic nativists. Felix Warburg, the investment banker, and Julius Rosenwald, the head of Sears, Roebuck, sent Judge Jonah Goldstein to see Levy, and to make him this offer: if Levy would donate Monticello to the United States as a memorial to Thomas Jefferson, on that same day they would personally and quietly deposit $500,000 in his bank account. Levy responded that he had refused $1,000,000 and laughed.[500]

When approached by the new TJMF, Levy initially asked more than the $500,000 that had been the standing price ever since 1914, but the Foundation's representatives refused to move from their offer: $100,000 in December of 1923, upon which title would pass to the TJMF; a second payment of $100,000 soon after by using the title for a mortgage given to a New York bank, and the balance of $300,000 to be paid off over a period of years with six percent bonds of the Foundation, secured by a second mortgage on the property. In order to persuade Levy to accept, Gibboney and Grossman advanced him $10,000 against the first payment by writing him personal checks.

To search the title, Kuper retained Thomas Jefferson Randolph IV, a Virginia lawyer and descendent of the original owner. According to Kuper, "the

New York, May 28th, 1923.

Thomas Jefferson Memorial Foundation, Inc.,
115 Broadway,
New York City.

Dear Sirs:-

In consideration of the sum of ten thousand (10,000) dollars cash to me in hand paid, I hereby give you an option to purchase Monticello and the personal property mentioned in the inventory upon the terms and conditions set forth in the annexed contract, provided, however, that said contract is signed and delivered by you on or before the fifteenth day of June, Nineteen hundred and twenty-three.

I further agree that the amount paid for this option shall be applied on account of the purchase price of the property if the option is exercised and the contract is signed on or before the date stated.

This agreement shall bind my heirs, executors, administrators, successors and assigns.

Yours very truly,

Letter from Jefferson Monroe Levy to Thomas Jefferson Memorial Foundation, 1923 (Thomas Jefferson Foundation).

abstract of the title was a superbly drawn document which he presented to the Foundation without any charge. The gift was all the more appreciated since Mr. Randolph was far from being one of the wealthier Jefferson descendents."[501]

We need not go into all the details of the monetary transfers. The Foundation had more than a little trouble raising the balance of the initial $100,000. But here the financial strength of the membership made the difference. Gibboney and Manny Strauss, a New York businessman and fundraiser who served as the chair of the Ways and Means Committee, obtained signatures from members and non-members who agreed to pay the difference between what had been raised and what was needed; they signed promissory notes of $1,000 or multiples; New York banker Herbert Lehman alone signed for more than $11,000. The Foundation failed to raise the money, and the officers had to call upon the underwriters to pay the promissory notes; every man did, and the Foundation was able to pay Levy the first $100,000; upon receiving title they took it to a bank, pledged it as collateral for a first mortgage, and gave him his

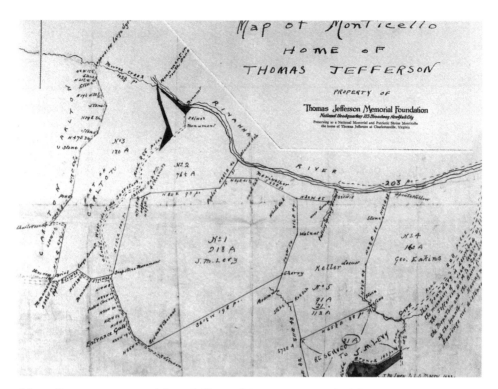

*Map of property conveyed from Jefferson Monroe Levy to the Thomas Jefferson
Memorial Foundation, 1923 (Thomas Jefferson Foundation).*

second $100,000, as well as the bonds for the remaining amount. Kuper
described the ceremony:[502]

> The cash and the bonds and the mortgage were delivered to Levy, and
> Levy signed the deed conveying full title to the property and all
> belonging to the Foundation. This was a very emotional scene and he
> burst out crying. He said that he never dreamt that he would ever part
> with the property.

A story later went around that Levy had personally contributed $100,000
of the purchase price reducing the actual amount the Foundation paid him to
$400,000. As Kuper later wrote, "I wish that the rumor had been true …. He did
not give one cent." Had he done so, Kuper claimed, the Foundation would have
been delighted to have erected a statue of Commodore Levy on the grounds at

Monticello. Instead, as we shall see, it immediately began erasing all evidence that the Levys had ever been there.

Jefferson Monroe Levy did not long outlive his ownership of Monticello. He died of heart failure three months later, on March 6, 1924, but his death did not affect the future of Monticello. The Foundation already had legal title to the property, and would retain it so long as it paid the debt it owed to his estate. His sister and heir, Amelia Mayhoff, confirmed that she would carry out her brother's wishes.[503]

The story of Jefferson Levy and his ownership of Monticello for nearly a half-century is complicated. On the one hand, everyone agrees that had he not put money and energy into restoring Monticello in the 1880s, the house would have deteriorated beyond repair, and today there would be no monument to Thomas Jefferson atop the little mountain. On the other hand, Levy made only a limited attempt to restore the interior of the house to Jeffersonian conditions. He saw it as his property, and as such had a right to furnish it and use it pretty much as he pleased. Given the primitive state of historic preservation at the time, we can hardly fault him for not living up to the standards of a later era. If he did not allow full and free access of everyone who wanted to enter the house or walk around the grounds, the record is clear that he gave permission to near-ly every one who applied.

That he loved the house and grounds is clear enough, but his behavior from the time Maud Littleton announced her "one wish" to the nation and the time he turned over title of Monticello twelve years later is confusing. He fought against being forced to sell, but once having agreed to do so he wavered between pushing the sale to its conclusion and doing all he could to thwart it. In the end a combination of events—his own obstinacy, the wariness of Congress in embarking upon this path, and the war which threw awry all plans unrelated to the defense—left him in control of Monticello long after most peo-ple expected him to have it. If it had not been for his reverses in the market, he might well have kept the place; with the Republicans in power in the 1920s, there would have been little push in Congress to buy Jefferson's home. In the end he sold, and while he did not know it at the time, the purchaser would prove a superb guardian of Mr. Jefferson's house.

Chapter Six

CODA: THE RETURN OF THE LEVYS TO MONTICELLO

"All my wishes end where I hope my days will end—at Monticello."
—THOMAS JEFFERSON[504]

The Thomas Jefferson Memorial Foundation had a difficult time raising the money to pay Levy's estate the remaining $300,000 it owed, as well as the funds to run Monticello. In its early years, Jews played an important role in the work of the Foundation, both in raising funds and on site; the first director of Monticello, in fact, was an immigrant Jew from Russia. Before very long, however, the information that a Jewish family had owned Monticello for nine decades—longer than Jefferson himself—faded into oblivion, and no mention of the Levys, either Uriah or Jefferson, could be heard on top of the little mountain. At first this erasure of the Levy legacy resulted from the Foundation's interpretation of its mission, "to preserve and maintain Monticello" as a national monument to the genius and patriotism of Thomas Jefferson, and as "a living and constant reminder of the immortal principles inscribed in the Declaration of Independence." Then other and less benign forces began to work, and despite the strenuous efforts of Jewish scholars like Malcolm Stern, the leadership of the Foundation refused to recognize the role that the Levys had played in saving Monticello. Not until the 1980s did the Levys finally "return" to Monticello.

❦

The original board of the Foundation included several Jews, including Manny Strauss, Moses H. Grossman, Rabbi Nathan Kraus, and financier Felix M. Warburg, and early fund-raising efforts relied heavily on Jewish contributions. Herbert

Theodore Fred Kuper (courtesy of Dennis Brock).

Lehman underwrote $11,000 of the pledges toward the initial $100,000 payment, and Warburg alone gave $45,000 to the campaign, by far the biggest donation.[505] The organizers deliberately reached out to get as broad a group as possible, northerners and southerners, Protestants, Catholics, and Jews, educational leaders as well as government officials. But the most creative appointment certainly had to be the naming of Theodore Fred Kuper first as the Foundation's lawyer and then as national director.

Born in Russia in 1885, Kuper's family migrated to the lower East Side of New York in 1891, and as a youngster he had his share of fights with neighboring Irish and Italian kids. He grew up street smart, went to law school, and had been doing moderately well until he got involved with a disastrous oil scheme in the early 1920s. In 1923 he went to work for the Foundation at fifty dollars a week "because I needed a job." His first assignment involved designing a letterhead for the new organization, and so he went to the library and pulled out several books on Jefferson. In one of them he found the phrase that would become the Foundation's motto in its early years: "All my wishes end where I hope my days will end—at Monticello." The Foundation and Monticello would become his life's work, and much of the burden of fund-raising and soliciting fell on his shoulders.

In December 1923, as soon as title had passed from Levy to the Foundation, Kuper and Stuart Gibboney went down to Virginia to examine their prize. They met Thomas L. Rhodes, whom Kuper later described as "a worshipper of Thomas Jefferson" as well as a devoted follower of the Lost Cause, and above his cottage right next to the big house flew a Confederate flag. After interviewing Rhodes,

Gibboney and Kuper decided to keep him on as caretaker of Monticello. Kuper then sat down with him to map out the ground rules.

Visitors would be charged fifty cents for admission, and given a receipt with Jefferson's signature stamped on it. For guides Kuper suggested using some of the local blacks whom Rhodes employed, and Kuper wrote out a brief lecture for them to give the guests. As for the Stars and Bars, Kuper asked Rhodes to replace it with an American flag; he could fly the Confederate banner inside his own house, but Monticello was an American shrine. To all this Rhodes agreed, and then took Kuper completely by surprise when he blurted out "But what are you going to do with the Niggers?"

It took Kuper a few seconds to realize that Rhodes meant rest room facilities, which throughout the South at that time were segregated by race. Perhaps only a northerner would have the temerity to tell Rhodes that at the home of the man who had written that "all men are created equal," there could be no racial segregation. The bathrooms were to be marked

(Left to right) Milton L. Grigg, Fiske Kimball, Frank K. Hampton, Henry A. Johnston, William S. Hilbreth (Thomas Jefferson Foundation).

"gentlemen" and "ladies." Monticello, at least in this respect, would be an island of integration until the rest of the South caught up more than thirty years later.[506]

Kuper must bear at least part of the blame for the original erasure of the Levys from Monticello. The Foundation had bought the estate to create a shrine to the nation's third president, and they saw Monticello and its history as tied to and limited by the years Jefferson lived there. In one of the very first fund-raising brochures put out by the Foundation and probably written by Kuper, there is absolutely no mention of the Levy years nor the role they had played in saving the house. The call for money was to help restore and furnish the mansion to the condition it had been in the early nineteenth century.[507] The Levys had become irrelevant.

Work began on Monticello shortly after title passed to the Foundation. In 1924 repairs were made to the roof framing and a new sheet metal roof installed. Workmen mended the north and south dependency stone walls and terrace walks. The real work of restoration began in 1938, after the appointment of Sidney Fiske Kimball, the distinguished art historian and director of the Philadelphia Museum of Art, as head of the restoration committee in 1925. Under his direction rotten beams throughout the house were replaced and a search begun for original furnishings. Very few of the pieces in the house that Levy had transferred to the Foundation could be authenticated as Jeffersonian, and the vast majority of the furniture clearly dated from a much later period. As a result, much of Levy's furniture was discarded or sold, and the house stood relatively bare for many years while the Foundation slowly acquired original Jefferson pieces.

As the Levy furniture left, so too did the Levys. While today historic preservationists would insist that the story of a house must be complete, in the 1920s the practice, as well as the intentions of the sponsors, focused on the period of the famous owner, in this case Thomas Jefferson. As the distinguished historian James G.

Restoration of Monticello, c. 1925 (Thomas Jefferson Foundation, gift of Lenore G. Watts).

Randall wrote at the time, Americans had too little sense of the past; in making Monticello into a shrine to Jefferson, the country would be able to cherish "the great political traditions associated" with his name[508]—with his name, not that of the Levys. People did not pay fifty cents to hear about Uriah Levy or his nephew; they wanted to hear about Mr. Jefferson. They trooped to his gravesite down the hill, ignoring the grave of Rachel Phillips Levy, which slowly sank into disrepair, the inscription on its headstone unreadable.

Rachel Levy's grave, 1973 (Thomas Jefferson Foundation, photo by Ed Roseberry).

Kuper stayed on with the Foundation for many years, helping to wipe out its debt and finally pay off the mortgage. During his tenure he helped develop a number of innovative educational programs, but he had little to do with the restoration work and the day-to-day operations. After his retirement the Foundation hired Curtis Thacker and then James A. Bear, Jr., whose visions were so focused on the house that according to Merrill Peterson even Jefferson the political philosopher, the entire reason for saving Monticello as a shrine to him, practically disappeared from view, to be replaced with the "relics of his domestic life and aesthetic vision."[509] This emphasis left little room for the Levys, who had for the most part disappeared before Thacker and Bear's tenures.

When Levy family members visited Monticello they felt unwelcome. Frances Lewis and her husband went there in the 1930s, the same place where as a young girl she had played every summer. They asked for the key to the gravestone of Rachel Levy, which stood behind a little fence. The people at Monticello said there was no one by that name buried there, and only after a great deal of persistence did they finally agree to look. Eventually someone came back with the key and said they could go in and take care of the grounds. "There was tremendous anti-Semitic feeling," the Lewises believed, "because of the fact that a Jew owned the house."[510]

The Lewises did not imagine the anti-Jewish sentiment; it existed. In 1962 Lewis Glaser, who supplied quill pens to Monticello, visited the estate and asked the superintendent, Curtis Thacker, who was buried in the badly neglected grave near the gift shop. According to Glaser, Thacker answered "some damn Jew." When Glaser said he was a Jew, Thacker quickly responded that he was "not like the rest of them." Glaser called him "a bigoted sonofabitch" and told him that he would no longer supply the quills to Monticello. A few years later, when James Bear had taken over, Glaser again went up the mountain, this time with a local architect in tow, to examine Rachel Levy's grave. The architect, Joseph Laramore (whose firm would do the restoration of the Levy Opera House), prepared a sketch for the refurbishment of the burial place, and Glaser offered to pay for the work himself. Bear declined and would soon find himself besieged by people insisting that the Levys deserved better treatment from Monticello.[511]

> **The Story of Monticello**—After Jefferson's death in 1826, Monticello was occupied by his daughter for two years. When her husband, Governor Thomas Mann Randolph, died in 1828, she felt she could no longer afford to remain at Monticello.
>
> The estate was then advertised in the 'Herald' of Alexandria, Va., as being worth $71,000, and containing 409 acres. It was sold, however to James L. Barclay for $7000. Four years later, it was acquired by Uriah Phillips Levy, of New York City, for $2500.00.
>
> In 1912, a movement was started to bring Monticello under public ownership as a National Shrine. Eleven years later, on Dec. 23, 1923, the Thomas Jefferson Memorial Foundation purchased the property from Jefferson M. Levy for $500,000.00.

Around 1953 Malcolm Stern, rabbi of Congregation Ohef Shalom in Norfolk, Virginia, and a historian of American Jewry, received a letter from one of his congregants, Mrs. Ben Paul Snyder, complaining about a new sign that had just been erected at the entrance to Monticello.[512] While one should not ascribe motives to whoever wrote the sign, it conveyed a message that sharp Jews had paid a few thousand for Jefferson's home and had made a killing when they sold it to the Foundation. The sign gave no indication that dollar values in 1834 differed significantly from values in 1923, or that Jefferson Levy had put perhaps as much as a million dollars into the property. Mrs. Snyder did not know what should be done, but she thought at the least the sign should be taken down. Stern sent the memo on to the Richmond office of the Anti-Defamation League, but there is no record of whether it filed a protest; after all, technically the facts were correct, but the implicit interpretation of them left an erroneous and nasty impression. Stern did, however, write a short article on the Levys that appeared in a regional historical journal;[513] at the time very few people knew of the role the Levys had played, and they certainly learned nothing about it when they visited Monticello.

In 1964 Stern moved to New York to take up a position as placement director for the Central Conference of American Rabbis, and to become even more active in American Jewish history. He did nothing more on the Levys until Irving Lipkowitz contacted him, sometime in the early 1970s. Lipkowitz worked as an attorney in the New York offices of the Philip Morris Tobacco Company, and for some reason he had become incensed by the way Monticello was treating the Levys. He began to bombard Bear with memoranda regarding the Rachel Phillips grave, signage, the information given by tour guides, as well as the material published by the Foundation.[514] He particularly objected to the version then current among historians and perpetuated by the Foundation that Monticello lay neglected and in ruin for the century between its founder's death and the purchase by the Foundation.[515] Bear recognized that some mention should be made of the role the Levys played in the house's history. He offered to meet with Lipkowitz, who went to Monticello in the summer of 1974. The New York attorney praised the Foundation for what it had done, and agreed that Monticello should be first and foremost a shrine to Jefferson. But he urged Bear to acknowledge the work of the Levys in saving the house; there should at the least be a marker at Rachel Levy's gravesite, and the sign regarding the prices paid by Uriah and received by Jefferson should either be explained, or better yet, removed.[516] Bear responded that "it is not that we wish to purposefully omit the Levy ownership, but we do not think it of enough interest to those who come here to reduce what we say about Jefferson, or to lengthen the tour by including Levy lore." A few weeks later Bear's assistant, Charles L. Granquist, told Lipkowitz that there were "many ambiguities about the Levys' role," but he hoped that as they learned more they could develop a better text.[517]

Bear kept his word, and as he worked on a revision of the basic Monticello guidebook, he peppered both Lipkowitz and Stern with specific questions, and the latter enlisted the help of Nathan Kaganoff, the librarian at the American Jewish Historical Society, and Leonard Gold, the librarian in the Jewish Division of the New York Public Library. Stern also wrote to his good friend, Saul Viener, a Richmond businessman and amateur historian who was active in both the American Jewish Historical Society and the Southern Jewish Historical Society, to see if they could maintain pressure on Bear through local people. Viener, in turn, approached Virginius Dabney, the well-known newspaper editor and historian.[518] Dabney expressed his surprise, since although he wrote widely on Virginia history, he knew little about the Levys nor that a Levy grave existed at Monticello. "It goes to show," Dabney wrote, "how the entire subject has been grossly neglected."[519] But although Stern praised Bear as "the first official who seems to be trying to ascertain the facts,"[510] very little changed. The offending sign did come down (thanks in large measure to the vigorous protest of Harold L. Lewis, who married a grand-niece of Jefferson Levy), and some mention of the Levys became part of the guidebook. But the guides remained unaware of them, and the weeds grew higher on Rachel Levy's grave.

Things began to change in February 1984 when the Thomas Jefferson Memorial Foundation named as its new president Dr. Daniel P. Jordan, a historian then teaching at Virginia Commonwealth University in Richmond. On the day the newspaper announced his appointment, those who had been involved in trying to get the Levys proper recognition began calling to find out where he stood on the issue. Jordan himself, as he later recalled, "started to hear from various Jewish friends—some were eminent scholars and some just had an interest in history—with the same message: that an important story was not being told at Monticello."[521]

Jordan promised that as soon as he had a chance to settle into his new job, which would not start until January 1985, he would look into the matter, and he did. Soon after Jordan's arrival at the Foundation, a working group of advisors was recruited to help the Foundation think about the issue. Members included Virginius Dabney, Irving Lipkowitz, Malcolm Stern and Saul Viener, as well as Rabbi Myron Berman. The first priority would be the gravesite, and in the spring of 1985 the Foundation's Board of Trustees enthusiastically and unanimously offered their support for the progress being made on refurbishing Rachel Levy's gravesite. On March 25, Jordan wrote a progress report to Viener, including the proposed text for a plaque to be placed at the gravesite:[522]

This is the grave of Rachel Phillips Levy (1769-1839), daughter of Jonas and Rebecca Machado Phillips of Philadelphia, and mother of Commodore Uriah P. Levy, USN (1792-1862), who purchased Monticello in 1836.

Rachel Levy's grave and plaque following restoration and dedication in 1985 (Thomas Jefferson Foundation, photo by H. Andrew Johnson).

An ardent admirer of Thomas Jefferson, Commodore Levy believed that the houses of great men should be preserved as "monuments to their glory," and he bequeathed Monticello in his will to the "People of the United States." The government relinquished its claim to the estate, however, and litigation over the will deprived Monticello for seventeen years of an owner to care for it.

In 1879 Jefferson Monroe Levy (1852-1924), who shared his uncle Uriah's admiration for Jefferson, gained clear title to Monticello and began to make badly needed repairs. After adding considerable land from the original Monticello tract, he sold the house and 662 acres to the Thomas Jefferson Memorial Foundation in 1923.

At two critical periods in the history of Monticello, the preservation efforts and stewardship of Uriah P. and Jefferson M. Levy successfully maintained the property for future generations.

A jubilant Viener called Malcolm Stern in New York to report that there would be a formal dedication of the gravesite in June, and that Stern would be invited to deliver a paper on the Levy role. Unfortunately Stern could not be in Charlottesville that day, but he wrote the paper, which Viener read for him.

June 7 turned out to be a glorious spring day, sunny but not too warm, and many of the invited guests—including more than sixty descendants and friends of the Levys—were almost delirious in their joy that the family had finally been recognized. In addition to remarks by Jordan and Viener (in his capacity as chairman of the board of the American Jewish Historical Society), Edgar Bronfman, the president of the World Jewish Congress, who owned a nearby estate, also spoke. After a memorial prayer by Rabbi Louis Gerstein of Shearith Israel in New York, Harley Lewis, Rachel's great-great-granddaughter, unveiled the plaque.[523]

Back in New York Malcolm Stern received reports of the day, and took more than a little satisfaction in the role he had played to make it happen. But as Irving Lipkowitz quickly reminded him, this was not the end, but only the beginning of the recognition of the Levys at Monticello.[524]

In October of 1985, a new permanent exhibition was opened on Jefferson and Monticello, with a large space devoted to Monticello after Jefferson's death, which prominently featured the history of the Levy stewardship. The Foundation also published (and then reprinted several times) a booklet of essays related to the dedication of Rachel Levy's gravesite. Further, Monticello's scholarly Curator, Susan R. Stein, joined the staff in 1986 and began to collect and to research systematically Levy materials and to make talks on the story throughout the country. Monticello's interpreters were also given in-depth briefings on the subject. A new Monticello guidebook published in 1998 describes the important role of the Levys in the preservation of Monticello and features a sidebar with a color photograph of Commodore Levy. Since 1985, the Foundation has hosted a number of individuals and groups who came to Monticello for the explicit purpose of learning more about the Levy years. This volume is another step in ensuring that the Levy role in saving Thomas Jefferson's house is not forgotten.

❦

The task of historians is to interpret the past so that we as a people can understand where we have been and how we have gotten to where we are today. While it is possible to identify certain objective "facts," most historical "truth" is subjective, and reflects not only the biases of the author but the times in which the historian writes. The Levys vanished from Monticello's history for more than a half-century because historians focused so much on Thomas Jefferson that, in their eyes, a Monticello without its builder could not have been anything but abandoned. That it served as the home of a family for nearly ninety years made little difference, since in their view the only proper role the house could play was as a shrine; people living there did not "save" Monticello, but desecrated it.

On the other hand, we actually know far more about the Levys than their defenders would acknowledge. The growth in American Jewish scholarship, as well as in the history of historic preservation, has given us a wealth of knowledge about Uriah Levy and his family, as well as the vicissitudes of Monticello. What we needed was not to ignore or to glorify the Levys, but to give them credit—as well as blame—for what they did. Monticello may be envisioned as a monument to Thomas

Jefferson, but its history is that of the Levys as well. That seems to be the position at which, after many years, the Thomas Jefferson Foundation has arrived, and it is one where both Jefferson admirers and Levy advocates can be comfortable.

In his magisterial biography of Thomas Jefferson, Dumas Malone talks about how Jefferson loved Monticello, and imagines his shade returning on soft summer nights to walk around the house and grounds, once again enjoying the clear cool air and the beauty of the distant Blue Ridge. One is tempted to believe that if Jefferson's ghost does appear on such an evening, he may well be accompanied by two other spirits, those of Uriah and Jefferson Levy, and as the three stroll around the lawn they share reminiscences of the house they all loved and cherished.

Appendix

Note that this document is quoted in its entirety but attributions to artists and furniture-makers (especially Thomas Jefferson) are now questioned by scholars.

**Inventory of Goods Transferred from Jefferson Monroe Levy to
the Thomas Jefferson Memorial Foundation***

MAIN HALL

1	8-day Tower clock and weights
1	Folding ladder (made by T. Jefferson for clock)
1	Bust, Washington (on bracket) composition
1	" Hamilton " " marble, by Powers
2	Davenports—upholstered
1	Marble top table (made by Thos. Jefferson)
1	Portrait Thomas Jefferson by Dick, wearing sable coat presented by Kosciusko
1	Statuette, Henry Clay
1	Marble bust, Franklin (on pedestal)
1	" " Washington " "
1	" " Thos. Jefferson, by Ceracchi (original) on pedestal of pillar and capitol (designed) of sheaf of wheat and tobacco " for capitol
1	Music stand, black walnut (made by T.J.)
2	Gate leg card tables, mahogany (T.J.)
1	Candelabrum (7 branches) bronze
3	Gilt chairs, upholstered
2	French mechanical lamps (on mantel)
1	Bronze lamp (Samson) on lift card table
1	Pr. brass andirons—fireplace
1	Gilt brass hanging lamp—4 extensions (T.J.)
1	Ink Stand (Boars Head) on R card table
1	Statuette, Henry Clay (by Ball) on R card table
1	Porcelain Vase (decorated) somewhat broken
4	Oriental rugs, small (1 of which oblong)
1	Jasper Door stop

SALON

1	Pompeian marble top table
1	Chandelier—6 branch—Candelabrum
2	Louis XIV mirrors from France by T.J.
1	(set—Clock; gilt bronze and 2 Vases, blue) on mantle
1	Cabinet, small (bronze coating)
1	Bust, Lotus Eater (on pedestal) marble
4	Five branch—Louis XV bronze wall candelabras
8	Louis XV gilt arm chairs, upholstered
2	small sofas " " " "
1	Pandora clock, Louis XV
1	Statue, Mary and her little lamb, on pedestal
6	Pairs Old Rose brocade hangings with the backs
1	bronze fireplace fender (lions)
1	small Oriental rug

DINING ROOM

1	Round extension table and leaves (mahogany)
2	Arm chairs, ebony & tapestry, fruits and birds
10	Straight chairs, " " " "
1	Sideboard, mahogany with T.J. crest
1	841 branch chandelier candelabrum (1 missing)
1	Side Service table, 1 drawer, mahogany
1	Chinese jar over door to breakfast room
1	pr. Sandwich Island battle clubs breakfast room
3	pieces Wedgwood ware on Mantle
2	Blue bronze vases on mantle
1	Lamp stand
1	set andirons (lions) bronze
1	blue rug

BREAKFAST ROOM

1	Round Roman gilt table containing lapus lazuli and other precious marbles, etc.
1	Bronze Wine Cabinet 4 decanters, 7 glasses (on round table)
1	nest of four tables
2	laquer fire screens
2	ebony and marble tables
1	small round checkerboard table (Palazzo dei Caesari Febbraio 1869)
1	gilt sofa upholstered with flower patterns
1	fireproof safe

RANDOLPH AND MRS. LEVY'S BEDROOM

1   Four-poster French Walnut Bedstead (complete) with velvet hangings and canopy

1   French walnut table

1   Straight chair—upholstered French walnut

1   Arm chair

1   Upholstered long stool

3   Pairs Velvet Portieres

1   Pair Brass Andirons

1   Blue and gilt clock on mantle

2   Four-branch Candelabra on mantle

2   small rugs

1   Wash stand in dressing room

1   Commode in dressing room

1   Standing Lamp

1   Ash tray (on mantle)

LIBRARY

1   Inlaid table exhibition (from Berlin)

1   Model of 1st Corliss Engine (on table)

1   Bell (on table) Inlaid (metal)

1   Corner lounge upholstered

1   Prayer chair   "

1   Arm   "   "

3   Straight "   "

1   Bust, Franklin (on bookcase)

1   Black Marble Clock with two side pieces (on bookcase)

1   Fechters Sword

1   Japanese   "

1   Large musical box

1   Piano—upright

1   Stool

1   Stool

2   Side mirrors and candle

1   Standing Lamp

3   Cases of books

1   Bronze Card Receiver (basket)

1   Mail Pouch

1   Hanging Lamp

CONSERVATORY
2   Bronze brackets "Peace" and "War"
13   pieces Miscellaneous Furniture
     Books

STUDY
1   Velvet and mahogany sofa, Library set
1   Arm Chair   "   "
1   Stool   "   "
2   Side Shelves made by Thos. Jefferson
1   Plan of Monticello, ground floor, framed, made by Thos. Jefferson's granddaughter, Cornelia J. Randolph, Sept. 21, 1808. Paper brought from France.
1   Empire Desk
1   swivel desk chair
1   Ink stand, bronze and rosewood (large)
1   Onyx Paper weight,   on desk
1   Small brass Candlestick, "   "
1   Chest of six drawers decorated
     slats used in bed by T.J. in alcove
     Gray blue carpet

JEFFERSON ALCOVE
     Gray blue carpet

THOMAS JEFFERSON'S BEDROOM
1   gilt Louis XIV bedstead and headpiece with blue & silver hangings
1   Arm Chair upholstered in blue silk
1   Straight Chair   "   "   "   "
1   Sofa   "   "   "   "
2   Pair of blue & silver portieres with tie backs
15   Chandelier Candelabrum with crystals
1   Pair Bronze Andirons
1   Road side table with 3 gilt legs
     Gray blue carpet

MADISON ROOM (BED) ABBÉ CORREA
1   white enamel bedstead
1   "   "   table
1   "   "   chiffonier (long stool)
1   White and upholstered arm chair
1   Upholstered arm chair

1   Small straight chair
1   Colonial Clock (with lion)
1   Crystal Lamp
    Alcove slats
       "   marble top washstand
3   Pair Portieres, brocade
1   Hat tree
1   Bronze Bacchus, from Rome, in hall near Madison Room

MONROE ROOM (BED)
2   bedsteads (twin) from King Ludwigh in Munich, used by "Mad King" and canopy
1   White Enamel Bureau
1   Sofa, white enamel and brocade
1   Straight chair, "   "   "
1   marble top washstand (alcove)
1   Crane Lamp
2   Small rugs
1   Bronze and glass altar piece

BUTLER'S PANTRY
    Refrigerator
2   tables
    chairs
    closets

LAFAYETTE ROOM (BED)
1   Franklin Grate
1   blue enamel bedstead with head piece and canopy
1   mahogany table made by T.J.
1   marble top washstand
1   blue enamel, chest of four drawers with mirror
1   "   "   straight chair
1   Picture of Empress Eugenie as a bride
1   Arm Chair
1   Rug
1   small square table
1   China Figure—Mozart
1   Ormolu and bronze side table
3   pairs Brocade Portieres

ADAMS ROOM (BED)

1 bedstead complete

1 Arm chair

1 Straight Chair

1 white enameled bureau

1 Wardrobe

1 Table

1 Clock

2 Pair Velvet Curtains

1 White Enamel Table (alcove)

1 washstand   "

GALLERY

1 Damask Flat Settee

1   "   " gilt

2 Bronze Figures on pedestals

1 Black flowered satin and gilt flat settee

1 Floor Lamp

SARAH RANDOLPH & MRS. MAYHOFF'S ROOM (BED)

 Bird's Eye Maple Set of Furniture

1 dressing table

1 dresser

1 desk

1 table

1 wardrobe

2 straight chairs

1 Upholstered Arm Chair

2 Brass bedsteads (twin) complete

1 Wash stand (in alcove)

1 Lamp

2 pairs Velvet Curtains

T.J. RANDOLPH BED ROOM

2 pairs Pink Brocaded Curtains

1 " " Portiere

1 White Enamel dresser

1 "   " dressing table

1 Upholstered arm chair

1   "   flat settee

1 straight upholstered chair

1   single brass bedstead (complete)

1   small round table

2   small rugs

1   chest in alcove—1 flag—1 rosewood chifferobe

HALL

1   Mahogany table
     Carpets in all halls

MAID'S ROOM (BED)

1   Franklin grate—with Prince of Wales feathers

1   Single brass bedstead (complete)

1   Birds Eye Maple Rocking Chair

1   Arm Chair—white enameled

1   Small table

1   White enameled Chiffonier

1   Gilt frame mirror

1   Painting "Pandora"

1   White enameled dresser

1   Embroidered Screen

BATH ROOM

2   Upholstered chairs—straight

1   Bath tub

1   Washstand

1   Clothes Hamper

1 Set of Flags of All Nations

THIRD FLOOR

1   Billiard Table

1   set of full armour

1   Lamp

1   Sewing table

1   Painting (spurious) Jefferson

1   Painting Jefferson

1   Body of gig in which T.J. rode from Monticello to Philadelphia to sign the
     Declaration of Independence

2   Bronze Lamps

1   Porcelain Vase

1   Model "White House"

2   Wall Paintings

1   Painting Gen. Beauregard and staff

1   Black flowered and gilt flat settee

1   painting—woods

1   painting—fence in woods

     It is hereby expressly understood and agreed that all personal property on the premises not included in the foregoing inventory is not included in this conveyance & sale.

*   "Exhibit A," Deed transferring Monticello to the Thomas Jefferson Memorial Foundation, 30 June 1923, Monticello Papers, Thomas Jefferson Foundation, Charlottesville, Virginia.

NOTES

[1] Thomas Jefferson to Maria Cosway, 12 October 1786, in John P. Kaminski, ed., *Jefferson in Love: The Love Letters between Thomas Jefferson and Maria Cosway* (Madison, 1999), 50.

[2] Development in the Charlottesville area threatened to mar this beauty, but fortunately necessary steps were taken to ensure the preservation of unmarred vistas. See Chiles T.A. Larson, "Alarm on 'Little Mountain'," *Historic Preservation* 43 (March/April 1991): 46-48.

[3] Although this study is primarily concerned with the *house* that Jefferson built, one needs to keep in mind that the building did not stand alone. It was the center of his plantation, which meant that it had economic and communal aspects that went well beyond it being his residence. Like other southern planters, Jefferson carried on a large-scale agricultural enterprise, growing and selling crops. More than 150 slaves labored at Monticello, not only on the farm, but making the nails, furniture, tools and other implements needed to sustain the plantation. This self-sustaining community revolved around the house and its dependencies, and one needs to keep in mind the intertwined role of house and plantation.

[4] Dumas Malone, *Jefferson the Virginian*, volume 1 of *Jefferson and His Time* (Boston, 1948), 143.

[5] B.L. Rayner, *Life of Thomas Jefferson* (Boston, 1834), 524, quoted in Susan R. Stein, *The Worlds of Thomas Jefferson at Monticello* (New York, 1993), 13.

[6] Jefferson to James Ogilvie, 20 February 1771, in Julian Boyd *et al.*, eds., *The Papers of Thomas Jefferson* (27 vols. to date, Princeton, 1950-), 1:63.

[7] *Id.*, 4:174.

[8] Malone, *Jefferson the Virginian*, 150.

[9] Frederick D. Nichols and James A. Bear, Jr., *Monticello* (Charlottesville, 1967), 13-14.

[10] Jack McLaughlin, *Jefferson and Monticello: The Biography of a Builder* (New York, 1988), 161. I am heavily indebted to this book, as well as to Stein, *The Worlds of Thomas Jefferson at Monticello,* for information on the architecture of the two Monticellos.

[11] Quoted in Malone, *Jefferson the Virginian*, 149.

[12] *Id.*, 148.

[13] Merrill D. Peterson, ed., *Visitors to Monticello* (Charlottesville, 1989), 11-12.

[14] Nichols and Bear, *Monticello,* 16.

[15] For the influence of these and other ancient buildings, see William L. Beiswanger, "Jefferson's Sources from Antiquity in the Design of Monticello," *Antiques* 144 (July 1993): 58-69.

[16] Dumas Malone, *Jefferson and the Ordeal of Liberty* (Boston, 1962), vol. 3 of *Jefferson and His Time*, 226.

[17] *Id.*, 227; see also Stein, *Jefferson at Monticello*, 18-40, for the influence of France on his taste, and the many purchases he made while there.

[18] For a description of the library, see Peterson, *Visitors to Monticello*, 58-60, 63-65.

[19] There is an elaborate description of Monticello "prepared by a member of Mr. Jefferson's family, who lived there for many years," in a work by his great-grand-daughter, Sarah N. Randolph, *The Domestic Life of Thomas Jefferson* (New York, 1871), 332-37; an overly fulsome contemporary description of the house and its furnishing is in B.L. Raynor, *Life of Thomas Jefferson* (Boston, 1834), 397-402.

[20] A visitor in 1809 described the dome room as "a noble and beautiful apartment, with 8 circular windows and a sky-light. It was not furnished and being in the attic story is not used, which I thought a great pity, as it might be made the most beautiful room in the house." Margaret Bayard Smith, *The First Forty Years of Washington Society*, ed. Galliard Hunt (New York, 1906), 71.

[21] Peterson, *Visitors to Monticello*, 34.

[22] McLaughlin, *Jefferson and Monticello*, 368 ff.; see also, Lucia C. Stanton, "Jefferson and the Amusements of Science," *Antiques* 144 (July 1993): 92-99.

[23] Peterson, *Visitors to Monticello*, 52. The reference is to "The Man in the Hill" in Henry Fielding, *Tom Jones*, Book VIII, chapters 10-15.

[24] Stein, *Worlds of Thomas Jefferson at Monticello*, 63.

[25] Malone, *Ordeal of Liberty*, 229.

[26] Jefferson to Benjamin H. Latrobe, 10 October 1809, quoted in Dumas Malone, *The Sage of Monticello* (Boston, 1981), volume 6 of *Jefferson and His Times*, 8.

[27] James A. Bear, Jr., "Monticello," in Merrill D. Peterson, ed., *Thomas Jefferson: A Reference Biography* (New York, 1986), 442

[28] *Forty Years of Washington Society*, 69.

[29] Peterson, *Visitors to Monticello*, 35.

[30] *Id.*, 95-96.

[31] Quoted in Marion Louise White, "Debt Unresolved: Jefferson and Monticello" (Unpublished masters thesis, University of Virginia, 1993), 1.

[32] Jefferson received $9,000 a year as ambassador to France, not enough to support him with all he purchased there. As secretary of state he received only $3,500 in salary.

[33] Jefferson to Martha Randolph, 5 January 1808, in Edwin Morris Betts and James A. Bear, Jr., *The Family Letters of Thomas Jefferson* (Columbia, Missouri, 1966), 319.

34   See Malone, *Sage of Monticello*, 34-42, for a discussion of Jefferson's assets and liabilities when he left office.

35   For extensive explanations of Jefferson's finances, see White, "Debt Unresolved," and Steven Harold Hochman, "Thomas Jefferson: A Personal Financial Biography" (unpublished doctoral dissertation, University of Virginia, 1987).

36   In addition to the two works cited above, see also Herbert E. Sloan, *Principle and Interest: Thomas Jefferson and the Problem of Debt* (New York, 1995).

37   Jefferson apparently had the right idea. John McCusker and Russell, *The Economy of British America, 1687-1789* (Chapel Hill, 1985), 304, suggest that the high cost of labor required for tobacco made wheat and other grains more profitable; Timothy H. Breen, *Tobacco Culture: The Mentality of the Great Tidewater Planters on the Eve of the Revolution* (Princeton, 1985), 180-82, believes the growing indebtedness of tobacco farmers forced them to seek more profitable crops. Whatever the reason, Jefferson correctly surmised that the old tobacco culture was failing.

38   Quoted in Hochman, "Personal Financial Biography," 201. The duke's only complaint was that Jefferson had failed to manure the fields properly.

39   For Jefferson's agricultural experiments, see Edwin Morris Betts, ed., *Thomas Jefferson's Farm Book* (Charlottesville, 1987).

40   Part of the problem here involved the economic dislocation caused by the war. He sold off 5000 acres of Wayles land for £5836, but because of the war could not get the British to accept bonds from these sales. Then Virginia took the money to prosecute the war, and so at the end Jefferson had neither the land nor the bonds, but still had the debt. Malone, *Jefferson the Virginian*, 163.

41   Hochman, "Personal Financial Biography," pp. 252 ff.; McLaughlin, *Jefferson and Monticello*, 377.

42   White, "Debt Unresolved," 66.

43   James A. Bear, Jr., and Lucia C. Stanton, eds, *Jefferson's Memorandum Books, Papers of Thomas Jefferson*, Second Series (2 vols., Princeton, 1997), xviii.

44   *Id.*

45   *Id.*, xix.

46   Nicholas to Jefferson, 19 April 1919, quoted in Malone, *Sage of Monticello*, 303.

47   Jefferson to Patrick Gibson, 30 July 1818, quoted in *id.*, 304.

48   Jefferson to Madison, 17 February 1826, in James Morton Smith, ed., *The Republic of Letters: The Correspondence between Thomas Jefferson and James Madison* (3 vols., New York, 1995), 3: 1965-66.

49   The section on Jefferson's financial problems has been drawn primarily from Malone, *Sage of Monticello*, and Hochman, "Jefferson: Personal Financial Biography," *passim*.

50 Hochman, "Jefferson: Personal Financial Biography," 278, 280; for details about Randolph's financial problems, see Elizabeth Langhorne, *Monticello: A Family Story* (Chapel Hill, 1987), 230-32.

51 *Id.,* 287.

52 Jefferson to Madison, 17 February 1826, in Smith, *Republic of Letters,* 3:1966.

53 Malone, *Sage of Monticello,* 474-78, 496.

54 Jefferson to Martha Randolph, 6 February 1808; Randolph to Jefferson, 2 March 1809, in Betts and Bear, *Family Letters,* 327, 386.

55 Malone, *Sage of Monticello,* 488.

56 Hochman, "A Financial Biography," 286-87.

57 McLaughlin, *Jefferson and Monticello,* 379; Peterson, *Visitors to Monticello,* 95, 112.

58 Mary Cable and Annabelle Prager, "The Levys of Monticello," *American Heritage* 29, no. 2 (1978): 32.

59 Adams, *Jefferson and Monticello,* 243.

60 Bear, "Monticello," in Peterson, ed., *Jefferson: Reference Biography,* 444.

61 *Richmond Enquirer,* 22 July 1828.

62 In contemporary terms, one might also describe Monticello as a "white elephant." All the idiosyncrasies that made the house so peculiarly Jefferson's and contributed to his comfort and taste did not necessarily appeal to many would-be occupants. He had eschewed the typical large staircase to the second floor in favor of two very narrow, cramped stairwells; the main bedroom was not large, the bed in an alcove with a small clothes closet; and because of the narrow stairwells, practically anything— including luggage—had to be hoisted to the second floor by way of the balcony.

63 Adams, *Jefferson and Monticello,* 244.

64 Paul Wilstach, *Jefferson and Monticello* (Garden City, 1925), 215-16.

65 Peterson, *Visitors to Monticello,* 114-19.

66 Unsigned newspaper article, 28 May 1830, Jefferson Transcripts, University of Virginia Library, Charlottesville, Virginia.

67 Virginia Randolph Trist to Ellen Randolph Coolidge, 23 March 1827, Jefferson Transcripts; Adams, *Jefferson and Monticello,* 244-45.

68 Bear, "Monticello," 445.

69 Apparently a house Barclay owned in Charlottesville also changed hands. The druggist claimed it was worth $4500 and wanted it to be part of the price he paid, but Jefferson Randolph desperately needed cash, not another property. In the end they

agreed on the value of the house, whatever that might be, to be subtracted from the purchase price.

70 "God's Noble Woman," *Wheeling Intelligencer,* 10 August 1908, in Barclay Materials, University of Virginia Library Special Collections; see also *Jeffersonian Republican* (Charlottesville), 25 January 1888, *id.,* Jefferson Transcripts. She also claimed that Washington had sent Thomas Barclay as first consul to France in 1785, a clear impossibility since Washington was not in the government at the time.

71 *Id.* James Bear, the former director of Monticello, seems to have accepted at least part of the Barclay story, and adds that the affluent Barclays brought with them a large amount of good furniture that blended in well with the items left behind by the Randolphs. Bear, "Monticello," 446.

72 Cable and Prager, "Levys of Monticello," 33.

73 William Taylor Barry to Susan Barry Taylor, 16 August 1832, William Taylor Barry Papers, University of Virginia Library, Charlottesville, Virginia.

74 John E. Semmes, *John H.B. Latrobe and His Times: 1803-1891* (Baltimore, 1917), 248-51.

75 Mrs. George Leiper (Eliza Showden Thomas) to her daughters, Elizabeth and Ann, 29 June 1832, Leiper and Patterson Family Papers, University of Virginia Library, Charlottesville, Virginia.

76 Advertisement in Atkinson's *Saturday Evening Post* (Philadelphia), 19 October 1833, reported in James A. Bear, Jr., "Accounts of Monticello, 1780-1878: A Selective Bibliography," *Magazine of Albemarle County History* 21 (1962-1963): 19.

77 Uriah Phillips Levy to John Coulter, November 1832, quoted in Donavan Fitzpatrick and Saul Saphire, *Navy Maverick: Uriah Phillips Levy* (Garden City, 1963), 128.

78 George Alfred Townsend, *Monticello and Its Preservation Since Jefferson's Death, 1826-1902* (Washington, 1902), 9. Scholars agree that Jefferson Monroe Levy either wrote or directed the writing of this work.

79 Paul Wilstach, *Jefferson and Monticello* (Garden City, 1928), ch. 14; William Gaines, "From Desolation to Restoration," *Virginia Cavalcade* (1952): 5.

80 Maud Littleton, *Monticello* (New York, 1912), 12.

81 Melvin I. Urofsky, *Commonwealth and Community: The Jewish Experience in Virginia* (Richmond, 1997), 1-4.

82 David and Tamar De Sola Pool, *An Old Faith in the New World: Portrait of Shearith Israel, 1654-1954* (New York, 1955).

83 Edwin Wolf 2nd and Maxwell Whiteman, *The History of the Jews of Philadelphia from Colonial Times to the Age of Jackson* (Philadelphia, 1957). The best study of American Jews in the colonial era is Eli Faber, *A Time for Planting: The First Migration, 1654-1820,* volume one of Henry Feingold, ed., *The Jewish People in America* (5 vols., Baltimore, 1992).

84 A majority, but not all, colonial Jews followed the so-called Sephardic or Spanish ritual. These were Jews whose ancestors had been driven out of Spain in 1492, and then had settled either in Spanish colonies in the Caribbean and South America, or in Holland. The remainder of colonial Jewry were Ashkenazim, or German, Jews who came from central and eastern Europe. While Sephardic Jews dominated communal life in the eighteenth and early nineteenth century, the great influx of German Jews after 1840 overwhelmed them. They still form a vibrant but small part of American Jewry.

85 Samuel Rezneck, *The Saga of an American Jewish Family since the Revolution: A History of the Family of Jonas Phillips* (Washington, 1980).

86 Jonas Phillips to the President and Members of the Convention, 7 September 1787, in Max Farrand, ed., *The Records of the Federal Convention of 1787* (4 vols., New Haven, 1966 ed.), 3:78-79.

87 Irving Lipkowitz to Virginius Dabney, 13 July 1984, Malcolm Stern Papers, American Jewish Archives, Cincinnati, Ohio; "Life Story of Jonas Phillips Levy," Lewis Family Papers, Hartsdale, New York.

88 Rezneck, *Saga of an American Jewish Family*, 81.

89 Michael Levy to Henry Deering, 21 September 1787, and to Dudley Woodbridge, 12 August 1788, both from Aux Cayes, Santa Domingue (Haiti), Uriah Phillips Levy Papers, American Jewish Historical Society, New York; memorandum, Ira Dye to Ruth Hoffman, 27 April 1998, Archival Collections of K.K. Mikveh Israel, Philadelphia.

90 Edward Davis, *The History of Rodeph Shalom Congregation Philadelphia, 1802-1926* (Philadelphia, 1927), 21, 23.

91 Mary Cable and Annabelle Prager, "The Levys of Monticello," *American Heritage* 29, no. 2 (1978): 33.

92 The main source for Levy's life is the statement he made before the appeals board in 1857. The full transcript of the hearings are in the National Archives, but Levy's statement is included in Jacob Rader Marcus, ed., *Memoirs of American Jews, 1775-1865* (3 vols., Philadelphia, 1955), 1: 76-116, and is hereafter cited as Levy Memoirs. Popular studies of Uriah Levy's life include Abram Kanof, *Uriah Phillips Levy: The Story of a Pugnacious Commodore* (Philadelphia 1949) and Fitzpatrick and Saphire, *Navy Maverick*. A popularized version highlighting the romance and drama is in Stephen Birmingham's *The Grandees: America's Sephardic Elite* (New York, 1971), primarily pp. 200-27 and 233-54. Regrettably neither *Navy Maverick* nor *The Grandees* has footnotes, and it is impossible to check out some of the facts and quotes used by the authors. An excellent although compressed version is the entry on Levy by Ira Dye in John A. Garraty and Mark C. Carnes, eds., *American National Biography* (24 vols., New York, 1999), 13: 553-55.

93 Levy Memoirs, 79.

94 Birmingham, *The Grandees*, 204. A *mezuzah* is a small container in which are copies, in Hebrew, of certain verses of the Torah. Observant Jews, following the biblical

command in Deuteronomy 6:9, nail them to the doorframes of their homes. Uriah would not, however, be the last to do so; three other brothers, Morton, Benjamin and Jonah also became merchant captains.

95 An official transcript of Levy's career in the navy, with all postings, courts-martial and promotions, is appended to Abram Kanof, "Uriah Phillips Levy: The Story of a Pugnacious Commodore," *Publications of the American Jewish Historical Society,* 39 (Sept. 1949), 1-66, at 55-60, and is hereafter cited as Official Transcript. Uriah was not the first Jewish officer commissioned into the navy during the War of 1812; that distinction belongs to Levi M. Harby of Charleston.

96 Ira Dye, *The Fatal Cruise of the* Argus: *Two Captains in the War of* 1812 (Annapolis, 1994), 273-74. Folklore has long held that Levy and other Americans spent their time as prisoners of war in the dreaded prison at Dartmoor; see, for example, Birmingham, *The Grandees,* 207-208. Captain Dye, however, has determined through official records that Levy went to Ashburton; while common seamen may have been sent to Dartmoor, officers would not have been treated that way. The rules of war being more civilized in those days, officers, on giving their promise not to escape, would be confined to a town, and would often partake in local social activities. Note in the previous chapter how Jefferson, as governor of Virginia, entertained captured Hessian officers at Monticello.

97 Levy Memoirs.

98 It is unnecessary to our story to go in detail on each of these events; see Kanof, *Pugnacious Commodore,* or Fitzpatrick and Saphire, *Navy Maverick,* for full accounts. The records of the courts martial are available in the National Archives on Microfilm Publication M273, "Records of General Courts-Martial and Courts of Inquiry of the Navy Department, 1799-1867."

99 Allan Nevins, ed., *The Diary of Philip Hone, 1828-1851* (New York, 1936), entries for 5 May 1831, p. 41, and 23 April 1835, p. 156.

100 Fitzpatrick and Saphire, *Navy Maverick,* 126-27; Crystal, "Uriah P. Levy: Savior of Monticello," *Albemarle Archives* [n.d.] 53. Levy held about twenty-five pieces of real property in New York at the time of his death in 1862; for an inventory see memorandum by Asahel Levy, 1 May 1863, in Uriah Levy MSS, Box 1.

101 Fitzpatrick and Saphire, *Navy Maverick,* 128.

102 Levy Memoirs.

103 This "darker side" of Jefferson has been explored in other areas as well. See, for example, Leonard W. Levy, *Jefferson and Civil Liberties: The Darker Side* (Cambridge, 1963), an admittedly revisionist tract, and Paul Finkelman, *Slavery and the Founders: Race and Liberty in the Age of Jefferson* (Armonk, 1996).

104 Dumas Malone, *Jefferson the Virginian* (Boston, 1948), 274.

105 Jefferson to Joseph Delaplaine, 25 December 1816, quoted in Eugene R. Sheridan, *Jefferson and Religion* (Charlottesville, 1998), 14.

[106] Jefferson to Smith, 6 August 1816, in Dickinson W. Adams, ed., *Jefferson's Extracts from the Gospels*, Papers of Thomas Jefferson, Second Series (Princeton, 1983), 376.

[107] Sheridan, *Jefferson and Religion*, 22.

[108] This is discussed extensively in *id.*

[109] 8 Code of Virginia § 57-1. The original draft, subsequent modification, and eventual passage—the latter credit going primarily to James Madison—is detailed in Malone, *Jefferson the Virginian*, ch. 20.

[110] *Id.*, 275.

[111] For various views on the importance and effect of the document, see Merrill D. Peterson and Robert C. Vaughn, eds., *The Virginia Statute for Religious Freedom: Its Evolution and Consequences* (New York, 1988).

[112] 8 Code of Virginia § 57-1.

[113] Jefferson to Madison, 16 December 1786, in James Morton Smith, ed., *The Republic of Letters: The Correspondence between Thomas Jefferson and James Madison* (3 vols., New York, 1995), 1: 458.

[114] In the debate over the bill several Virginia counties petitioned for tolerance of Jews, and Amherst County repudiated its 1779 plea for the exclusion of "Jews, Turks and Infidels" from public life. Thomas J. Curry, *The First Freedoms: Church and State in America to the Passage of the First Amendment* (New York, 1986), 145.

[115] Frederic Cople Jaher, *A Scapegoat in the Wilderness: Origins and Rise of Anti-Semitism in America* (Cambridge, 1994), 100.

[116] Carol Ely, Jeffrey Hantman, and Phyllis Leffler, *To Seek the Peace of the City: Jewish Life in Charlottesville* (Charlottesville, 1994), 3.

[117] Jefferson to Isaac Harby, 6 January 1826, in Joseph Blau and Salo Baron, eds., *The Jews of the United States, 1790-1840: A Documentary History* (3 vols, New York, 1963), 3:704-705. The University of Virginia was the first school of higher education in the country to hire a Jew, James Joseph Sylvester, to teach a secular subject, but the anti-Semitism of faculty and students forced him to leave. The University, however, has ever since the beginning of the twentieth century had a significant number of Jewish students.

[118] Jefferson to Mordecai M. Noah, 28 May 1818, in Abraham Karp, ed., *The Jewish Experience in America* (5 vols., Waltham, 1969), 1:359-60.

[119] See, for example, in addition to the letter to Noah in *id.*, Jefferson to Joseph Marx, 8 July 1820, in Blau and Baron, *Jews of the United States*, 1:13, and to Jacob de la Motta, 9 September 1820, *id.*, 3:704.

[120] "Syllabus of an estimate of the merit of the doctrines of Jesus compared to those of others," Jefferson to Benjamin Rush, 21 April 1803, Paul Leicester Ford, ed., *The Works of Thomas Jefferson*, 12 vols. (New York, Federal edition, 1905), 9: 461.

[121] Jefferson to Joseph Priestly, 9 April 1809, *id.,* 458n.

[122] Jefferson to John Adams, 13 October 1813, citing Johann Jacob Brucker, *Historia critica philosophiae,* (6 vols., 1742-1767), in Albert Ellery Bergh, ed., *The Writings of Thomas Jefferson,* 20 vols. (Washington, 1903-1904), 13: 388-389.

[123] Jefferson to Ezra Stiles, 25 June 1819, *id.,* 15: 203.

[124] Malone, *Sage of Monticello,* 404-05.

[125] Levy, Memoirs, 108-109.

[126] Charles Pond to Benjamin Butler, 12 December 1857, Transcript of the Proceedings of the Court of Inquiry, November-December 1857, 109, original in National Archives, copy in Uriah Levy MSS.

[127] Official Transcript, 59.

[128] Fitzpatrick and Saphire, *Navy Maverick,* 131.

[129] Robbins to Levy, 27 May 1834, cited in Fitzpatrick & Saphire, *Navy Maverick, 132.*

[130] Gales & Seaton's *Register of Debates in Congress,* 23d Cong 1ˢᵗ Sess, 27 June 1834, Vol. X. Part 4, 4787.

[131] Jonas P. Levy to Justin Morrill, 15 July 1876, Papers of Jonas Phillips Levy, American Jewish Historical Society, New York.

[132] Letter to the Editor by Leslie M. Freudenheim, *New York Times,* 5 January 1995; Freudenheim bases the story of Levy charging admission and feeding the poor on reports in *The New York Evening Post* of 19 and 28 February 1834.

[133] Theodore Fred Kuper to Saul Viener, 25 April 1976, Malcolm Stern MSS; Fitzpatrick and Saphire, *Navy Maverick,* 128; James A. Bear, Jr., "Monticello," in Merrill D. Peterson, ed., *Thomas Jefferson: A Reference Biography* (New York, 1986), 447.

[134] Henry N. Ferguson, "The Man Who Saved Monticello," *American History Illustrated,* vol. 14, no. 10 (1980): 23; William Taylor Barry to Susan Barry Taylor, 16 August 1832, William Taylor Barry Papers, University of Virginia Library, Charlottesville, Virginia.

[135] *Atkinson's Saturday Evening Post* (Philadelphia), 19 October 1833, copy in Samuel Sobel, *Intrepid Sailor* (Philadelphia, 1980), 30.

[136] Fitzpatrick and Saphire, *Navy Maverick,* 133ff. A number of other works written afterwards, such as Sobel, *Intrepid Sailor,* rely on this account.

[137] *The Niles Register,* [n.d.] quoted in William Howard Adams, *Jefferson's Monticello* (New York, 1983), 246. Another piece of evidence that the earlier date is accurate is that *Martin's Gazeteer of Virginia,* published in Charlottesville, noted in 1835 the wretched condition of the house while Barclay owned it, and declared that the new owner, Lieutenant Levy, intended to restore the house to its full beauty. Quoted in

Townsend, *Monticello and Its Preservation,* 10. I have found no evidence of any "inheritance" to Levy; his father had died a number of years earlier, and his mother was still alive at this time. Any money he had came from his real estate ventures.

[138] Although Levy paid $2,700 as opposed to the $4,500 Barclay had paid, he received an estate only 40 percent as large. Barclay had gotten 552 acres, Levy only 218. On an acreage cost, Levy paid Barclay about three percent less than Barclay had paid to the Jefferson family.

[139] Bear, "Monticello," 447; Indenture of sale, Barclay to Uriah Levy, 21 May 1836, Uriah Levy MSS, Box 1. The deed describes the property "by reference to a plat made by A. Broadhead in pursuance of an order of survey of the Circuit Superior Court of Law and Chancery for Albemarle County."

[140] Charles Hosmer, *Presence of the Past* (New York, 1965), 153.

[141] Fitzpatrick and Saphire, *Navy Maverick,* 128.

[142] *Id.,* 141.

[143] Theodore Fred Kuper to Saul Viener, 25 April 1976, Stern MSS.

[144] The following section is drawn from several sources, including Charlotte Crystal, "Uriah P. Levy: Savior of Monticello," *Albemarle Archives* [n.d.], 52; Fitzpatrick and Saphire, *Navy Maverick,* 141-42; Adams, *Jefferson's Monticello,* 246-47; and Ferguson, "The Man Who Saved Monticello," 23.

[145] Like many slaveholders, Levy established warm personal relations with a few servants. In 1858 he wrote that he had received news "of the death of my faithful servant Peggy. I shall miss her very much for she is identified with Monticello and was much attached to me as I to her." Levy to George Carr, 17 September 1858, Papers of George Carr, University of Virginia Library, Charlottesville, Virginia.

[146] Rachel Levy's grave would later become the source of much controversy; see below, ch. 6.

[147] William H. Sager to Jacob Rader Marcus, 5 October 1949, Uriah Levy Materials, American Jewish Archives.

[148] Fitzpatrick and Saphire, *Navy Maverick,* 142.

[149] Memoirs of George Blatterman, ca. 1902, University of Virginia Library, Charlottesville, Virginia.

[150] Fitzpatrick and Saphire, *Navy Maverick,* 144.

[151] Uriah Levy to John P. Sampson, 29 December 1839, in Carr MSS. Sampson replied on 10 January 1840, and on 14 January Uriah accepted his offer of the land at $10 per acre.

[152] Levy to Carr, 3 April 1838, *id.*

[153] Levy to Carr, 17 September 1858, *id.*

[154] Levy to Carr, 4 June 1858, *id.*

[155] "Life Story of Jonas Phillips Levy," Lewis Family Papers. For a recounting of his life, see Samuel Reznick, "The Maritime Adventures of a Jewish Sea Captain, Jonas P. Levy, in Nineteenth-Century America," *The American Neptune,* vol. 37, no. 4 (Oct. 1977): 239-252.

[156] There existed some controversy about the marriage, since Virginia Lopez was Uriah's niece and one-third his age; for more on her and on the marriage, see next chapter.

[157] "Reminiscences of Virginia Lopez Levy Rée," *The American Hebrew* (10 April 1925), p. 739. Malcolm Stern has termed these memoirs, written when Mrs. Rée was near 90, as "highly romantic and historically questionable."

[158] *Id.,*743. Mrs. Rée said this prank was done by a cousin, but other sources say Levy himself did it. *Jewish Week,* 20 December 1985.

[159] Noted in James A. Bear, Jr., "Accounts of Monticello, 1780-1878: A Selective Bibliography," 21 *Magazine of Albemarle County History* (1962-1963): 20.

[160] J.S. Buckingham, *The Slave States of America* (2 vols., London, 1842), 2: 401-402.

[161] John P. Walters to F. Walters, 27 October 1851, Jefferson Transcripts.

[162] Benson J. Lossing, "Monticello," *Harper's New Monthly Magazine,* Vol. VII, No. 38 (July 1853): 148-50. Lossing described the capital as plaster, but the one that came down to the Thomas Jefferson Foundation, and which is believed to be the same one, is made of stone.

[163] "A Visit to Monticello," hand-written and initialed by "J.R." and "J.D.T.," 20 May 1856, University of Virginia Library, Acc. 8105; a transcription is available in John Barnwell, "Monticello: 1856," *Journal of the Society of Architectural Historians,* vol. 34 (1975): 280-85. The graveyard, as noted above, did not pass with the sale of Monticello but remains to this day in Jefferson family hands. So many people commented on the poor condition of the grave site that Congress finally appropriated money to have it restored; see below, ch. 4.

[164] Merrill D. Peterson, ed., *Visitors to Monticello* (Charlottesville, 1989), 125,

[165] "Reminiscences of Virginia Rée," 739.

[166] See below, ch. 6.

[167] Adams, *Jefferson's Monticello,* 247.

[168] F.D. Nichols and James A. Bear, Jr., *Guidebook to Monticello* (Charlottesville, 1967), 71.

[169] Levy to David Caddington, 1 December 1842, Monticello materials, Thomas Jefferson Foundation, Charlottesville, Virginia.

[170] For the development of naval rules, see Leland P. Lovette, *Naval Customs: Traditions and Usages* (Annapolis, 1939). Lovette notes that normally a commander could not

order more than twelve lashes without approval of a superior officer, and that a serious crime required a court martial.

[171] Official Transcript, 59.

[172] Copy in Uriah Phillips Levy MSS, Box 1; Harold D. Langley, who has done the most thorough research on reform in the Navy, argues that Levy did not write the articles contained in the pamphlet, even though he took credit for it. *Social Reform in the United States Navy, 1798-1862* (Urbana, 1967), xx.

[173] *Congressional Globe,* 31st Cong., 1st Sess., Vol. XIX, Part 2, 2057-60.

[174] 9 Stat. at Large 513, 515, 28 September 1850.

[175] For naval reform in this context, see Langley, *Social Reform in the Navy,* ch. 7, "The End of Flogging."

[176] "An Act to Promote the Efficiency of the Navy," 10 Stat. at Large 616, 28 Feb. 1855

[177] Transcript of the Proceedings of the Court of Inquiry.

[178] This is not the infamous Benjamin F. "Beast" Butler who was one of the Union's cruelest generals during the Civil War.

[179] *Memorial of Uriah P. Levy, late Captain in the Navy, to the Congress of the United States, complaining of the Action of the Board of Naval Officers ...* (New York, 1855).

[180] "An Act to Amend ...," 11 Stat. at Large 152, 16 Jan. 1857.

[181] This narrative is based on the Transcript of Proceedings; Birmingham, *Grandees,* 248-52; and Kanof, "Uriah Phillips Levy," *passim.*

[182] The testimonials in Levy's behalf are available in Benjamin F. Butler, *Defense of Uriah P. Levy, Before the Board of Inquiry Held at Washington City, November and December 1857* (New York, 1858)

[183] Levy, "Memoirs," 84-85.

[184] Quoted in Birmingham, *Grandees,* 252.

[185] Levy, "Memoirs," 116.

[186] Official Transcript, 60.

[187] James Tertius de Kay, *Chronicles of the Frigate* Macedonian (New York, 1995), 275.

[188] Diary of James Finn, entry of 16 September 1859, copy in Levy Materials, American Jewish Archives.

[189] Uriah Levy to George Carr, 4 June 1858, Carr MSS.

[190] Levy to Carr, 17 September 1858, *id.*

[191] *Id.*

192 Levy to Welles, 15 June 1861, quoted in Fitzpatrick and Saphire, *Navy Maverick,* 243.

193 *The American Hebrew,* 15 May 1925; Kanof, "Uriah Phillips Levy," 60.

194 Last Will and Testament of Uriah Phillips Levy, Probate Court Records, Liber 141 of wills, 254, Surrogate Court of Court of New York, Hall of Records, County Court House, Chambers Street, New York.

195 File on the probate proceedings of Uriah Levy, *id.*

196 In Victorian England the deceased often made bequests to specific family and friends of rings to serve as a memento of the departed; in Uriah's case he left the style of the ring to be chosen by the mourner.

197 Uriah Levy, "Last Will and Testament." In the original there are no paragraphs; I have broken the text so as to make it easier to read.

198 Charles B. Hosmer, Jr., *Presence of the Past: A History of the Preservation Movement in the United States before Williamsburg* (New York, 1965), ch. 2.

199 John S. Patton and Sallie J. Doswell, *Monticello and Its Master* (Charlottesville, 1925), 58-59.

200 "Inventory of Personal Estate of Uriah Phillips Levy," [n.d.], Papers of Uriah Phillips Levy, American Jewish Historical Society, New York, Box 1.

201 Property and Tax Listings, *Id.*

202 *Levy v. Levy,* 40 Barbour (N.Y. Superior Court) 585, 588 (1863).

203 Stephen Birmingham, *The Grandees: America's Sephardic Elite* (New York, 1971), 246.

204 Memoirs of George Blatterman, ca. 1902, University of Virginia Library.

205 Jonas P. Levy to Robertson & Southall, 10 February 1868, Jonas Phillips Levy Papers, American Jewish Historical Society, New York.

206 William J. Robertson to Jonas Levy, 13 February 1868, *id.* As Robertson explained, the Code of Virginia (ch. 109, §§ 1, 2) did prohibit such marriages, but it made them voidable, not void *ab initio,* that is, a legal action would have to be undertaken to nullify the marriage. Without such action the marriage remained valid. In addition, Uriah had married his wife in New York, where such a bar did not exist. Section 2 of the law prohibited people from going to another state to evade the ban and then returning to live in Virginia. Someone had apparently filed a complaint and the grand jury had looked into the marriage under this provision. The panel had decided that the Levys were not really residents of Virginia but of New York, where they lived the majority of the year, and so declined to bring an indictment.

207 "Reminiscences of Virginia Lopez Levy Rée," *The American Hebrew* (10 April 1925), 739.

208 Birmingham, *The Grandees,* 254; James Tertius de Kay, *Chronicles of the Frigate Macedonian* (New York, 1995), 276.

[209] Birmingham, *The Grandees*, 255.

[210] Had there been heirs, that is, if she and Uriah had had children, then even if she broke the will, the dower would have remained a life interest, eventually going to the children.

[211] "Life Story of Jonas Phillips Levy," Lewis Family Papers; Samuel Reznick, "The Maritime Adventures of a Jewish Sea Captain, Jonas P. Levy, in Nineteenth-Century America," *The American Neptune*, vol. 37, no. 4 (Oct. 1977): 239-252. It is difficult to tell just how accurate the memoirs are, since they are riddled with contradictions. For example, Levy claims that he and his "family" escaped, but he did not marry until November 1848, and his first child was not born until December 1849.

[212] Jonas Phillips Levy, Petition to Congress, 26 January 1852; Memorandum of Comptroller's Office, 31 March 1855; Jonas Levy, Memorial to Congress, January 1882, all in Jonas Phillips Levy MSS. In response to an 1873 petition, the Senate Committee on Foreign Relations recommended rejection; Senate Report No. 432, 43rd Cong., 1st Sess., 11 June 1874.

[213] George E. Downey, Comptroller, to Jefferson Monroe Levy, 14 December 1914; Henry M. Goldfogle to Levy, 23 December 1920; H.R. 15671, "A Bill for the Relief of the Heirs of Captain Jonas P. Levy," 66th Cong., 3rd Sess., introduced 11 January 1921; all in the Papers of Jefferson Monroe Levy, American Jewish Historical Society, New York.

[214] This section is based on Samuel Rezneck, "The Strange Role of a Jewish Sea Captain in the Confederate South," *American Jewish History* 68 (September 1977): 64-73.

[215] The only source for this is Townsend, *Monticello and Its Preservation since Jefferson's Death*, which, as noted earlier, may have been written by Jonas's son, Jefferson Levy.

[216] Jonas P. Levy to George Carr, 7 June 1861, George Carr Papers, University of Virginia Library, Charlottesville, Virginia.

[217] Rezneck, "Strange Role," 69.

[218] Levy to Hill, 14 April 1862, cited in *id.*

[219] Levy to Carr, 5 July 1862, Carr MSS.

[220] Alexander Rives to Levy, 23 October 1864, Jonas Levy MSS.

[221] Rezneck, "Strange Role," 70.

[222] *Id.*, 71-72.

[223] Fred Kuper believed that the Confederacy intended to convert Monticello into a residence for its president, but the conduct of the war soaked up whatever resources the government might have applied to this task. Kuper to Saul Viener, 10 April 1976, Malcolm Stern Papers, American Jewish Archives, Cincinnati, Ohio.

224 *Richmond Daily Examiner,*1 November 1863; Adams, *Jefferson's Monticello,* 256. One story has it that Ficklin immediately signed over ownership of the estate to the Commonwealth of Virginia.

225 Leonard Carmichael and J.C. Long, *James Smithson and the Smithsonian Story* (New York, 1965), 14. Congress proved equally hesitant in dealing with another gift a century later. When Oliver Wendell Holmes, Jr., died in 1935 he left his estate to the government, and although Congress accepted, did not know what to do with it. Nearly two decades passed before Congress established the Oliver Wendell Holmes Devise to underwrite a comprehensive, multi-volume history of the Supreme Court.

226 *Congressional Globe,*37ᵗʰ Cong., 3ʳᵈ Sess., 3 March 1863, Vol. XLI, Part 2, 1495.

227 Resolution No. 38, 12 Stats. at Large 830-31, 3 March 1863.

228 Asahel Levy to T.J. Coffey, 18 February 1864, Record Group 60, Department of Justice, Records of the Attorney-General's Office, Letters Received 1809-1870, National Archives, Washington, D.C.

229 E. Delafield Smith to Edward Bates, 16 March 1864, *id.*

230 Bates to Hannibal Hamlin, 29 March 1864, *id.*

231 See below, ch. 5.

232 37 Hen. VIII, c.4.

233 Gareth H. Jones, *History of the Law of Charity, 1532-1827* (London, 1969), 13.

234 9 Geo. II, c.36.

235 Jones, *History of the Law of Charity,* 109.

236 Robert Ludlow Fowler, *The Law of Charitable Uses, Trusts, and Donations in New York* (New York, 1896), 38.

237 3 Ch.Cas. 1 (1682). The notion of the rule had, however, been gestating for several decades, and various unrefined notions coalesced in this case into an identifiable legal doctrine.

238 Lawrence M. Friedman, *A History of American Law* (New York, 1973), ch. v.

239 There were some, of course, such as Kings (later Columbia) College, chartered in 1754, the Society for the Hospital of the City of New York (1775), and some schools and colleges.

240 The attack by New York courts on charitable bequests is detailed in Stanley Katz, Barry Sullivan and C. Paul Beach, "Legal Change and Legal Autonomy: Charitable Trusts in New York, 1777-1893," 3 *Law and History Review* 51, 59-72 (1985).

241 *Williams v. Williams,* 8 N.Y. 525 (1853).

242 4 Wheat. 1 (1819).

243 *Vidal v. Girard's Executors*, 2 How. 127 (1844).

244 Friedman, *History of American Law*, 166-78.

245 1 N.Y. Rev. Stat. 727 (1829)

246 Act of 13 April 1860, N.Y. Laws of 1860, ch. 350.

247 Carl Zollman, *American Law of Charities* (Milwaukee, 1924), 31-32.

248 *Levy v. Levy*, 40 Barbour 585, 587 (N.Y., 1863). One bit of evidence suggesting collusion is the fact that Asahel's father, Isaac, was one of the family members contesting the will; since this would raise a conflict of interest, Asahel would normally have been expected to resign from the case and let the other executors carry the litigation. He did not resign.

249 Uriah had two other siblings, his brothers Louis and Benjamin, who were dead at this point and had no surviving family.

250 40 Barbour at 592. In New York then as now, the Supreme Court is the lowest court in the state, while the Court of Appeals is the highest.

251 *Id.*

252 *Id.* at 596.

253 *Id.* at 599.

254 *Id.* at 604.

255 Bradford cited *Philadelphia Baptist Association v. Hart's Executors*, 4 Wheat. 1 (1819), and *Inglis v. Trustees Sailors' Snug Harbor*, 3 Peters 99 (1830). Prior to the reformation of the Supreme Court's docket in 1825, the tribunal served as court of last resort in all types of cases, including matters that traditionally fell within the purview of state law and could by no means be considered constitutional.

256 40 Barbour at 611, 612.

257 *Id.* at 619.

258 *Id.* at 620.

259 *Id.* at 622, 623.

260 *Id.* at 625.

261 *Id.* at 616. This rule, first enunciated here, would be confirmed by the New York Court of Appeals in its review of this case, and reaffirmed in *In re will of Charles Fox*, 52 N.Y. 530 (1873), *In re will of Merriam*, 136 N.Y. 58 (1892), and also by the Supreme Court in *United States v. Fox*, 94 U.S. 315 (1876).

262 Harold M. Hyman and William M. Wiecek, *Equal Justice under Law: Constitutional Development, 1835-1875* (New York, 1982), 403-404.

[263] 40 Barbour at 617, italics in the original.

[264] *Levy et al. v. Levy et al.*, 33 N.Y. 97, 101 (1865).

[265] *Id.* at 103.

[266] *Id.* at 107.

[267] *Id.* at 117.

[268] *Id.* at 123-24.

[269] *Id.* at 124-34.

[270] *Id.* at 134-36.

[271] *Id.* at 136-37.

[272] *Id.* at 137-38.

[273] *Id.* at 138.

[274] Fowler, *Law of Charitable Uses, passim.*

[275] *Tilden v. Greene,* 130 N.Y. 29 (1891).

[276] Asahel Levy to George Carr, 31 January and 17 May 1866, Carr MSS.

[277] "In the matter of the final accounting of Virginia Rée, administratrix ...," 28 August 1869, Surrogate Court Records.

[278] Jonas Levy to Secretary of the Treasury, 29 July 1867, Jonas Levy MSS.

[279] William Robertson to Jonas Levy, 6 May 1868, *id.*

[280] Robertson & Southall to Jonas Levy, 4 February 1868, *id.*

[281] Levy to Robertson & Southall, 10 February 1868, *id.* Asahel Levy concurred in his uncle's choice of lawyers, and wrote separately to Robertson to urge him to make sure that the case also resolved any questions of title to the surrounding land. Asahel Levy to Robertson, 18 February 1868, *id.*

[282] Robertson to Levy, 18 March 1868, *id.*

[283] Levy to Robertson, 28 September 1868, and Robertson to Levy, 21 December 1868, *id.*; see also Gouverneur Tillotson to George Carr, 25 June 1869, Carr MSS. Tillotson represented "a claim against Mrs. Rée ... which she has proposed to pay by an assignment of her interests in the Commodore's Virginia property."

[284] Decision of the Circuit Court of the City of Richmond in the case of Jonas P. Levy & Fanny his wife and Eliza Herricks against Mary Jane Hastings *et al.*, 30 November 1868, copy in Carr MSS.

[285] Notes by George Carr [n.d., probably 1869], *id.*

286 Robertson to Levy, 18 March 1869, Jonas Levy MSS.

287 Levy to Carr, 18 and 28 December 1868, Carr MSS

288 George Carr to Jonas Levy, 23 December 1868, *id.*

289 Robertson to Levy, 21 December 1868, Jonas Levy MSS; Carr to Levy, 23 December 1868, Carr MSS.

290 Carr to Levy, 22 January 1869, Jonas Levy MSS.

291 Edwin Blair Smith to Carr, 8 March 1869; other expressions of interest came from A.J. Ford on 20 February 1869, James G. Barrish, 22 April 1869; and Randolph Caldwell on 2 April 1869, all in Carr MSS.

292 Carr to Levy, 22 March 1869, Jonas Levy MSS.

293 Robertson to Levy, 9 April 1869, *id.* The provision is found in Code of Virginia, ch. 80, § 2 (1860).

294 Robertson to Levy, 19 April 1869, *id.*

295 Edward G. Corcoran to Asahel Levy, 16 July 1869, *id.*

296 Robertson to Levy, 2 August 1869, 11 and 14 October 1869, *id.*

297 Robertson to Levy, 28 May 1870 and 6 June 1870; James Alfred Jones to Levy, 7 Nov. 1870, , *id.*

298 *Commonwealth v. Levy*, 23 Gratton (64 Virginia) 21 (1873); only one judge, Waller R. Staples, dissented from this portion of the opinion, arguing that the action of the United States did not bind Virginia.

299 *Id.* at 37, 38.

300 Carr to Levy, 4 April 1873, Jonas Levy MSS.

301 Levy to Carr, and Levy to Robertson, both 7 April 1873, *id.*

302 Carr to Levy, 7 May 1873, *id.*

303 Robertson to Levy, 7 and 11 June 1873, 25 November 1873, 15 December 1873; Carr to Levy, 21 November 1875, all in *id.*

304 See next chapter.

305 Apparently Joseph Levy had left his interest in Monticello to someone Jonas either did not care for or who would not work with him, and Jonas contemplated a suit to break Joseph's will. Robertson, however, talked him out of it. The contest would be "expensive and troublesome," and would have to be pursued as a separate litigation from the Monticello suit. Robertson to Levy, two letters, 2 March 1874, Jonas Levy MSS.

306 Levy to Justin Morrill, 15 July 1876; Memorial from Jonas P. Levy to Congress [n.d. 1876], *id.*

[307] Jefferson M. Levy to George Carr, 15 June 1877, and Jonas P. Levy to Carr, 20 September 1877, Carr MSS.

[308] Jefferson Levy to Carr, 15 April and 6 May 1878, *id.*

[309] Levy to Carr, 5 June 1878, *id.*

[310] Levy to Carr, 16 December 1878, *id.*

[311] Unsigned chronology, Monticello Levy files (Thomas Jefferson Foundation).

[312] Public notice of sale, n.d.; certificate of sale, 20 March 1879, *id.*

[313] Final decree, 7 July 1881, *id.*

[314] George Alfred Townsend, *Monticello and Its Preservation Since Jefferson's Death, 1826-1902* (Washington, 1902), 26.

[315] Diary of Sarah Strickler, 1 August 1864, Fife Papers, University of Virginia Library, Charlottesville.

[316] Theodore K. Davis, *Harper's Weekly,* 2 June 1866.

[317] Thomas L. Rhodes, *The Story of Monticello* (Washington, 1928), 91-92; Paul Wilstach, *Jefferson and Monticello* (Garden City, 1925), 217-18; Frank R. Stockton, "The Later Years of Monticello," *Century Magazine,* vol. 34, no. 5 (September 1887): 657.

[318] *Journal of Commerce* (New York), 8 March 1869, enclosed with Jonas Levy to George Carr, 9 March 1869, George Carr Papers, University of Virginia Library.

[319] Carr to Levy, 22 March 1869, Jonas Phillips Levy Papers, American Jewish Historical Society, New York.

[320] Levy to Carr, 7 April 1873. and Carr to Levy, 28 April 1873, *id.*

[321] Carr to Levy, [June] 1873, *id.*

[322] Robertson to Levy, 21 February 1874, *id.*

[323] Rental agreements between Joel Wheeler and George Carr, as Commissioner, various dates from 1873 to 1878, Carr MSS.

[324] Jefferson Levy to Carr, 15 April 1878, *id.*

[325] Levy to Carr, 6 May 1878, *id.* The letter is transcribed exactly as written, with only a minimal of punctuation and capitalization. Indecipherable words are indicated as [*].

[326] Levy to Carr, 5 June 1878, *id.*

[327] Levy to Carr, 27 June 1878, *id.*

[328] Levy to Carr, 16 December 1878, *id.*

[329] Basic biographical information can be found in the obituary that appeared in *The New York Times,* 7 March 1924, and the entry in Lyon Gardiner Tyler, *Encyclopedia of Virginia Biography* (5 vols., New York, 1915), 5: 1038.

[330] In his entry in the *Biographical Dictionary of the American Congress, 1774-1996* (Washington, 1997), 1389, Levy claimed to have graduated from NYU Law School, but there is no other evidence for this assertion. In the same entry he also wrote that he inherited Monticello from his uncle.

[331] There seems to have been close ties between Potter and the Levy family. Jefferson's sister Isabella and her husband Markus named their only son Clarkson Potter Ryttenberg.

[332] *New York Herald,* 27 July 1902; *New York Tribune,* 1 February 1903. Many of the newspaper articles referred to can be found in the scrapbooks Levy kept. He, like many other prominent men of the time, subscribed to a clippings service. The scrapbooks are in the Jefferson Monroe Levy Papers, American Jewish Historical Society, New York.

[333] Memoirs of Frances Levy, typescript (1960), Lewis Family Papers.

[334] Annabelle Prager, "Extract of Interview with Frederick Rhodes," June 1976, Monticello Papers, Thomas Jefferson Foundation, Charlottesville, Virginia.

[335] *New York Times,* 4 September 1912. Ms. Wilson had been a defender of his ownership of Monticello against Maud Littleton; see next chapter.

[336] He chose not to run for re-election in 1900 and 1914. Apparently he considered running for Congress as early as 1893, but could not garner enough party support. Levy to Basil Brown Gordon, 23 August 1893, Basil Brown Gordon Papers, Virginia Historical Society, Richmond, Virginia.

[337] *New York Press,* 1 March 1916.

[338] Jefferson M. Levy, *Elector's Handbook, or Digest of the Election Laws of the State of New York, Applicable to the City of New York* (New York, 1895).

[339] Bureau of Municipal Research, *Memorandum of Matters Relating to New York City's Debt…* (New York, 1908); Bureau of Municipal Research, *New York City's Debt* (New York, 1909). Such bureaus were commonly the weapons of good government reformers in most American cities.

[340] Remarks in the House of Representatives, 4 March 1915, *Congressional Record,* 63rd Cong., 3rd Sess., Vol. 52, Part 6, 647-49.

[341] For the evolution of the system from private to public, see H. Parker Willis, *The Federal Reserve System* (New York, 1923).

[342] See, for example, *New York Times,* 29 March and 10 April 1916.

[343] Naomi W. Cohen, *Not Free to Desist* (Philadelphia, 1972), 3-5; the papers of the National Relief Committee are in the Jefferson Levy Papers at the American Jewish Historical Society.

[344] Speech of M. Jefferson M. Levy, *Réception de la Statue de Thomas Jefferson ... par Hon. Jefferson M. Lévy, Citoyen Américain* (Angers, 1905), 10.

[345] Theodore Fred Kuper to Saul Viener, 10 April 1976, Malcolm Stern Papers, American Jewish Archives, Cincinnati; Wilstach, *Jefferson and Monticello*, 219.

[346] *Congressional Record*, 45th Cong., 2nd Sess. (13 April 1878), p. 2494. Hardenbergh had visited Monticello to investigate the condition of Jefferson's grave, discussed below.

[347] Frank R. Stockton, "The Later Years of Monticello," *The Century Magazine*, 34 (September 1887), 657.

[348] Trist to Septimia Meikleham, 4 August 18—, Meikleham Family Papers, University of Virginia Library.

[349] Mortgage executed on Monticello, 30 December 1911, filed in Albemarle County Court House 11 March 1912, describing parcels and dates of purchase, Shakelford Family Papers, University of Virginia Library.

[350] Deed of trust conveying land, 9 March 1905, Jefferson M. Levy Legal Papers in Duke Family Papers, University of Virginia Library.

[351] Jefferson Levy to Mrs. William C. Story, 7 December 1916, House Committee on Public Buildings and Grounds, *Purchase of Monticello, Hearings ... on H.J. Resolution 269*, 64th Cong., 1st Sess. (Washington, 1917), 17.

[352] Testimony, 15 December 1916, *id.*, 28.

[353] Brooklyn (N.Y.) *Times*, 16 October 1914.

[354] *Purchase of Monticello*, 27. Cable and Prager say that the firm declined his invitation and told him that any addition would ruin Jefferson's design. "The Levys of Monticello," 36. McKim, Mead & White had no similar compunctions when the University of Virginia invited the firm to remodel Jefferson's Rotunda, and completely altered the building's interior. In the 1970s the University restored the Rotunda to the original Jeffersonian design.

[355] Stockton, "Later Years of Monticello," 657. The same charges were not made against Uriah because furniture styles had not changed that much when he took over the house from what they had been in Jefferson's time.

[356] See Norman Tyler, *Historic Preservation: An Introduction to Its History, Principles, and Practices* (New York, 2000), *passim*.

[357] Mary Cable and Annabelle Prager, "The Levys of Monticello," *American Heritage*, vol. 29, no. 2 (1978), 35-36; Malcolm Stern, "Memorandum: Ownership by JML," Stern MSS

[358] Thomas L. Rhodes, *The Story of Monticello* (Washington, 1928), 91.

[359] Henry N. Ferguson, "The Man Who Saved Monticello," *American History Illustrated*, vol. 14, no. 10 (February 1980), 25; the claim is repeated in Samuel Sobel, *Intrepid Sailor* (Philadelphia, 1980), 52.

[360] Unsigned, undated memorandum, Monticello Papers, Thomas Jefferson Foundation, Charlottesville, VA.

[361] "Exhibit A," 1923, *id.* George Blatterman exploded when he heard that Jefferson Levy had offered some of Jefferson's furniture to the 1900 World's Fair in St. Louis, saying he knew as a fact that Levy did not own a stick of Jefferson's furniture. Clearly Blatterman erred. Blatterman Memoirs, University of Virginia Library.

[362] Anna Barringer, "Pleasant It Is," *The Magazine of Albemarle County History* (vol. 27 or 28), 53; William Howard Adams, *Jefferson's Monticello* (New York, 1983), 258.

[363] Annabelle F. Prager, "Extracts of Interview with Frederick Rhodes," June 1976, Monticello MSS.

[364] Jefferson was very proud of his uncle, and took slight if he thought Uriah's honor had been impugned. When a writer to the *Hebrew Standard* questioned Uriah's role in abolishing flogging and his claim to be called "Commodore," Jefferson immediately fired off several letters to the paper defending his uncle. Levy to Editor of *Hebrew Standard,* 31 January and 20 February 1911, Jefferson Levy MSS.

[365] Neither the model of the *Vandalia* nor the portraits of Uriah and Jefferson were transferred to the Memorial Foundation in 1923; an inquiry of the Lewis family disclosed that its members did not know of the disposition of these items.

[366] Cable and Prager, "The Levys of Monticello," 36; Barringer, "How Pleasant It Is," 56.

[367] Maud Howard Peterson, "The Home of Jefferson," *Munsey's Magazine,* 20 (1899), 618; similar and even more striking pictures contrasting the Victorian furniture during Levy's time and the restoration as it looks today can be found in Cable and Prager, "The Levys of Monticello."

[368] In the 1920s the Thomas Jefferson Memorial Foundation began selling off items that it could not authenticate as coming from the Jeffersonian era. A woman in Nashville purchased the lions and gave them to the owner of the Belle Meade plantation (a local historic house); the lions were later donated to the Cheekwood Museum and Gardens in Nashville, Tennessee, where they stand today. Chad Wollerton to Susan Stein, e-mail of 21 September 2000, forwarded to author by Ms. Stein on 22 September.

[369] Prager, "Interview with Frederick Rhodes;" Wilstach, *Jefferson and Monticello,* 219.

[370] F. Berger Moran (née Jeannie Blackburn), "In Memoriam, Fanny Mitchell Levy," in *Miss Washington of Virginia: A Semi-Centennial Love Story* (Philadelphia, 1893), 9.

[371] Anna Barringer, "Pleasant It Is," refers to her as "Mrs. von Mayhoff." Although her husband Charles had been born in Germany, it is doubtful that he was entitled to use this form of name usually reserved for nobility. In a file in the Jefferson Levy MSS there are some papers in which she is addressed as "Mrs. Mayhoff" and in others as "Mrs. von Mayhoff."

[372] There were a number of year-round employees under Rhodes's direction, including two handyman brothers, Willis and James Henderson; Thomas Coleman, the

oxteam driver, and his wife Elizam the gatekeeper (James Henderson married the Colemans' daughter); and Dora Richter, a German cook. Servants who came down from New York included Willie McGushin, a valet; his brother Jack, a butler; a Miss Cameron, who was Monroe Mayhoff's governess; and the laundress, Maria McManus, she of "beautiful Irish eyes and black hair," whom Al Smith, a Charlottesville plumber, avidly courted. Prager, "Interview with Frederick Rhodes."

[373] Frances Wolff Levy, "The Approach to Monticello," *Jacobi School Magazine* (March 1908), Lewis Family Papers.

[374] "Gran's Yesterdays," written in 1960 by a much older Fanny, now Frances Lewis, for her children and grandchildren, Lewis Family Papers.

[375] Adams, *Jefferson's Monticello*, 259; see also the anti-Semitic rantings of George Blatterman, Blatterman Memoirs.

[376] Townsend, *Monticello and Its Preservation*, 13; Marc Leepson, "The Levys of Monticello," *Preservation*, 50 (March/April 1998), 49.

[377] Moran, *Miss Washington of Virginia*, 10.

[378] Barringer, "Pleasant It Is," 58.

[379] Rental agreement between Jefferson Levy and E. Reinhold Rogers, 3 September 1907, Jefferson M. Levy Legal Papers.

[380] Two rental agreements between Levy and Burnley, Smith & Co. 23 October 1903, *id.*

[381] Rental agreement between Levy and J.A. Burgess, 5 November 1903, *id.*

[382] Rental agreement between Levy and Thomas W. Wiseman, 3 March 1910, *id.*

[383] Rental agreement between Levy and G.R.B. Michie, 1 October 1896, *id.*

[384] Levy to R.T.W. Duke, Jr., 12 June 1916, *id.*

[385] Theodore Fred Kuper, comments on 1959 article by Malcolm Stern, Stern MSS.

[386] See, for example, R.T.W. Duke, Jr., to S.V. Southall, 20 June 1900, and Isabella Leitch to Levy, 8 February 1899, Levy Legal Papers.

[387] Townsend, *Restoration of Monticello*, 39. According to Townsend, Levy said that Blaine "ought to have been President. He was the ablest of the Republicans."

[388] Jefferson Club Association of St. Louis, *The Pilgrimage to Monticello ... October 10 to 14, 1901* (St. Louis, 1902).

[389] Undated letter of Frances Wolff Levy, Lewis Family Papers.

[390] Frances Levy, "Gran's Yesterdays," *id.*

[391] Frances Wolf to Lillian Levy, 31 May 1902, *id.*

[392] "Gran's Yesterdays;" Frances Levy to Lillian Levy, 6 June 1902, *id.*

[393] Fanny Mitchell Levy to Louis Napoleon Levy, 4 July 1881, *id.*

[394] Fanny Mitchell Levy to Marcus Ryttenberg, 24 July 1881, *id.*

[395] *New York Times,* 10 December 1912.

[396] Merrill D. Peterson, *The Jeffersonian Image in the American Mind* (New York, 1960), 237.

[397] *Congressional Record,* 45th Cong., 2nd Sess.,(13 April 1878), 2493-94.

[398] Thomas L. Rhodes, *The Story of Monticello* (Washington, 1928), 87-88.

[399] Paul Wilstach, *Jefferson and Monticello* (Garden City, 1925), 220; Peterson, *Jeffersonian Image,* 238. The remnants of the original obelisk now sit on the campus of the University of Missouri.

[400] *Charlottesville Daily Progress,* 19 July 1904, 10 July 1909.

[401] Maud Howard Peterson, "The Home of Jefferson," *Munsey's Magazine,* 20 (1899), 618; the story of the entrance fee going to charity is also reported in Mary Cable and Annabelle Prager, "The Levys of Monticello," *American Heritage,* Vol. 29, no. 2 (1978), 36.

[402] William Howard Adams, *Jefferson's Monticello* (New York, 1983), 259; Peterson, *Jeffersonian Image,* 381.

[403] Charlotte Crystal, "Uriah P. Levy: Savior of Monticello," *Albemarle Archives* [n.d.], 56.

[404] Erroll Dunbar, letter to the editor, *New York Herald,* 17 November 1912.

[405] Annie Nathan Meyer, letter to the editor, *New York Times,* 22 November 1912.

[406] *Brooklyn* (N.Y.) *Times,* 16 October 1914.

[407] Amos J. Cummings, "A National Humiliation," *New York Sun,* 24 August 1902.

[408] Townsend, *Monticello and Its Preservation,* 3-4.

[409] Bryan to Levy, Richmond *Dispatch,* 9 April 1897, and Levy's response, 15 April 1897, *id.*

[410] Quoted in Peterson, *Jeffersonian Image,* 238.

[411] *Congressional Record,* 45th Cong., 2nd Sess. (13 April 1878), 2494.

[412] Dumas Malone, *Jefferson the Virginian* (Boston, 1948), vol. 1 of *Jefferson and His Time,* 280-85.

[413] See Dumas Malone, *The Sage of Monticello* (Boston, 1981), vol. 6 of *Jefferson and His Time,* chs.16-19. For explications of Jefferson's educational views, see James B. Conant, *Thomas Jefferson and the Development of American Public Education* (Berkeley, 1962).

[414] The Association sponsored Albert Ellery Burgh, ed., *The Writings of Thomas Jefferson* (20 vols., Washington, 1907); the other edition was edited by Paul Leicester Ford, *The Works of Thomas Jefferson* (12 vols., New York, 1905).

[415] Quoted in Patricia West, *Domesticating History: The Political Origins of America's House Museums* (Washington, 1999), 103. This book, as well as Charles B. Hosmer, Jr., *Presence of the Past: A History of the Preservation Movement in the United States before Williamsburg* (New York, 1965), are invaluable in putting the Monticello debate into a larger context of both politics and preservation.

[416] *The Pilgrimage to Monticello by the Jefferson Club of St. Louis* (St. Louis, 1902), 7.

[417] Michael Kammen, *A Machine That would Go of Itself: The Constitution in American Culture* (New York, 1986).

[418] For the purchase of Mount Vernon, see Hosmer, *Presence of the Past*, ch. 2.

[419] John Higham, *Strangers in the Land: Pattens of American Nativism, 1860-1925* (New Brunswick, 1955), 26-27.

[420] Stephen Steinberg, "How Jewish Quotas Began," *Commentary*, 52 (September 1971): 71; Gerald Sorin, *A Time for Building: The Third Migration, 1880-1920* (Baltimore, 1992), *passim*.

[421] Norman Tyler, *Historic Preservation: An Introduction to Its History, Principles, and Practice* (New York, 2000), 35-36.

[422] Charlottesville *Daily Progress*, 12 April 1909.

[423] Maud Littleton, *"One Wish"* (Privately printed, 1911).

[424] *New York Times*, 19 March 1913.

[425] West, *Domesticating History*, 102.

[426] *United States v. Gettysburg Electric Railway Company*, 160 U.S. 668, 681 (1896).

[427] Jefferson Levy to Martin Littleton, 3 February 1912, Jefferson Levy Papers, American Jewish Historical Society, New York.

[428] *New York Times*, 4 April 1912.

[429] Senate Concurrent Resolution 92, in, U.S. Congress, 62nd Cong., 2nd Sess., Senate Committee on the Library, *Public Ownership of Monticello, Hearings ...*, 9 July 1912 (Washington, 1912), 3.

[430] *Id.*, 4-52.

[431] *Id.*, 7.

[432] *Id.*, 31, 48.

[433] *Id.*, 50.

[434] Beck to Mrs. Littleton [n.d.], *id.*, 50-52.

[435] U.S Congress, 62nd Cong., 2nd Sess., *Public Ownership of Monticello. Hearings before the House Committee on Rules ...*, July 24, 1912 (Washington, 1912), 36.

[436] *Id.,* 37.

[437] *Id.,* XXX.

[438] Statement [n.d.] released by Levy, Jefferson Levy MSS.

[439] *New York Times,* 8 August 1912.

[440] *Washington Post,* 11 August 1912.

[441] Hosmer, *Presence of the Past,* 168.

[442] Appleton to Littleton, 28 October 1912, quoted in West, *Domesticating History,* 101.

[443] Appleton to Littleton, 4 November 1912, quoted in Hosmer, *Presence of the Past,* 167.

[444] Statement [n.d., November 1912], Jefferson Levy MSS.

[445] "Who Shall Have Monticello?" *Harper's Weekly,* XX (27 July 1912), 20. The journal then went on to reprint the Lossing article of 1853, although to what purpose it is unclear, since Lossing had for the most part been favorably impressed with Uriah Levy's care.

[446] *Washington Herald,* 9 December 1912, and other papers.

[447] Randolph to Levy, provided by Levy to papers, *New York Times,* 8 December 1912.

[448] See, for example, letters to the editor in the *New York Herald,* 17 November 1912, and New York *Evening Sun,* 26 November 1912.

[449] Resolution passed by Albemarle Chapter of DAR, 13 November 1912, Jefferson Levy MSS. Levy used the statement to ask other women's groups to pass similar resolutions; *Brooklyn Daily Eagle,* 19 November 1912. At least one group did, the Louisa Adams Chapter of the DAR in Washington passed a resolution praising Levy on 10 December 1912; Grace Porter Hopkins to Jefferson Levy, 11 December 1912, Levy MSS.

[450] *Richmond Journal,* 6 December 1912.

[451] *Brooklyn Daily Eagle,* 19 November 1912.

[452] "Patriot" to editor, *New York Herald,* 16 November 1912; a response on 26 November confirmed the blatant commercialism of Mount Vernon.

[453] *Congressional Record,* 62nd Cong., 3rd Sess., 9 December 1912, 347.

[454] *Id.,* 347, 348.

[455] *Congressional Record,* 348, 349.

[456] James M. Lindgren, *Preserving the Old Dominion: Historical Preservation and Virginia Traditionalism* (Charlottesville, 1993), 212-13.

[457] *Congressional Record,* 349.

[458] *New York Times,* 10 December 1912. The same paper on 12 December identified the potential donor as Thomas Fortune Ryan, and said that Ryan would be willing to pay up to $750,000 for Monticello.

[459] Jefferson Levy to William Hodges Mann, 11 December 1912, *New York Times,* 12 December 1912.

[460] Hosmer, *Presence of the Past,* 170-71; Patricia West disagrees with this analysis, and thinks Hosmer is too harsh on Mrs. Littleton, *Domesticating History,* 101-102.

[461] *New York Herald,* 11 November 1912.

[462] Mortgages executed on 30 December 1911, and filed in Albemarle County Court House on 11 March 1912, Shakelford Papers, University of Virginia Library.

[463] *New York American,* 28 December 1912; Statement of Mrs. Littleton to newspaper editors and members of Congress, [n.d., probably late December 1912], *id.*

[464] For historic preservation as a political statement, see Lindgren, *Preserving the Old Dominion, passim.*

[465] Maud Littleton to Downing Smith, 31 December 1912, Monticello Papers, Thomas Jefferson Foundation.

[466] *New York Times,* 19 March 1913.

[467] Levy, address to Empire State Society, Sons of the American Revolution, Waldorf-Astoria Hotel, 15 April 1913, Levy MSS.

[468] *New York Times,* 17 and 26 February 1914.

[469] Dorothea Dix, "Monticello—Shrine or Bachelor's Hall?" *Good Housekeeping* 58 (April 1914), 538-39.

[470] See chapter 2.

[471] Dix, "Monticello," 541.

[472] Fairfax Harrison to Frederic A. Delano, 13 July 1914, Fairfax Harrison Papers, Virginia Historical Society, Richmond, Virginia.

[473] *New York Herald,* 18 March 1914; *Atlanta Constitution,* 20 March 1914. See also U.S. House Committee on Rules, 63rd Cong., 2nd Sess., *Hearings on Purchase of Monticello ...* (Washington, 1914).

[474] Bryan to Levy, 23 September 1914, in Committee on Rules, U.S. House of Representatives, 63rd Cong., 2nd Sess., *Purchase of Monticello ... Hearings* (Washington, 1915), 7-8.

[475] *New York American,* 6 October 1914.

[476] *New York World,* 6 October 1914.

[477] *New York Evening Telegram,* 15 October 1914.

[478] *Saginaw (Mich.) Courier-Herald,* 25 October 1914.

[479] *Louisville Post,* 24 October 1914.

[480] *Boston Transcript,* 6 October 1914; *Christian Science Monitor,* 9 October 1914; *New York Evening Telegram,* 15 October 1914; *Birmingham (Ala.) Age,* 8 October 1914.

[481] Hosmer, *Presence of the Past,* 174.

[482] Committee on Rules, U.S. House of Representatives, 63rd Cong., 2nd Sess., *Purchase of Monticello ... Hearings* (Washington, 1915), 7.

[483] *Id.,* 10.

[484] Woodrow Wilson to Oscar W. Underwood, 16 January 1915, in Arthur S. Link *et al.,* eds., *Papers of Woodrow Wilson* (69 vols., Princeton, 1966-1992), 32: 82. Underwood had responded that he fully supported the measure.

[485] House Committee on Public Buildings and Grounds, 64th Cong., 1st Sess., *Purchase of Monticello. Hearings ...* (Washington, 1916); Woodrow Wilson to Daisy Allen Story (president–general of the DAR), 27 July 1916, *Wilson Papers,* 37: 482; Washington *Post,* 8 December 1916.

[486] Hosmer, *Presence of the Past,* 176; Levy to Mrs. Story, 7 December 1916, in *Purchase of Monticello,* 15 December 1916, 17-18.

[487] Undated note, Monticello Files, Thomas Jefferson Foundation.

[488] Subcommittee of the Committee on Public Buildings and Grounds, U.S. Senate, 64th Cong., 2nd Sess., *Purchase of Monticello. Hearings ...* (Washington, 1917).

[489] *Charlottesville Daily Progress,* 7 January 1917; *New York Herald,* 29 January 1917; *Roanoke Times,* 30 January 1917.

[490] Wilson to Albert Sidney Burleson, 9 February 1917, *Wilson Papers,* 41: 179-80; Wilson to Claude Swanson, 15 February 1917, *id.,* 234.

[491] Wilson to Mrs. Story, 2 March 1917, *id.,* 310-11.

[492] Hosmer, *Presence of the Past,* 179; *Washington Post,* 29 July 1921.

[493] H.J. Res 117, 67th Cong., 1st Sess., 12 May 1921.

[494] H.J. Res. 121, 67th Cong., 1st Sess., 16 May 1921.

[495] *New York Times,* 29 June 1920, 3 November 1922; Theodore Kuper believes that Levy, when he could not get a private buyer for Monticello, played an active hand in creating this organization. Kuper, Comments on Stern article, Stern MSS.

[496] Wilson to M.M. Andrews, 6 April 1923, and to A.S. Hotchkiss, 9 November 1923, in *Wilson Papers,* 68: 320-21, 464-65; West, *Domesticating History,* 107.

497 Editorials in Richmond *Times-Dispatch* and *News-Leader*, both on 10 October 1922.

498 The following section relies primarily on Hosmer, *Presence of the Past*, 180-84, who in turn relied heavily on his interviews with Fred Kuper; I have also used memoranda prepared by Kuper recalling his dealings with Levy.

499 *New York Times*, 28 July 1921.

500 Kuper, Comments on Stern article.

501 Fleming, "Monticello's Long Career," 66.

502 Hosmer, *Presence of the Past*, 183.

503 *New York Times*, 7 and 11 March 1924.

504 Thomas Jefferson to George Gilmore, 11 August 1787, Albert Ellery Bergh *et al.*, eds., *The Writings of Thomas Jefferson*, (20 vols., Washington, 1907), 6: 265.

505 Thedore Fred Kuper, Comments on Stern article, Malcolm Stern Papers, American Jewish Archives, Cincinnati, Ohio.

506 *Id.*; Thomas Fleming, "Monticello's Long Career—from Riches to Rags to Riches," *Smithsonian Magazine*, Vol. 4, no. 3 (June 1973), 62-69.

507 *The Story of the Thomas Jefferson Memorial Foundation* (New York, 1925).

508 James G. Randall, "When Jefferson's Home was Bequeathed to the United States," *South Atlantic Quarterly*, 23 (January 1924), 39.

509 Merrill D. Peterson, *The Jefferson Image in the American Mind* (New York, 1960), 387.

510 Marc Leepson, "The Levys of Monticello," *Preservation* 50 (March/April 1998), 50.

511 Lewis Glaser to Saul Viener, 21 February 1974, Uriah Levy Materials, Beth Ahabah Museum and Archives, Richmond, Virginia.

512 Memorandum, "Monticello and the Levy Family," [n.d., 1953], Stern MSS.

513 Malcolm Stern, "Monticello and the Levy Family," *Journal of the Southern Jewish Historical Society*, vol. 1, no. 2 (October 1959): 19-23.

514 Copies of these memoranda, as well as correspondence between Stern and Lipkowitz, are in the Stern MSS.

515 See, for example, Thomas Fleming, "Monticello ... would moulder through a hundred years of abuse and decay," *The Man from Monticello* (New York, 1969), 381.

516 Irving Lipkowitz to James Bear, 21 August 1974, *id.*

517 Bear to Lipkowitz, 1 October 1974; Granquist to Lipkowitz, 14 November 1974, *id.*

518 Stern, Notes for a speech delivered at the Jewish Historical Society of New York, 13 October 1985, *id.*

[519] Virginius Dabney to Irving Lipkowitz, 16 June 1984, *id.*

[520] Stern to Leonard Gold, 6 January 1976, *id.*

[521] Leepson, "Levys of Monticello," 50.

[522] Daniel P. Jordan to Saul Viener, 25 March 1985, Stern MSS.

[523] *The Levy Family and Monticello: A Commemorative Ceremony* (Charlottesville, 1985).

[524] Notes for speech, Stern MSS.

BIBLIOGRAPHY

I. Manuscript Collections

James Turner Barclay Materials, Alderman Library, University of Virginia, Charlottesville, Virginia.

William Taylor Barry Papers, Alderman Library, University of Virginia, Charlottesville, Virginia.

George Walter Blatterman Papers, Alderman Library, University of Virginia, Charlottesville, Virginia.

George Carr Papers, Alderman Library, University of Virginia, Charlottesville, Virginia.

Records of General Courts-Martial and Courts of Inquiry of the Navy Department, 1799-1867. Microfilm M273, National Archives, Washington, D.C.

Fairfax Harrison Papers, Virginia Historical Society, Richmond, Virginia.

Records of the Department of Justice, Record Group 60, National Archives, Washington, D.C.

Basil Brown Gordon Papers, Virginia Historical Society, Richmond, Virginia.

Thomas Jefferson Transcripts, Alderman Library, University of Virginia, Charlottesville, Virginia.

Leiper and Patterson Family Papers, Alderman Library, University of Virginia, Charlottesville, Virginia.

Jefferson Monroe Levy Papers, American Jewish Historical Society, New York, New York.

Jefferson Monroe Levy Legal Papers, in Duke Family Papers, Alderman Library, University of Virginia, Charlottesville, Virginia.

Jonas Phillips Levy Papers, American Jewish Historical Society, New York, New York.

Uriah Phillips Levy Papers, American Jewish Historical Society, New York, New York.

Uriah Phillips Levy Materials, American Jewish Archives, Cincinnati, Ohio.

Uriah Phillips Levy Materials, Congregation Beth Ahabah Museum and Archives, Richmond, Virginia.

Lewis Family Papers, in the possession of Harley and Richard Lewis, Hartsdale, New York.

Meikleham Family Papers, Alderman Library, University of Virginia, Charlottesville, Virginia.

Archival Collections of K.K. Mikveh Israel, Philadelphia, Pennsylvania.

Probate Court Records, Surrogate Court of New York, Hall of Records, County ourt House, New York, New York.

Shakelford Family Papers, Alderman Library, University of Virginia, Charlottesville, Virginia.

Malcolm H. Stern Papers, American Jewish Archives, Cincinnati, Ohio.

Sarah Strickler Diary, Alderman Library, University of Virginia, Charlottesville, Virginia.

Thomas Jefferson Memorial Foundation Papers, Alderman Library, University of Virginia, Charlottesville, Virginia.

Thomas Jefferson Memorial Foundation, Monticello Records, Monticello Research Center, Charlottesville, Virginia.

2. Books, Pamphlets and Theses

Adams, Dickinson W. *et al.*, eds. *Jefferson's Extracts from the Gospels.* The Papers of Thomas Jefferson, 2nd Series. Princeton: Princeton University Press, 1983.

Adams, William Howard. *Jefferson's Monticello.* New York: Abbeville Press, 1983.

Baron, Robert C. *Jefferson the Man: In His Own Words.* Golden: Fulcrum/Starwood, 1993.

Bear, James A. *Jefferson at Monticello.* Charlottesville: University Press of Virginia, 1967.

——— and Lucia C. Stanton, eds. *Jefferson's Memorandum Books.* The Papers of Thomas Jefferson, 2nd Series. Princeton: Princeton University Press, 1997.

Bergh, Albert Ellery, *et al.*, eds. *The Writings of Thomas Jefferson.* 20 vols. Washington: Thomas Jefferson Memorial Association, 1907.

Betts, Edwin Morris, ed. *Thomas Jefferson's Farm Book.* Charlottesville: University Press of Virginia, 1987.

———, and James Adam Bear, Jr., eds. *The Family Letters of Thomas Jefferson.* Columbia: University of Missouri Press, 1966.

Birmingham, Stephen. *The Grandees: America's Sephardic Elite.* New York: Harper & Row, 1971.

Blau, Joseph, and Salo Baron, eds. *The Jews of the United States, 1790-1840: A Documentary History.* 3 vols. New York: Columbia University Press, 1963.

Boyd, Julian *et al.*, eds. *The Papers of Thomas Jefferson.* 27 vols to date. Princeton: Princeton University Press, 1950- .

Breen, Timothy H. *Tobacco Culture: The Mentality of the Great Tidewater Planters on the Eve of the Revolution.* Princeton: Princeton University Press, 1985.

Buckingham, James Silk. *The Slave States of America.* 2 vols. London: Fisher, Son & Co., 1842.

Bureau of Municipal Research. *Memorandum of Matters Relating to New York City's Debt.* New York: Bureau of Municipal Research, 1908.

——. *New York City's Debt.* New York: Bureau of Municipal Research, 1909.

Butler, Benjamin F. *Defense of Uriah P. Levy, Before the Board of Inquiry Held at Washington City, November and December 1857.* New York: Bryant, 1858.

Carmichael, Leonard, and J.C. Long. *James Smithson and the Smithsonian Story.* New York: Putnam, 1965.

Cohen, Naomi W. *Not Free to Desist.* Philadelphia: Jewish Publication Society, 1972.

Davis, Edward. *The History of Rodeph Shalom Congregation Philadelphia, 1802-1926.* Philadelphia: Congregation Rodeph Shalom, 1927.

De Kay, James Tertius. *Chronicles of thye Frigate Macedonian, 1809-1922.* New York: Norton, 1995.

De Sola Pool, David, and Tamar De Sola Pool. *An Old Faith in the New World: Portrait of Shearith Israel, 1654-1954.* New York: Columbia University Press, 1955.

Dye, Ira. *The Fatal Cruise of the* Argus: *Two Captains in the War of 1812.* Annapolis: Naval Institute Press, 1994.

Ely, Carol, Jeffrey Hantman, and Phyllis Leffler. *To Seek the Peace of the City: Jewish Life in Charlottesville.* Charlottesville: Hillel Jewish Center, 1994.

Faber, Eli. *A Time for Planting: The First Migration, 1654-1820.* Baltimore: The Johns Hopkins University Press, 1992.

Farrand, Max, ed. *The Records of the Federal Convention of 1787.* 4 vols. New Haven: Yale University Press, 1966 ed.

Fitzpatrick, Donovan, and Saul Saphire. *Navy Maverick: Uriah Phillips Levy.* Garden City: Doubleday & Co., 1963.

Ford, Paul Leicester, ed. *The Works of Thomas Jefferson.* 12 Vols. New York: Federal Edition by Putnam's, 1905.

Fowler, Robert Ludlow. *The Law of Charitable Uses, Trusts, and Donations in New York.* New York: Diossy Law Book Company, 1896.

Friedman, Lawrence M. *A History of American Law.* New York: Simon & Schuster, 1973.

Higham, John. *Strangers in the Land: Patterns of American Nativism, 1860-1925.* New Brunswick: Rutgers University Press, 1955.

Hochman, Stephen Harold. "Thomas Jefferson: A Personal Financial Biography." Unpublished dissertation, University of Virginia, 1987.

Hosmer, Charles B., Jr. *The Presence of the Past: A History of the Preservation Movement in the United States before Williamsburg.* New York: Putnam's, 1965.

Hyman, Harold M., and William M. Wiecek. *Equal Justice under Law: American Constitutional Development, 1835-1875.* New York: Harper & Row, 1982.

Jaher, Federic Cople. *A Scapegoat in the Wilderness: The Origins and Rise of Anti-Semitism in America.* Cambridge: Harvard University Press, 1994.

Jefferson Club Association of St. Louis. *Pilgrimage to Monticello. . . October 10 to 14, 1901.* St. Louis: Curran Publishing Co., 1902.

Jones, Gareth H. *History of the Law of Charity, 1532-1827.* London: Cambridge Univesity Press, 1969.

Kammen, Michael G. *A Machine that Would Go of Itself: The Constitution in American Culture.* New York: Knopf, 1986.

Kaminski, John P., ed. *Jefferson in Love: The Love Letters beween Thomas Jefferson and Maria Cosway.* Madison: Madison House, 1999.

Kanof, Abram. *Uriah Phillips Levy: The Story of a Pugnacious Commodore.* Philadelphia: Jewish Publication Society, 1949.

Karp, Abraham, ed. *The Jewish Experience in America.* 5 vols. Waltham: American Jewish Historical Society, 1969.

Langhorne, Elizabeth. *Monticello: A Family Story.* Chapel Hill: Algonquin Books, 1987.

Langley, Harold D. *Social Reform in the United States Navy, 1798-1862.* Urbana: University of Illinois Press, 1967.

The Levy Family and Monticello. Charlottesville: Thomas Jefferson Memorial Foundation, 1985.

Levy, Jefferson M. *Elector's Handbook, or Digest of the Election Laws of the State of New York, Applicable to the City of New York.* New York: W.P. Mitchell, 1895.

———-. *Réception de la Statue de Thomas Jefferson . . . par Hon. Jefferson M. Lévy, Citoyen Americain.* Angers: Privately printed, 1905.

Levy, Uriah P. *Memorial of Uriah P. Levy, late Captain in the Navy, to the Congress of the United States, complaining of the Action of the Board of Naval Officers. . . .* New York: Bryant, 1855.

Lindgren, James M. *Preserving the Old Dominion: Historic Preservation and Virginia Traditionalism.* Charlottesville: Unversity Press of Virginia, 1993.

Link, Arthur S. et al., eds. *The Papers of Woodrow Wilson.* 69 vols. Princeton: Princeton University Press, 1966-1994.

Littleton, Maud. *Monticello.* New York: Privately printed, 1912.

——, *"One Wish."* New York: Privately printed, 1911.

Lovette, Leland P. *Naval Customs: Traditions and Usages.* Annapolis: United States Naval Institute, 1939.

McLaughlin, Jack. *Jefferson and Monticello: The Biography of a Builder.* New York: Holot, 1988.

Malone, Dumas. *Jefferson and His Times.* 6 vols. Boston: Little, Brown & Co., 1948-1981.

Moran, F. Berger. *Miss Washington of Virginia: A Semi-Centennial Love Story.* Philadelphia: Lippincott, 1893.

Nevins, Allan, ed. *The Diary of Philip Hone, 1828-1851.* New York: Dodd, Mead, 1936.

Nichols, Frederick D., and James A. Bear, Jr. *Monticello: A Guidebook.* Monticello: Thomas Jefferson Memorial Foundation, 1967.

Patton, John S., and Sallie J. Doswell. *Monticello and Its Master.* Charlottesville: The Michie Company, 1925.

Peterson, Merrilld D. *The Jefferson Image in the American Mind.* New York: Oxford University Press, 1960.

——, ed. *Thomas Jefferson: A Reference Biography.* New York: Charles Scribner's Sons, 1986.

——, ed. *Visitors to Monticello.* Charlottesville: University Press of Virginia, 1989.

——, and Robert C. Vaughn, eds. *The Virginia Statute for Religious Freedom: Its Evolution and Consequences.* New York: Cambridge University Press, 1988.

Randolph, Sarah N. *The Domestic Life of Thomas Jefferson.* New York: Harper, 1871.

Raynor, B.L. *Life of Thomas Jefferson.* Boston: Lilly, Wait, Colman & Holden, 1834.

Rezneck, Samuel. *The Saga of an American Jewish Family since the Revolution: A History of the Family of Jonas Phillips.* Washington: University Press of America, 1980.

Rhodes, Thomas L. *The Story of Monticello.* Washington: American Publishing Company, 1928.

Semmes, John E. *John H. Latrobe and His Times, 1803-1891.* Baltimore: Norman, Remington Co., 1917.

Sheridan, Eugene R. *Jefferson and Religion.* Charlottesville: Thomas Jefferson Memorial Foundation, 1998.

Sloan, Herbert E. *Principle and Interest: Thomas Jefferson and the Problem of Debt.* New York: Oxford University Press, 1995.

Smith, James Morton, ed. *The Republic of Letters: The Correspondence between Thomas Jefferson and James Madison.* 3 vols. New York: W.W. Norton, 1995.

Smith, Margaret Bayard. *First Forty Years of Washington Society, Portrayed by the Family Letters of Mrs. Samuel Harrison Smith from the Collection of her Grandson, J. Henley Smith.* Gaillard Hunt, ed. New York: Charles Scribner's Sons, 1906.

Sobell, Samuel. *Intrepid Sailor.* Philadelphia: Cresset Publishers, 1980.

Sorin, Gerald. *A Time for Building: The Third Migration, 1880-1829.* Baltimore: The Johns Hopkins University Press, 1992.

Stein, Susan R. *The Worlds of Thomas Jefferson at Monticello.* New York: Harry N. Abrams in association with the Thomas Jefferson Memorial Foundation, 1993.

Stern, Malcolm H. *First American Jewish Families.* 3rd ed. Rev. Baltimore: Ottenheimer Publishers, 1991.

Thomas Jefferson Memorial Foundation. *The Story of the Thomas Jefferson Memorial Foundation.* New York: Thomas Jefferson Memorial Foundation, 1925.

Townsend, George Alfred. *Monticello and Its Preservation since Jefferson's Death, 1826-1902.* Washington: Gibson Brothers, 1902.,

Tyler, Norman. *Historic Preservation: An Introduction to Its History, Principles, and Practice.* New York: W.W. Norton, 2000.

Urofsky, Melvin I. *Commonwealth and Community: The Jewish Experience in Virginia.* Richmond: Virginia Historical Society, 1997.

West, Patricia. *Domesticating History: The Political Origins of America's House Museums.* Washington: Smithsonian Institution Press, 1999.

White, Marion Louise. "Debt Unresolved: Jefferson and Monticello." Unpublished masters thesis, University of Vrginia, 1993.

Willis, H. Parker. *The Federal Reserve System.* New York: Ronald Press, 1923.

Wilstach, Paul. *Jefferson and Monticello.* Garden City: Doubleday & Co., 1925.

Wolf, Edwin, 2nd, and Maxwell Whiteman. *The History of the Jews of Philadelphia from Colonial Times to the Age of Jackson.* Philadelphia: Jewish Publication Society, 1957.

Zollman, Carl. *American Law of Charities.* Milwaukee: Bruce Publishing Co., 1924.

3. Articles and Chapters in Books

Barnwell, John. "Monticello 1856." *Journal of the Society of Architectural Historians* 34 (1975): 280-85.

Barringer, Anna. "Pleasant It Is." *The Magazine of Albemarle County History, vol. 27 or 28.*

Bear, James A., Jr. "Accounts of Monticello, 1780-1878: A Selective Bibliography." *Magazine of Albemarle County History* 21 (1962-1963).

Beiswanger, William L. "Jefferson's Sources from Antiquity in the Design of Monticello." *Antiques* 144 (July 1993): 58-69.

Blanford, B.W. "Commodore Uriah P. Levy, Adventures and Experiences Including Hitherto Unpublished Reminiscences by His Widow—Former Chatelaine of Monticello." *American Hebrew* 116 (1925): 694, 739, 743, 770, 784, 786, 807, 822.

Cable, Nary, and Annabelle Prager. "The Levys of Monticello." *American Heritage* 29 (Feb/Mar 1978): 30-39.

Crystal, Charlotte. "Uriah P. Levy: Savior of Monticello." *Albemarle Archives* [n.d.] 46-57.

Dix, Dorothea. "Monticello—Shrine or Bacherlor's Hall." *Good Housekeeping* 58 (April 1914): 538-44.

Ferguson, Henry N. "The Man Who Saved Monticello." *American History Illustrated* 14 (February 1980): 20-25.

Fleming, Thomas. "Monticello's Long Career—From Riches to Rags to Riches." *Smithsonian Magazine* 4 (June 1973): 62-69.

Gaines, William H., Jr. "From Desolation to Restoration: The Story of 'Monticello' Since Jefferson." *Virginia Calvacade* 1 (Spring 1952): 4-8.

Hosmer, Charles B., Jr. "The Levys and the Restoration of Monticello." *American Jewish Historical Quarterly* 52 (March 1964): 219-252.

Kanof, Abram. "Uriah Phillips Levy: The Story of a Pugnacious Commodore." *Publications of the American Jewish Historical Society* 39 (1949): 1-66.

Katz, Stanley N., Barry Sullivan, and C. Paul Beach. "Legal Change and Legal Autonomy: Charitable Trusts in New York, 1777-1893." *Law and History Review* 3 (1985): 51-89.

Larson, Chiles T.A. "Alarm on 'Little Mountain'." *Historic Preservation* 43 (March/April 1991): 46-48.

Leepson, Marc. "The Levys of Monticello." *Preservation* 50 (March/April 1998): 44-51.

Levy, Uriah P. "Defense of Uriah P. Levy . . . ," (1858) in Jacob Rader Marcus, ed., *Memoirs of American Jews, 1775-1865* (Philadelphia: Jewish Publication Society, 1955), 76-116.

Lossing, Benson J. "Monticello." *Harper's New Monthly Magazine* 7, no. 38 (July 1853): 145-160.

Nicolay, J.G. "Thomas Jefferson's Home." *The Century Magazine* 34, no. 5 (September 1887): 643-53.

Peterson, Maud Howard. "The Home of Jefferson." *Munsey's Magazine* 20 (1899): 608-19.

Randall, James G. "When Jefferson's Home was Bequeathed to the United States." *The South Atlantic Quarterly* 23 (January 1924): 34-39.

Rezneck, Samuel. "The Maritime Adventures of a Jewish Sea Captain, Jonas P. Levy, in Nineteenth-Century America." *The American Neptune* 37, n. 4 (October 1977): 239-52.

——. "The Strange Role of a Jewish Sea Captain in the Confederate South." *American Jewish History* 68 (September 1977): 64-73.

Stanton, Lucia C. "Jefferson and the Amusements of Science." *Antiques* 144 (July 1993): 92-99.

Steinberg, Stephen. "How Jewish Quotas Began." *Commentary* 52 (September 1971): 67-76.

Stern, Malcolm H. "Monticello and the Levy Family." *Journal of the Southern Jewish Historical Society* 1, no. 2 (October 1959): 19-23.

Stockton, Frank R. "The Later Years of Monticello." *The Century Magazine* 34, no. 5 (September 1887): 653-58.

4. Government Publications

Committee on the Library, U.S. Senate, 62nd Cong., 2nd Sess. *Public Ownership of Monticello. Hearings on S.J. Res. 92.* Washington: Government Printing Office, 1912.

Committee on Public Buildings and Grounds, U.S. House of Representatives, 64th Cong., 1st Sess. *Purchase of Monticello. Hearings on H.J. Res. 269.* Washington: Government Printing Office, 1916.

Committee on Rules, U.S. House of Representatives, 62nd Cong., 2nd Sess. *Public Ownership of Monticello. Hearings on S. Con. Res. 24, July 24, 1912.* Washington: Government Printing Office, 1912.

Committee on Rules, U.S. House of Representatives, 63rd Cong., 2nd Sess. *Purchase of Monticello. Hearings pursuant to H.J. Res. 390, H.J. Res. 418, and a Substitute Therefore.*

Washington: Government Printing Office, 1915.

Commonwealth v. Levy, 23 Gratton (Virginia) 21 (1873).

Congressional Globe.

Congressional Record.

Levy et al. v. Levy et al., 40 Barbour 585 (N.Y. 1863).

Levy et al. v. Levy et al., 33 N.Y. 97 (1865).

Register of the Debates in Congress (Gales and Seaton).

Statutes at Large.

Subcommittee of the Committee on Public Buildings and Grounds, U.S. Senate, 64th Cong., 2nd Sess. *Purchase of Monticello. Hearings on S.J. Res. 153, a Bill Directing the Secretary of the Treasury to Acquire by Purchase the Estate Known as Monticello . . . .* Washington: Government Printing Office, 1917.

Index

Numbers in italics indicate pages containing illustrations.